Museum Architecture in Frankfurt

Museum Architecture in Frankfurt 1980-1990

Edited by
Vittorio Magnago Lampugnani

with
Volker Fischer and Heike Lauer

with contributions by
Roland Burgard, Hilmar Hoffmann,
Vittorio Magnago Lampugnani
and Wolfgang Pehnt

with commentaries by
Dieter Bartetzko, Kenneth Frampton,
Falk Jaeger, Heinrich Klotz,
Michael Mönninger, Peter Rumpf,
Manfred Sack, Mathias Schreiber
and Monika Zimmermann

Prestel

First published in conjunction with the exhibition
'Museumsarchitektur in Frankfurt 1980–1990'
at the German Architecture Museum, Frankfurt am Main,
from 1 September 1990 to 2 January 1991

Edited by Vittorio Magnago Lampugnani
on behalf of the Dezernat für Kultur und Freizeit
Amt für Wissenschaft und Kunst der Stadt Frankfurt am Main
German Architecture Museum

Translated from the German by Eileen Martin
English edition edited by Ian Robson

Cover: Museum of Decorative Arts (photo Ivan Nemec)
Frontispiece: Schirn Art Gallery (photo Hans Georg Göllner)

Endpapers: Frankfurt am Main, view from the air
© Bollmann-Bildkarten-Verlag, Braunschweig

© 1990 Prestel, Munich
© of texts by the authors, see p.199
Photocredits see p.199

Prestel-Verlag, Mandlstrasse 26, D-8000 Munich 40,
Federal Republic of Germany
Tel. (89) 381 7090; Telefax (89) 38 17 09 35

Distributed in continental Europe by Prestel-Verlag,
Verlegerdienst München GmbH & Co KG,
Gutenbergstrasse 1, D-8031 Gilching, Federal Republic of Germany
Tel. (08105) 21 10; Telefax (8105) 55 20

Distributed in the USA and Canada by te Neues Publishing Company,
15 East 76th Street, New York, NY 10021, USA
Tel. (2 12) 2 88 02 65; Telefax (2 12) 5 70 23 73

Distributed in Japan by YOHAN-Western Publications Distribution Agency,
14-9 Okubo 3-chome, Shinjuku-ku, J-Tokyo 169
Tel. (3) 2 08 01 81; Telefax (3) 2 09 02 88

Distributed in the United Kingdom, Ireland and all other countries by
Thames & Hudson Limited, 30–40 Bloomsbury Street, London WC1B 3QP, England
Tel. (71) 6 36 54 88; Telefax (71) 6 36 47 99

Color separations: Reproduktionsgesellschaft Karl Dörfel mbH, Munich
Typesetting , printing and binding: Passavia Druckerei GmbH Passau
Printed in Germany

ISBN 3-7913-1101-8 (German edition)
ISBN 3-7913-1096-8 (English edition)

Contents

Preface

Between 1980 and 1990 thirteen new museums were created in Frankfurt am Main. Some were new buildings, some reconstructions of or extensions to existing buildings. Taken together, they constitute something like a cross-section of the history of international architecture in the past decade – naturally not a full history, but representative in many ways.

The new cultural buildings in Frankfurt manifest not only the more or less successful compromises that necessarily resulted from the confluence of the various ideas and requirements of the architects, users and politicians involved, they also illustrate in a nutshell the development of contemporary architecture, with its parallel and often contradictory currents and tendencies. The new museums are astonishingly pure materializations of the architectural approaches of their creators. Often enough, though, they have also become individualistic, strongly characterized, and in some cases definitely uncompromising spatial constructions whose artistic autonomy is in stark contrast to their practical usefulness.

There is another and very important aspect to the new museum buildings in Frankfurt. They demonstrate the serious desire to maintain and repair the fabric of the city that has replaced the mostly haphazard reconstruction after the Second World War and put a stop to the irresponsible treatment of the historical city. Here the new buildings have acquired a double function: on the one hand they have helped to preserve a part of the city that was facing demolition, in that old buildings have been converted to new uses, and on the other they are figureheads of a new public consciousness, to the spread of which they are making a courageous contribution. They constitute a cultural opposition to the advancing commercialization of the city, a subtle but determined opposition which has not only given the people of Frankfurt a new sense of urban living, but also prompted other cities to rethink and to copy Frankfurt's example.

This book traces the "micro-histories" of all thirteen of the new Frankfurt museum buildings, from the first sketch of an idea to the realization. The intermediate stages generate more material than the average museum visitor or citizen might imagine: innumerable drawings, working-models, alternative designs, presentation-models, detailed blueprints, and of course whole mounds of working-plans. A selection of these is presented for each building, beginning with the Jewish Museum on the north bank of the Main and following an imaginary itinerary to end up at the Liebieghaus on the south bank. Short editorial texts provide the technical and functional data. In critical essays, respected architectural theorists put the buildings into the context of current architectural debate through commentary and evaluation. The photographs do the same, if in a rather less obvious way; all the buildings were photographed by leading architectural photographers. Four introductory essays deal with the cultural, philosophical, urbanistic and architectural aspects of the museum ensemble, with special reference to the now internationally famous riverside strip.

So this is not pure documentation; it is rather a friendly and critical appreciation, as befits an experiment that bravely sets out to explore new paths in order to give culture, architecture and the city a significant and lasting impulse.

Vittorio Magnago Lampugnani

Vittorio Magnago Lampugnani

The Historical City: Completion, Reinterpretation, Maintenance

When in 1694 Giuseppe Lanza, duke of Camastra and vicar-general of Val Demone and Val di Noto, founded a new city about seven kilometres from the ruins of Noto Antica, which had been completely destroyed by an earthquake the previous year, he followed a very simple procedure. On the dry earth of the hill in south-eastern Sicily that he had chosen for his "città di fondazione" he drew the lines of a rational city plan based on an orthogonal grid, on a scale of 1:1. He then allotted the sites thus created to various settlers, with the proviso that they must erect at least the street facades immediately. This is how Noto Nuova, one of the most beautiful and most enigmatic new towns of the eighteenth century, was built.

So runs the legend; the facts of the matter are less straightforward. The story, however – semifictional and greatly simplified – demonstrates better than an accurate report the principles of the baroque urban utopia, of which Noto is a very spectacular example. The first principle was a geometrical plan, as elegant a composition as possible. The second was uniform facade architecture, as rich as possible. The third principle resulted from the first two: a clearly defined, manageable urban space where people could live.

Urban Planning Today: An Exercise in Prudence

A glance at the history and present-day state of urban planning and we will see that – surprising though it may seem at first – these three principles, in rather more general terms, have applied to all cities at all times. The recipe for a beautiful city seems inalterable: a good plan, several specimens of good architecture to give it concrete form, and resulting therefrom a system of good public spaces, coupled with building dense enough to enable the whole to fill with life. Only the emphases may shift: Berlin's Südliche Friedrichstadt, for instance, laid out by Philipp Gerlach in the 1730s, is based on a single sophisticated plan, but the facades that line its streets are comparatively insignificant; the central Renaissance area of Rome has a rather indifferent plan, and it is only the supreme quality of the individual buildings that makes this a grandiose part of the city.

So much for the historical city. And the modern city? Our way of life has changed fundamentally over the last hundred years. Millions of cars have made the urban migration to and from work first easier, and then again

more difficult; new means of telecommunication and automation have begun to make this migration unnecessary. Our shopping habits have undergone a notable change, our leisure-pursuits a virtual revolution. Quite new types of livingarrangement are available for quite new types of family. In view of these changing conditions, can we still speak of the same city as a hundred years ago; does it not have to adapt and undergo fundamental changes?

Ever since the modernists began to polemize against the nineteenth-century city, architectural culture has been producing truly "new", utopian cities, bold ideas yet doomed to failure. From the "ville contemporaine" to the "plug-in city", they have all foundered on the fact that people may have changed their ways of life but they have not changed their basic needs and habits. The revolutions expected to follow from the mass availability of new technology have not come about. Radio has not replaced the concert-hall, nor has television replaced the theatre and the cinema. Telephone and telefax have not eliminated personal conversation, with all its nuances of interpersonal communication, from the twinkle in the eye to the twitch of the corner of the mouth. Nor have we seen the radical changes so often forecast in the whole scenario of urban living: we drive our cars, but we walk as well, and we use public transport; we work at home, but of course we also work in the office; we shop in supermarkets but also (and with increasing pleasure) at the cornershop; we spend part of our leisure time within our own four walls but we go out as well. In the home, new forms of living together have been tried out, but traditional family life has also survived. In our cities coexist a wide variety of social forms, the radical as well as the orthodox, often enjoying equal status. So people today need the traditional urban spaces as well as the new, because they want to do no different from what they have been doing for hundreds and thousands of years – stroll around, see and be seen, meet other people and communicate with them. The activities are as old as the public streets and communal areas they require.

There is another factor that helps to explain why we still need the historical urban space. Europe's cities exist, and it is neither possible nor necessary to pull them down and rebuild them. At most we can prudently renew them, modify them and extend them. The urban planner and the architect of today no longer need to plan a city from scratch, as the duke of Camastra did three centuries

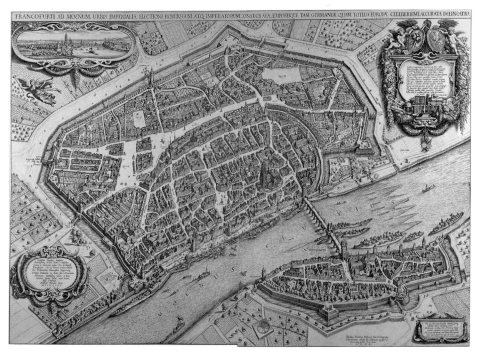

Plan of the Imperial City of Frankfurt am Main, copperplate engraving by Merian, 1628

ago. Their task – only ostensibly of it a more modest one – is creatively to preserve an existing city; they have not to construct but to repair and maintain.

So urban planning today derives from the permanent friction between the idea of a new city and the substance of an old one. This makes it not only more complex but also more ambitious; for the idea has to be strong enough to withstand the clash with existing reality, and at the same time modest enough to respect what already exists. Admittedly there is no patent remedy for the happy medium; it has to be discovered anew each time specific according to the conditions of the case. Nevertheless, for all the particular problems of the contemporary world, the fundamental urban planning principles that can be derived from the parable of Noto remain valid today.

Learning from the Past (Grand Scale)

The study of architectural history is not without its pitfalls. On the one hand it provides a wealth of proven and incontrovertible solutions to the problem of relating buildings to human life, and on the other, precisely because of this vast repertory, it can easily tempt us to be satisfied with what we and not look for anything beyond. The only way out of the conflict between a resigned imitation of the past and an over-eager search for novelty for its own sake would appear to be the critical approach: reflection, as unprejudiced and profound as possible, on how far the reconstruction of the past points to the best conceivable way for the future, and how far the construction of what has never been before will really lead to utopia, in both the narrower and the wider sense.

In the first place, all new architecture needs to be derived from the given structural premise of the city. The existing pattern of streets and open spaces in the historical city forms the basis for all new measures, which should clarify and complete this pattern. Where it is geometrically, spatially and functionally appropriate, the reconstruction should restore the urban structure of the past; where it is not appropriate, a new order needs to be created, extrapolated from the existing structure with the objective of creating a better city than the historical one was. The given structure includes everything that was ever built in the city and is still standing. So there are no "good" and "bad" historical periods, there are only good and bad buildings in relation to a complex urban order. The selection of what should and what should not be preserved and taken into consideration is thus based not on philological criteria but only on urbanistic maxims.

In the second place, the new buildings should obscure as little as possible the history of the city, the "geological" stratification of sediments of human life. A city is, among other things, a didactic formation, which narrates from its own memories. Without degenerating into a mere formal academic review of the past, the new city has to relate architecturally to the events that were significant for the old city, that destroyed it or helped it flourish, shook it to its foundations or strengthened it – events, in short, that formed it in various ways. Nothing that can be carried over into the future as experience should be relegated to oblivion: a place consists of what has been.

Creatively to transform what has been into a new rational unity is the task of every architectural town planning operator.

Sensitivity (Individual Scale)

Besides the grand scale, modern urban planning also needs to remember the individual level. The maintenance principle, the antithesis of the "demolish-and-start-again" principle, particularly demands sensitivity: sensitive understanding of what already exists, sensitive adaptation and modification, sensitive supplementation and continuation. This requires that love of detail that cannot come from theory but only from practice. The great idea, if it is really great, can of course stand many a cutback and many a compromise; but it is a matter of great import how the idea is realized in practice. In architecture and urban planning the material realization can never be seen divorced from the concept; the one conditions the other. One and the same house is a different house according to whether it is faced with plaster or with stone. One and the same city is a different city if its streets are asphalted rather than paved.

In public spaces particularly, which are largely perceived unconsciously, detail plays a major part. People often notice the lamps, benches, flowerboxes, railings, fences, kerbstones and pavings more than the monuments, street facades and perimeter architecture. Like the policeman in Edgar Allan Poe's *Purloined Letter*, they overlook the big things and notice the small ones. All the more carefully must the small things of the city be designed, drawn and realized.

The Face of the City

But where is all this to lead? To what overriding objective must the great and small ideas, the decisive and the prudent interventions in the historical city, be subordinated? In what direction should it change? Every historical European city has its own face. It has been formed over the centuries of its history, is the result of innumerable political, social and architectural events, and presents itself, so to speak, as the latest (but never the final) crystallization thereof.

It is the writers, film directors and painters who are better able than the architects to recognize this, the strangers better than the inhabitants. It cannot be precisely described; the city does not wear its face on its sleeve. But Franz Hessel has painted an unmistakable portrait of the Prussian capital in his book of *Spazieren in Berlin* ("Walks through Berlin"); Jean-Luc Godard has given us a very sharp profile of Paris in several of his films; and Giorgio de Chirico brought out the quintessence of Turin in many of his early pictures.

Urban planning, if it is not to be purely technocratic, must respect this face of the city. What matters is not an abstract utopia but a complex, subtle and often hidden reality. This needs to be recognized, developed and, where it appears meaningful, modified – with care and consideration, for this reality consists not only of build-

View of Frankfurt, copperplate engraving by Aveline, 1750

ings, streets, squares, houses, monuments, parks, lamps, hoardings and paving-stones, but also and above all of memories, experiences, dreams: in short, life itself.

Historical Awareness in Working with the City: The Example of Frankfurt's Museum Landscape

The "Museumsufer" of Frankfurt is part of this new architectural and urbanistic culture; it emerges from it.

Firstly, it is based on a great idea, namely that of a related sequence of educational and recreational institutions that ideally add up to a multiple and complementary panorama of showplaces for art and history. And the project is indeed not small in the material sense: thirteen new buildings or conversions have been accommodated directly on or near the banks of the Main.

Then again, it is deeply aware of history. For the museum project entailed a spectacular operation, through it was carried out with no great pomp and circumstance – the rescue of patrician villas threatened with demolition, whose original substance was adapted more or less skilfully to new uses (and to new architectural concepts). This applies to the German Architecture Museum, the German Film Museum, the Museum of Decorative Arts, the Museum of Ethnology and the Jewish Museum; it also applies to the Museum for Prehistory and Early History (although here it is not a villa but a church that has been preserved), the German Postal Museum (which includes an old building in its area of use) and the Portikus Exhibition Hall (which lurks mischievously behind a ruined portico). The Icon Museum is a converted interior anyway, the extensions to the Städel and the Liebieghaus museum basically annexes. But all, without exception, recall historical events.

Finally, the Museumsufer constitutes a new cityscape that has emerged from the preservation, renovation and adaptive re-use of an old cityscape. The historical structure and the substance that fills it have remained basically unchanged, and have merely been judiciously corrected, supplemented, reinterpreted; the streets and

View of Frankfurt from Mühlberg hill, coloured etching, 19th century

open spaces are for the most part still there – only details have been changed. The houses, villas and church have been preserved; they are just being used differently. The city has not been reinvented but has undergone a maintenance operation.

And yet, modest and cautious though the operation was, the face of the city of Frankfurt has changed. The Museumsufer with its quality architecture is the flagship; it has inspired other buildings of quality, both public and private. Overall, the standard of the city's architecture has been raised.

But the city is becoming more and more similar to that ("the name is not important") which Robert Musil foresaw back in the 1930s: "Like all big cities it consisted of irregularity, change, foresliding, not-keeping-in-step, clashes of things and affairs, unfathomable instants of silence in between, of tracks and the untracked, of a great rhythmic pulse and the eternal untuning and shifting of all rhythms against each other, and on the whole resembled a seething bubble resting in a vessel made of the permanent material of houses, laws, ordinances, and historical traditions."

This is of course the traditional city (still the only place where urban life in the truest sense can unfold) as city of contradiction, but also city of tolerance. Perhaps the variegated buildings standing one beside the next along the Main are images of just that: the coexistence of different views of life and ways of living. If they are, they represent nothing less than the profile that today's city should present to tomorrow.

Hilmar Hoffmann

Frankfurt's New Museum Landscape

The History, Development and Perspectives
of an Ambitious Cultural Programme

The museum scene in Frankfurt is unique in its reflection of changing attitudes over the years towards the museum both as cultural institution and as architectural element in the urban landscape. Historically, a particular aspect of the numerous Frankfurt museums is that none of them owes its existence to a princely *uomo universale* and his collection of works of art or other valuables or curiosities. (The Free Imperial City was never the capital of a dukedom or kingdom, apart from one brief episode, nor was it even the favourite residence of a princely family.) It was single items or – much more rarely – private collections built up by members of the patrician class that were presented to the public to form the basis for a museum, or it was the estate of a burgher – a scholar or an artist – that was declared "property of the people" (some of these estates are still under the scholarly general administration of private associations).

When Johann Friedrich Städel, a citizen of Frankfurt, made his will in 1815, he appended to it the "Deed of Foundation of the Städel Institute of Art", as a result of which two years later the foundation stone was laid for what was to be the most important museum in Frankfurt. The museum had to change its location several times before in 1878 it was housed in a specially erected building on the bank of the River Main. The Städel, particularly, is exemplary of the very specific development of the museum scene in Frankfurt: in his deed, Städel stipulated that the foundation should be administered by five "worthy persons from among the local citizenry, who should not need to consult any authority or obtain any approval"; the municipal administration was to be responsible only for balancing and auditing the books.

Städel's foundation had to face numerous difficulties right from the start. In 1817 civil proceedings began that were to last eleven years altogether, in which Städel's heirs contested his will and so made the building up of the collection extremely difficult. Due to a purchasing policy that concentrated on art-historical rarities, contemporary art, which had accounted for a considerable part of Städel's original collection, came to be increasingly neglected. Thanks to the bequest of Ludwig Josef Pfungst of Worms in 1907 it was possible to found a municipal gallery, attached to the Städel as an associated institute, which was to focus on the collecting of contemporary art – a tradition that is being continued today with the establishment of the new Museum of Modern Art in Braubachstrasse. At the same time as the munici-

pal gallery was founded, the sculpture collection was transferred to the villa of Baron Heinrich von Liebieg, which had been built in 1896 by Romeis and extended in 1909 by Kanold. More than eight years after it was opened a new wing was added, to plans by the Frankfurt architects Scheffler and Warschauer; together with the renovated old gallery tract, it was inaugurated in May 1990. The new building was created on the basis of old ideas that had remained unrealized, and it is sensitively oriented to the requirements of the collection and the existing buildings, without denying its own identity. The concept of "building in the historical context" – one of the main ideas of the riverside museum project – has been given its most emphatic formulation with this noble building.

But let us return to the Städel. As pioneering as the Städel institution itself, which combined a school and an art collection, the first building also reflected a major stage of development in museum architecture. The very typology is revealing: the architect Oscar Sommer clearly oriented himself to the type of museum that Gottfried Semper had built in Dresden. We can today see this as the deliberate propagation of the idea of the museum as monument, indeed, as the attempt to contest the hegemony of the Prussians with their Berlin museum buildings. The frontispiece is decorated with statues of the heroes of the German Renaissance, Dürer and Holbein (the adjoining streets are also named after them). All in all this was not a specifically regional or municipal architecture, it was a deliberate embracing of the "iconology of German museum architecture at the beginning of the Second Empire", as Otto Martin entitled his thesis for Mainz University, in which the new Städel building is also reviewed.

The extension to the Städel that soon became necessary, and was begun in 1915 to plans by Hermann von Hoven and Franz Heberer, was delayed by the war and its aftermath until 1926. Only then could the display facilities be enlarged and the imposing foyer added. The general appearance of the building was not altered, and it was also respected in Johannes Krahn's rebuilding after the Second World War, which is characterized by the same noble, restrained simplicity as his rebuilding of the Paulskirche. The Städel is a congenial expression of the spirit prevailing in late-nineteenth-century Frankfurt, when the city really began to develop its museum landscape. The imposing presence of this architecture is not diminished by the extension begun in 1987 to plans by the Viennese architect Gustav Peichl, but is complemented by the congenial implementation of contemporary architectural ideas. Peichl's building opened in the autumn of 1990.

Frankfurt's most famous citizen was indirectly involved in the foundation of the Städel, in that his essay "On Art and Antiquity" (*Über Kunst und Altertum*), published in 1816, urges that the art-works dispersed among the houses of prosperous citizens should be gathered under one roof and made accessible to the general public. And Goethe was no doubt also the *spiritus rector* of the establishment of the largest German museum of natural history, the Senckenberg Museum. In 1763 Dr Johann Christian Senckenberg had endowed a foundation with the aim of establishing a hospital, an "anatomical theatre", a chemical laboratory, a botanical garden, a science library and a natural history collection. The list alone shows how various disciplines of natural science were already being practised in Frankfurt at that time.

To illustrate the variety of the museum scene in Frankfurt, we may be excused for quoting a few statistics: up to the beginning of the Second World War Frankfurt boasted twenty-two museums or similar institutions, of which seventeen alone owed their existence to private initiative. Naturally, the city also had a duty to cultivate and increase this valuable heritage.

Of course, after the destruction brought by the Second World War, Frankfurt, like other cities, first had to concern itself with other and more urgent tasks, above all housing the homeless. Ernst May, who had aroused worldwide attention with the housing-estates he built at the end of the 1920s, had set a standard that was not quite to be reached again in the Dornbusch estate and the Nordweststadt, the two largest postwar housing projects.

Then came the requirements of traffic and the related infrastructure. Frankfurt was passed over as capital of the new republic, but in compensation was given the Federal Bank; other large corporations were attracted by the city's central location, and the city council concentrated on developing Frankfurt into a major business centre. Today, 320 banks and large insurance companies and many multinational concerns have their offices here. This was bound to have far-reaching consequences: the city, which before the war had been the biggest village in the German Reich, with more half-timbered buildings than any other comparable city and a street network in the centre that was almost as it had been in the Middle Ages, became after 1970 "Bankfurt", or "Mainhattan", the oft-cited example of the negative effects of an urban planning guided exclusively by economic considerations. Not for nothing did Alexander Mitscherlich evolve his concept of the "hostile city" here.

And culture? While the theatre and the opera were given a representative home relatively early, in 1964, and began to establish a reputation beyond the city limits,

the museums were still nowhere near regaining their prewar standing. Frankfurt was not unique in this respect: throughout the Federal Republic new museum buildings were few and far between. Museums had not changed much since before the war; indeed, some had degenerated to a level they had already surpassed in the nineteenth century. This was evident not only in their architecture but even more so in their actual functioning as organs of collecting, preservation and research; their traditional role of "educational" institution was increasingly alienating the potential visitor. To find a way out of this stagnation it was first necessary to reassess the concept of the museum; and it was not difficult to see what was keeping people away.

The Historisches Museum in Frankfurt played a pioneering role in the development of new attitudes. It is probably no coincidence that this almost universal type of museum set the ball rolling for that democratization of culture which meant in the first place that museums tried to attract the social groups which had traditionally been inclined to shun their hallowed portals. With the heterogeneous inventory of its collections, a regional museum of cultural history was best placed to perform the new functions that at the end of the 1960s were assigned to the museum as promoter of culture: to cease specialization and the isolated presentation of material, to open its doors to everyday culture, and to develop a new didactic approach that would cater to visitors of no more than average education who were unfamiliar with the communication-rituals of practised museum visitors. A new light was cast on the museum as a vehicle of enlightenment, as a "place of learning", and in Frankfurt, too, this became the motto of the cultural programme.

This didactic charge, to which the Historisches Museum responded with an ambitious but perhaps overzealous programme, was something quite new in the museum world, and teething troubles were bound to occur. Presentation was at first determined by a too one-sided preference for verbal argumentation, which went

Städel Art Institute, interior

over the heads of precisely those groups of the population whose interest in museums first needed to be awakened. Then there was a further and perhaps even more serious problem. The main argument for abandoning the isolated presentation of a work of art or a historical fragment had always been that "real" historical contexts could be established only if the visitor had a degree of prior knowledge that was rarely encountered. Since Walter Benjamin, a deep mistrust of the "aura" of the original had filled the enlightened museum didacticians; collecting was equated with fetishism, and in the end, the emphasis on the imparting of knowledge led to a tragic misunderstanding. The museum often became a substitute for school and university, for newspaper and television, indeed it was all of a sudden supposed to make up for the shortcomings of these media both in historical awareness and in visual communication. Above all, themes were taken up that could have been tackled just as well, and put across better, using other media – a series of books, a university project-group, a film or an adult education course, for instance. The specific quality of the museum, which becomes apparent only in relation to a historical object, was not adequately taken into account. After all, the exhibit itself is first and foremost a witness to history, and it affords an experience that cannot be offered by any other medium – though this experience does not necessarily ensue automatically, without the aid of a catalyst.

The big thematic exhibitions that attracted crowds of visitors in the 1970s – on the Staufer dynasty, Prussia, the gold of the Thracians, or the masks of Tutankhamun – must have made one thing clear to even the most obdurate critics of such "mass culture tourism": there is evidently a new interest in history, however superficial this interest might be in some visitors. The opportunity to see with one's own eyes, to "communicate" with an original, a witness to a bygone age – even if it is only a lifeless object – exerts a strong fascination; such exhibitions provide chances that might never occur again.

A further explanation for the popularity of the new German museums with architecture fans and general public alike lies in the desire of the municipal and state authorities who commission these buildings to acquire an architecture that the people can once more identify with, at least partially understand, and – why deny it? – that will also boost the image of the city in the outside world. Frankfurt, Stuttgart, Mönchengladbach and Munich figure on the itineraries of the international culture tourists not least on account of their museum buildings. In the 1980s, the larger and smaller German municipalities seemed to be vying with each other to possess the most spectacular museum architecture, although the peak of the enthusiasm for establishing new museums is probably now over. This enthusiasm was not so misplaced, for statistical comparisons show that it is the most controversial new museum buildings that have attracted the most visitors in recent years. So the novel, aesthetically interesting architecture of the museums has

Historisches Museum, Frankfurt am Main, interior

played a considerable part in increasing the motivation of potential visitors, even when it is often an architecture that is not particularly esteemed, or is indeed decried, by insiders in the art and architecture scene.

The newly awakened interest of circles that had hitherto been more or less indifferent has also brought about a radical change in attitudes to visiting museums. Opening nights, particularly, are major society events: people come with their friends or the whole family, the museum becomes a meeting-place, the starting-point for an evening on the town – a far cry from the culture ritual of the learned art-connoisseur. In this function the museum is merely the appropriate setting for exclusive social gatherings, exclusive in the sense that there is, even today, an invisible barrier that keeps many people outside the doors. But the museum has also become an institution for leisured society, and this is quite legitimate in my view when one considers the realistic prognosis that in the year 2000 only every third adult will be in paid employment.

With the Schaumainkai, whose new appellation *Museumsufer* ("riverside museum promenade") has now come to be used for the Untermainkai as well, the city of Frankfurt has been able to open up an area that uniquely meets the needs I have outlined. The left bank of the Main, between the Eiserner Steg and the Holbeinsteg bridges, and the right bank, popularly known as the "Nizza", are without parallel in other German cities, apart from the Rhine promenade in Düsseldorf or the Brühl terraces in Dresden. (It remains to be seen whether Berlin, with the integration of the museum landscape of the once divided city, will become a serious competitor to Frankfurt.) Moreover, on the Sachsenhausen side of the river a whole series of patrician villas have been preserved from the last century. These buildings, in their park-like gardens, were once a famous feature of Frankfurt, and it is uncontested today that they should be preserved as historic monuments. The villas, above all the Villa Metzler, the oldest and most famous, are embedded in a park landscape that may be small but is unique on account of its proximity to the city centre.

Museum of Decorative Arts, interior

Before discussing the individual buildings, I should like to say a few words on the political background to the Museumsufer project. In the mid 1970s a citizens' initiative was started by the Frankfurt architect Till Behrens, grandson of the famous Expressionist architect Peter Behrens; he wanted to see an expansion of the existing museums on the south bank of the Main, as an enhancement of the urban landscape. My party, the SPD, adopted this proposal in modified form as part of its political programme. In the 1978 local elections, however, the CDU obtained the majority and Walter Wallmann, from Marburg, became the new mayor of Frankfurt. Heinrich Klotz, the future director of the German Architecture Museum, also from Marburg, Frankfurt cultural critic Peter Iden, who was at the time founding director of the planned Museum of Modern Art, and I were able to convince Wallmann, relatively quickly and easily and without recourse to party political tactics, that he should take a personal interest in this concept for a Frankfurt museum landscape. Thus, it was in effect a coalition of Christian Democrats and Social Democrats that sponsored the programme, and this explains how it was possible for the individual projects to be realized so pragmatically and in such rapid succession. To be fair, I must also mention the then city architect, Hans-Erhard Haverkampf, and his assistant Roland Burgard, without whom the projects could not have been realized so efficiently.

What made the Frankfurt museum architecture of the 1980s so well known was the competitions: they helped to promote that new and still controversial architecture that has been given the somewhat vague appelation "postmodern". For all their differences in form and concept, these buildings provided something for the eye, a sharp contrast to the inarticulate helplessness of "late modern" architecture.

The first of these competitions produced the most spectacular of the buildings: the extension to the Museum of Decorative Arts. Containing one of the most important specialist collections in Germany, the museum had until then been housed in very inadequate conditions in the Villa Metzler, already mentioned, a neo-classical building designed as a private residence and naturally not at all suited to the needs of such a collection. The architect who won the international competition, the American Richard Meier, produced a design that integrated the various possible approaches to the case in point. One of the stipulations was that the still intact park landscape should be preserved; and it was around the Villa Metzler that the whole concept was to revolve. For what makes the Museumsufer a paradigm for urban planning and respect for the historical patrimony is the fact that every new museum and almost every extension built has been able to incorporate as its core one of the patrician villas that line the riverbank. Thus, the villas have been given a new use and preserved as historic monuments.

Meier's building, which is now regarded as one of the finest museums in the Federal Republic of Germany, angles itself around the historical core, which not only has been left as an independent entity but also recurs as the determinant module in the elevation and plan of the extension. Seen from the street, the external walls, clad with gleaming, white-enamelled panels, form a harmonious whole with the Villa Metzler. The new building, although it is much larger, is not monumental; it adapts to the historical scale. A variety of features links the interior with the exterior, integrating the ensemble of buildings quite organically into the park, which, with its systems of paths, gate designs and fountain is like a continuation of the museum in the urban space. Inside, a series of ramps conducts the visitor informally around.

After the long and sometimes controversial debate about the Museum of Ethnology, on the other side of the little Schaumainkai park, it was I think right to commission Richard Meier again to design the extension to this building. Along the same aesthetic lines as his Museum of Decorative Arts, this sizable structure will be set back from the other riverside buildings in order preserve as much as possible of the park and its fine trees, some of which are very rare. Meier's new building will fill one of the most serious gaps in the panorama of the museum landscape. It is not only that one of the largest ethnological collections in the Federal Republic, containing about 65,000 items, will at last have sufficient display space, but public interest in the cultural encounter with the Third World will now be adequately reflected in Frankfurt, venue of international trade fairs. Ethnological museums have long grown out of their old role as depositories for the spoils of colonialism, and they are also much more than collections of curiosities that only encourage a voyeuristic interest in the exotic. We will now be able to see in their proper ethnographic contexts the shrunken head and the totem pole that we encountered with a thrill of horror in our juvenile reading. Today, more than ever, the relationship between the highly industrialized countries and the civilizations of the "old" and "new" worlds needs redefining, because more than nodding acquaintance with foreign cultures is of great importance not only for the present but also for the future.

Before the new building for the Museum of Decorative Arts was erected, two institutions opened in mid-1984 that enriched the Frankfurt museum scene as new establishments in a very particular way: the German Film Museum and the German Architecture Museum. Their special cultural significance lies in the fact that it was the first time in the Federal Republic that two of the most important media were granted museum status.

Film, entirely a child of the twentieth century, had hitherto been neglected as a museum candidate because it was supposedly "not historical enough"; architecture, perhaps the oldest form of artistic expression known to man, directly affects every one of us today, often in a negative way – that may be the reason why it never occurred to anyone to create a museum of architecture. Well, hardly anyone, for way back in the 1920s Ernst May here in Frankfurt had the idea of a museum of town planning.

Now it is certainly not entirely easy to establish a museum for which there are hardly any precedents. And the critics were particularly quick to jump on the idea of an architecture museum. One of the chief objections was that architecture, which is in principle three-dimensional and so can really be experienced only "in the flesh", could not be properly conveyed with the means available in a museum. To counteract this argument right at the outset, it was decided at the planning stage to enlist the aid of a powerful ally: architecture itself.

The architect commissioned to build this museum, Oswald Mathias Ungers, oriented his plans right from the start on the idea of allowing the building itself to provide examples of those spatial relationships that people experience unconsciously every day with the architecture that surrounds them – but only unconsciously.

The museum comprises three types of building: a narrow glass-roofed hall, as high as the base of the old building which it encloses, a large rear hall, erected over part of the former garden of the villa, and finally, in the centre, the original building itself. This is therefore a "house within a house", whose five storeys illustrate the basic principles of architectural design: supports and loads, walls and space, and, finally, the archetype of the house. So architecture here becomes instructive; it is an entity in itself, not just a container for works of art.

Museum for Prehistory and Early History, interior

Both the Architecture Museum and the Film Museum exemplify the leitmotiv that governs the planning of the riverside strip and indeed of all the new Frankfurt museums: the unity of past and present.

Whereas Ungers, even more than Richard Meier, has made the old the point of departure for his considerations, reacting to the existing buildings in his new designs, Günter Behnisch has followed an entirely different concept in the new German Postal Museum, a little way along from the Architecture Museum: confrontation. Erected alongside a villa in English neo-renaissance style, his building is based on architectural principles quite different from those of the historical edifice. Old and new are equal partners for Behnisch. The main part of the exhibition-space is located below ground, under the garden and the old and new buildings, so that despite the large amount of space needed by the Postal Museum an effect of grandiosity has been avoided. The characteristics of the postal and telecommunications services find symbolic expression in the architecture.

The extension to the Städel, to plans by the Viennese architect Gustav Peichl, opened in the autumn of 1990. It became necessary because, fifty years after the city's art collection was decimated by the confiscation by the Nazis of nearly 500 "degenerate" works by modern artists, the Municipal Gallery has again built up a sizable stock of pictures.

On the basis of a progressive design that takes careful account of the requirements of a modern gallery, a building has been put up along Holbeinstrasse that not only pays homage to the tradition of a Gottfried Semper or an Oscar Sommer but is also distinguished by a contemporary, indeed highly individual architectural idiom. From the outside the extension seems very restrained, and the

Jewish Museum, interior

old building still dominates the scene. Like not much more than a garden wall, and aesthetically quite consistent with the effect of the material employed, reddish-yellow sandstone, it follows a scale that for all its monumentality is adapted to human proportions. The interior galleries are designed as unobtrusively as the exterior. The architecture does not dominate the works of art it houses but leaves the viewer room, allowing him to take his time and enter into a creative dialogue with the works on display.

So not only has the urgently needed space been created for an adequate presentation of the masterpieces of the twentieth century, but the building has also set an accent in urban design that restores to the overall complex of the Städel the unity that was inherent in its basic concept.

Through their relation to history, the Frankfurt museum-buildings have become paradigmatic not only for museum architecture but for architecture as a whole; this is also well exemplified by the recent buildings that strictly speaking do not form part of the Museumsufer. Two new museums were built in 1987 on the other side of the Main. The building for the museum that was particularly important to the people of Frankfurt met with spontaneous approval worldwide: it is the conversion of the Rothschild Palais, built in 1821 by Johann Friedrich Hess, into the Jewish Museum. The complex on Untermainkai consists of two buildings that were still fairly well preserved, their interior decoration also being of historical interest; thus, architectural intervention had to be conservative, within the framework of adaptive reuse. But what might seem to be a minimal architectural operation can be particularly difficult. The architect who was commissioned to carry out this conversion, Ante Josip von Kostelac, handled the job with great subtlety, and his new interior plan allows the museum to perform its didactic function adequately within the historical ambience.

While the new use of the Rothschild Palais has preserved an ensemble of buildings that was important for the historical atmosphere of the riverside area, the con-

German Architecture Museum, "house within the house"

version of and extension to the Carmelite monastery (which possesses one of Frankfurt's greatest art treasures in the restored mediaeval murals by Jörg Rathgeb) was a case of "urban repair" right from the start. The building now houses the Museum for Prehistory and Early History, which used to be accommodated in the little Holzhausen Palais and in the basement of the Culture Department building. The area around the ruin of the Carmelite monastery had sustained severe war damage, and had also suffered under subsequent urban planning that seemed to be concerned only with ensuring the smooth flow of motorized traffic. There were also untidy gaps between the buildings. Josef Paul Kleihues, the winner of the international competition for a new design, restored to the entire site its historical unity.

For the interior and the exterior a calm, pleasing architectural vocabulary was chosen that fits elegantly into its surroundings without subordinating itself. The architect has both upgraded the street outside as a zone of experience and created a communicative museum interior. The extension leaves the historical architecture almost untouched but adds to it what is in my view a very successful detail: the (originally wooden) late Gothic roof-structure with its elegant net-vault has been congenially recreated with modern means and materials.

In addition to these conversions and extensions, with their exciting combination of new and historical architecture, we also have exhibition-buildings that are entirely new. The largest of these is the Schirn, which forms a major element in one of the most important areas of Frankfurt – the Römerberg in the heart of the city. The construction of this communication centre was intended to meet one of the most urgent requirements of the Frankfurt exhibition scene: the need for a hall that would be flexible enough to accommodate the specialist in-depth exhibitions that nowadays appear to be an essential adjunct to the museums' own presentations. The reshaping of such a key area was not a matter to be decided on the toss of a coin; only after several competitions, numerous public discussions and much argument for and against was the design by Bangert, Jansen, Scholz & Schultes chosen for execution. The present and historical importance of the site, which lies between the Römer (where the kings of the Holy Roman Empire were elected) and the cathedral (where they were crowned from the sixteenth century onwards), was to be honoured in that the ensemble would consist of traditional types of building. Through a long arcade one reaches a glass-roofed rotunda, whose elevation quotes well-known models of centrally planned buildings, and which serves as an access lobby for the various wings of the complex. The actual exhibition area is a long gallery, while the concert-hall-cum-theatre with its barrel-vault is the embodiment of a quite different kind of room.

Conflict of opinions also surrounded the genesis of the Museum of Modern Art. Just as the establishment of the Municipal Gallery at the beginning of this century was intended to document what was then contemporary art, today we need a domicile specifically for current art, or art that has just become historical. Here, too, competition was held, and the Viennese architect Hans Hollein was the winner. In this building art is not only to be housed, it is also to be interpreted. An inner-city site was available, whose distinctive triangular shape has already earned the building the nickname "piece of cake". As the adjoining roads carry heavy traffic, the exterior is very solid-looking. The significance of the building as a museum whose contents centre upon the world-famous

German Film Museum, interior

Ströher collection of Pop Art is declared to the outside world by programmatic sculptural details.

In the spring of 1990 an icon museum, a branch of the Museum of Decorative Arts, was opened in the Deutschordenshaus, former headquarters of the Teutonic Knights. The severe, rationalistic conversion by O.M. Ungers occupies two storeys of one of the wings flanking the courtyard. And to round off our survey, we must not forget the Portikus Exhibition Hall. If in size and in aesthetic conception somewhat at odds with the general picture, this intriguing little building certainly offers its own solution to the problem of "ancient and modern".

The year 1990, with the opening of five new museums, sees an ambitious project almost completed, a project whose overall idea is not only to preserve the urban landscape on both sides of the Main but to upgrade it culturally, to make Frankfurt an exciting place to visit and to live in, where facilities for leisure and learning – in the most enjoyable way – are integrated on a high level. Those who explore Frankfurt's museum landscape will not be overwhelmed by its "monumentality". Unlike such cities as Paris, with its major projects ranging from the Centre Pompidou to the new Musée d'Orsay, or Cologne, which recently acquired a gigantic double museum, or Munich with its German Museum, Frankfurt has not aimed for the grand structure that combines a variety of media under one roof. The Frankfurt museums are more individual, more specific, but they are not isolated: they form a landscape. This is not a heroic, ideal landscape, it is more like a genre painting, dotted with scenes of everyday life. These are not always brightly coloured, do not always harmonize "agreeably", but they are exciting, and an encounter with them is always worth while.

Wolfgang Pehnt

A Stroll through the Museum Landscape

The continuing boom in museum building is truly astonishing. Not only in the public sector: in recent years private initiative has been making itself felt to an increasing extent. Even small provincial towns such as Weil, Schwendi or Kornwestheim are benefiting, as local patronage steps in where the municipal budget is not big enough. Frankfurt's share in this trend is eminently respectable, in quantity, concept and quality. It is hard to believe that such a radical about-turn took place in the course of just a few years: in 1967, hardly a decade before the rediscovery of the museum, the German Museum Association was lamenting the malaise of the museums in the Federal Republic; today the Association has to warn its members not to let prestige-hungry architects and local politicians monopolize the field.[1]

The old definition in the *Handbook of Architecture* was always a firm tenet of those who practised the politics of culture: "Museums ... are essential institutions in the state and the community, both for the edification and general education of the people and for the furtherance of serious study by scholars and artists."[2] But the classic formulation of the tasks of the museum – to preserve, to care for, to make accessible, to display – was clearly not enough to mobilize sufficient forces to solve the problems the museums were obviously facing. The reference to the educational value of museums, their function as a "counterweight to the growing superficiality of our times",[3] seemed hopelessly old-fashioned. What on earth, so soon after these prophecies of doom, impelled so many to embark upon the tiring trudge through institutions that offered nothing but lifeless objects? And what on earth induced the municipal, state, and finally federal politicians to devote considerable sums from their budgets to erecting buildings that seemed to offer no return at all?

There are many reasons; they are interconnected, and Frankfurt will serve as a good example of all of them. In view of the shortages in the first decade after the war, local authorities were not in a position to invest money equally in all sectors of building; they had to concentrate on housing as the first priority, then came schools, hospitals and public service buildings, which left very little to spare. Frankfurt was also staking its claim to be designated federal capital, which involved a sizable outlay of funds, and then there were the city's commitments as regards the new university buildings. Early cultural projects, like the rebuilding of St. Paul's Church and the

Goethe House – optimistic symbols of a cultural renaissance, a will to higher things – were by no means hailed on all sides: the city records for the winter of 1946/47 reveal that the reconstruction of St. Paul's was expressly bound up by council resolution with the rebuilding of one of the bombed-out housing-estates on the periphery, in order to assuage popular criticism of what was apparently a waste of money, labour and materials.[4]

What was absolutely essential was done for the Städel Art Institute and the Liebieghaus, but no more. As elsewhere, the theatre was given higher priority. The old playhouse was restored and enlarged in 1950 to serve as the main theatre and opera house, and a new playhouse, a workshop-theatre and a common foyer were added a decade later. With the reconstruction of the old opera house as a concert-hall, the people of Frankfurt fulfilled one of their dearest wishes, and this formed the spectacular overture to the rediscovery of history in Frankfurt am Main. The first major new museum building, the Historical Museum (1969–72), apparently did not count as a historical building, despite the fact that it incorporated genuinely historic elements with the Rententurm, the Bernusbau, the Burnitzbau, the *palas* from Staufer times, and the Saalhof chapel: the (moderate) concrete brutalism of the new wing appeared to have killed for a long time any enthusiasm the Frankfurters might have felt for museum building.

A similar sequence can be traced for the Federal Republic as a whole. Above and beyond their specific purposes, churches and theatres satisfied both the creative urge and the awakening need for prestige and display. The 1950s and 1960s saw the building of churches whose huge interiors would never be full, except perhaps at Christmas, and theatres and concert-halls whose most striking innovations were the planning of the foyer and interval facilities and the tiers that projected like open drawers or sloped down into the stalls. Gottfried Böhm's huge cathedral in Neviges and Hans Scharoun's Berlin Philharmonic Hall, where walkways and bridges lead the guests precariously down into the crater of the auditorium, marked the peak and end of developments in this genre.

The museum, on the other hand, did not at first seem to offer comparable opportunities for self-presentation to the masses who were now discovering that they constituted a "society": visiting a museum is something for the individual or the small group. Where new museums were built they did not nearly arouse that public interest – apart from Manfred Lehmbruck's Lehmbruck Museum in Duisburg (1959–64) and Mies van der Rohe's New National Gallery in Berlin (1965–68) – which the municipal theatres in Münster and Gelsenkirchen, the Liederhalle concert-hall in Stuttgart, the Philharmonic Hall in Berlin or the Beethoven Hall in Bonn were enjoying. It almost seems as if it were left to us of a later day to discover the qualities inherent in the early postwar buildings – Rudolf Schwarz's homely and at the same time sober and dignified Wallraf-Richartz Museum in Cologne (1951–57, now the Museum of Applied Art) or Hans Döllgast's creative reconstruction of the Alte Pinakothek gallery in Munich (1959–64). Only when the cycle of municipal and state prestige buildings was completed, when the town halls, theatres, sports arenas and multi-purpose halls had been built, did the museum really get its chance.

In the 1960s – but before the 1968 upheavals, in fact – the mission of the museums began to be redefined. The museum as a place of learning took precedence over the temple of culture. The time of the "dark museums" began, the black boxes in which the instructive but also exciting presentation could be mounted without distraction by the architecture that made it possible. Natural light was not desired – views of the outside world would only be confusing. The structural frame of the building would be in the way and should be concealed as far as possible. In Germany, the extensions to the Stiftung Preussischer Kulturbesitz museum in Berlin's Dahlem to accommodate non-European cultures (1964–70) and the Romano-Germanic Museum in Cologne (1967–74) were built as theatres in which gifted producers could "stage" exhibitions in the truest sense of the word. It was a concept that made these closed boxes, standing aloof from their environment, a questionable enrichment of the urban landscape. The most important presentation aid was the spotlight with its pointing pedagogical finger, and second most important was comprehensive explanatory material in the form of illuminated charts or taped commentaries. Frankfurt's Historisches Museum became notorious for its verbalization strategy, in which the exhibit was used to illustrate a preformulated thesis.

The strategy of the cultural institutions was also determined for years to come by another key word of the day: communication. Who was to communicate with whom about what, was by the by; the main thing was that communication should take place. This desideratum was based on the forecasts of a continuously rising productivity of labour that would result in people having more leisure time. The prophecies of the French sociologist Jean Fourastié little more[5] of a general reduction in working hours made a strong impression at the time on planners in the cultural sector. More leisure was equated with increasing demands on educational and cultural facilities and a growing level of knowledge. As a result,

Historisches Museum, Frankfurt am Main

institutions were needed that would provide information, further social integration, and promote creativity and cultural activity, so that all this would be made as pleasurable and undemanding as possible.

The first architectural requirement was to remove the psychological barriers that were felt to surround the traditional temples of culture, with their symbols of majesty, sweeping approach-steps, colonnades, pediments, ceremonial staircases and domed roofs. Now culture was to be something that anybody could enjoy, without in effect realizing that it was "culture". The best museum was the one people strayed into without noticing it. The architectural pattern was the public pathway that led through the museum complex, flanked by restaurants, cafeterias, and quite possibly shops and boutiques too. Every now and then there should be a window or peephole to give a glimpse of the temptingly displayed museum-treasures. Although attitudes were already beginning to change again, such pathways of enticement are found in most museums built in the 1970s and 1980s, in Mönchengladbach, Cologne, Hanover, Stuttgart, Düsseldorf. In Frankfurt such feeder routes, complete with restaurants, are a feature of the Schirn, with its rotunda in the public domain, and Richard Meier's Museum of Decorative Arts, which is intersected by a park axis parallel to the riverbank.

Another architectural consequence was the concept of the communication-centre, which ideally should combine everything under one roof. This universalist approach to culture was a first reaction against the functionalism of the Modern Movement, in which each function was to be catered for specifically: the school as a school, the church as a church, the theatre as a theatre, the museum as a museum. It was only later realized that this new trend also amounted to a sort of functionalism, and that the ideology of the centre as opposed to the intricacy of daily use would also lead to an isolation of the urban elements, only now in the shape of much larger units. The people would fare no better in these cultural centres than in the sports, shopping or school centres.

But since funds became available to improve the cultural facilities of the cities only after the more pressing social and commercial needs had been met, most municipalities did not have to make the decision: the cultural centre had by then been dropped from the agenda. Frankfurt's "Centre Pompidou", planned for the most attractive site in the city, between the Römer and the cathedral, was jettisoned. The first-prize-winners in the competition of 1962–63 had proposed a "comprehensive integrated complex", in which the floor area was parcelled out among no fewer than eleven different uses, including an art-gallery and exhibition-rooms, all rubbing shoulders with each other.[6] Not much of this programme survived to be incorporated in the later Schirn culture centre, which comprises separate, well-defined institutions, each with its own entrance, not the hodge-podge that the "communication" thesis of the 1960s would have required.

The "new" public that has made the new museums possible, and in turn been conditioned by them, evidently differs from the "culturally oriented" public as traditionally understood. But it is not the information-hungry, knowledge-thirsty "communication set" the 1960s theorists had in mind as clientele. These people come in trainers and bermuda shorts, baggy sweaters and anoraks, carry their babies in slings, and do not keep the older children on the leash. They believe in taking things easy, have no wish to be culturally "browbeaten".

"Most people visit a museum to be entertained and to enrich their general knowledge a little, without having very specific ideas of what they want to learn," as the museum sociologist puts it, pointing to the increased spontaneity and improvisation in leisure planning. Often the decision to visit a museum is made only at the breakfast table on the day in question, or is a sudden impulse when passing the entrance.[7]

The museum as an institution is oriented towards spontaneity. It is able to induce both the "feelings of solemnity" with which the eighteen-year-old Goethe entered the art-gallery in Dresden, and the feeling of being in a "fairground" of which Wilhelm Heinrich Wackenroder's "art-loving monk" complained, also a couple of centuries ago. Unlike the more conventionalized theatre and concert visits, for which tickets have usually to be purchased in advance so that people generally have to plan ahead, they can go to the museum any time, unless there happens to be a cult-show on, such as a Velázquez or Van Gogh exhibition. Theatre performances and concerts last for a specific length of time, but the visitor to a museum can decide for himself how long he wants to stay. The popularity museums are now enjoying has a lot to do with this greater spontaneity and flexibility, and also with curiosity, the desire to see what is currently being talked about. The architectural sensations of the new buildings have certainly sent the number of visitors shooting up, for a time at least – for curiosity is rarely an indicator of abiding worth.

That more people *want* to visit museums is also partly because more of them *can*. The slogan "Culture for all" meant so much to Hilmar Hoffmann, long-time head of Frankfurt's Culture Department and museum initiator, that he chose it as the title for a book:[8] it does apply, but only with reservations. Not everyone is a potential museum visitor, though certainly more people now come than used to; the level of formal education – still a criterion of the probability of a museum visit – has risen, and more people than ever before have A levels or a degree. Greater time-flexibility also benefits the museums: one-third of the visitors to German museums come in the morning.[9]

The museums react by providing rest-areas and refreshment rooms, reading niches and outdoor relaxation zones, to make the longer visit as pleasant as possible. Out-of-town museums, such as the Louisiana in Copenhagen or the Hombroich Island near Neuss, aim to give their guests a total tourist experience in which art is just one of many components, and this strategy has also rubbed off on the inner-city museums. Frankfurt's museum zone suggests the idea of an inner-city recreational landscape as idyllic setting for the temples of the Muses, and this idea is in fact realized up to a point on the south bank of the Main.

The criticism that the buildings often did not present their exhibits in the best possible way in museum-terms, sometimes indeed exposing them to detrimental influences, carried little weight with their builders. But even the German Museum Association, to which more than two thousand museums in the Federal Republic are affiliated, is now aware of the discrepancies between the ambitions of the urban planners and the needs of the museum curators. It is quite evident that these buildings were not created primarily for the exhibits they display, but for a public that seeks therein a synaesthetic experience composed of many ingredients – art being only one. Only when the overall form is original enough is it permissible to make the interior conventional, as in the upper storey enfilade of Stirling's Stuttgart State Gallery or the unendingly long gallery of the Frankfurt Schirn.

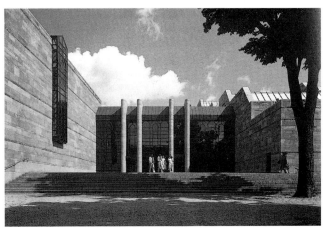

Neue Pinakothek, Munich

The museum as public institution is a child of the Age of Enlightenment. The right of free access to art was not the least significant of the demands formulated in the period leading up to the French Revolution. That feudal collectors permitted their possessions to be viewed and actually fixed regular opening-hours was one of the stages on the way to bourgeois emancipation. A further stage was the establishment and endowment of art or natural history collections by private citizens. In the former Free Imperial City of Frankfurt, Johann Christian Senckenberg, with his 1763 foundation that included a natural history collection, and Johann Friedrich Städel were part of this tradition. The deed of foundation for the Städel Art Institute, delivered in 1815, breathes the spirit of enlightenment when it provides that five worthy citizens should administer the institute "without recourse to authority or the need for official approval".

The development of the museum is that of increasing public access to art, and in this respect Hilmar Hoffmann's democratization campaign was also a legacy of the Age of Enlightenment. The Historisches Museum, with its inclusion of everyday culture and its emphasis on the didactic mission, was one of the last true "museums of enlightenment", representative of a philosophy which – even though adapted to the new attitudes of the 1968 generation – was by now falling more and more into disrepute.

Even the later museums founded or rehoused in Frankfurt do not break totally with the tradition. Their promotors have jumped on a new cultural bandwagon, which does not however mean returning to square one. Somehow the slogans of "emancipation" and "equality of opportunity" no longer really apply. Free and informal contact with aesthetic objects, the process of edification

Staatsgalerie Stuttgart

and instruction through the observation of scientific specimens and instruments, the broadening of the mind through encounters with the artefacts of other cultures or with the paraphernalia of modern communication techniques, all this is neither the exclusive nor the central motive of a visit to a museum today; the main thing is to participate in a "theatrical" experience.

The Frankfurt museum planners reacted to these premises. As a pendant to the "Who's who in art" presented by the collections, they compiled a "Who's who in architecture" by offering the public exciting architectural dramas by prominent personalities in the profession. "An art gallery, too, should be a unified work of art in itself":[10] this ideal was formulated in the nineteenth century, and it is only natural in our day and age, when architecture has become fully accepted as an art in itself, that the building of museums should be such a popular activity. But the late 1970s and the 1980s went further than the typified museum architecture of the nineteenth century. Even before the visitor has an opportunity to become familiar with the contents, the show has already started with the first glimpse of the building. Independent of the exhibitions shown within their walls, the museums themselves constitute a permanent exhibition. Architecture, as the painter Markus Lüpertz complains, is trying to be "more artistic than art".[11]

Although the Frankfurt competitions and the commissions that resulted were never officially declared to be an exhibition of architecture, they did add up to a sequence of events that tacitly, and at times quite explicit, competed with the International Building Exhibition that was running at the time in Berlin. The culture centre on the cathedral-Römerberg site, the subject of the 1962–63 competition, was to have been built by a local team of architects, Bartsch, Thürwächter & Weber; and the City Architect's Department had itself taken charge of the new building for the Historisches Museum in 1969. But with the awarding of the first commissions for the south bank of the Main, top names in the German and international architectural scene entered the arena: Günter Behnisch, Hans Hollein, Josef Paul Kleihues, Richard Meier, Gustav Peichl, Oswald Mathias Ungers, and – if one includes the buildings on Saalgasse and other urban projects – Norman Foster, Adolfo Natalini, Charles Moore and Robert Venturi. The inviting of specific architects to submit proposals, the composition of the juries, the cultural ambitions of Walter Wallmann, mayor of Frankfurt from 1978 to 1989, the enthusiasm of the city departmental heads concerned (besides Hoffmann, city architect Hans-Erhard Haverkampf), and the influence of Heinrich Klotz as founding director of the German Architecture Museum all guaranteed that the international standard was maintained. Newcomers to the scene, like the first-prize-winners for the Museum of Ethnology, praised by the jury for the "complex logic and the relaxed, almost light-hearted approach" of their design, had to bow out when Richard Meier's success with the Museum of Decorative Arts became apparent and he was called on to repeat it on the neighbouring site.

Varied as the styles of the architects involved may be, the changed conditions of museums and their visitors today are reflected in all the new buildings. Theatrical elements figure prominently. None of the buildings is based – as Oscar Sommer's Städel gallery of 1874–78 was – on a familiar type, a popular cliché, such as in the nineteenth century would have entailed a ceremonial approach, an imposing frontage worthy of a cultural institution, a hierarchical arrangement of rooms, and an axial plan for the top-lit galleries. The new museums each defined their premises for themselves, and the best of them did so with an eye to neighbouring buildings and the whole environmental situation. Surprises are to be expected; the unpredictability of the architectural experience is virtually part of the programme. The compulsion to be original must have weighed heavily on all the architects: nothing might be as it already was elsewhere – at best parallels were permitted only with their own work. It is all right for a Richard Meier building to look like a Richard Meier, but not like a Peter Eisenman or an Arata Isozaki, unless its creator wants to risk being expelled from the architectural Hall of Fame.

Unlike the glass museum of the 1960s, whose physical transparency was intended to draw attention to its contents – the exhibits – the museums of the last fifteen years or so, in Frankfurt and elsewhere, rely on the attractiveness of their buildings. The model here is not the display-case but the treasure-chest. Not so long ago rejected as being a deterrent to the prospective visitor, the threshold has been reintroduced, but at the same time the idea of crossing it has been made more intriguing.

Entrance areas are less clearly defined: at the German Architecture Museum one has to search for the doors of the porch among the piers of the arcade before one can enter; at the Museum of Decorative Arts the entrance is tucked away at the side of the courtyard, on the right between two projecting parts of the building; at the Museum for Prehistory and Early History one sees visitors wander right round the museum and monastery complex before they decipher the message of the library wing that projects obliquely on stilts – "this way in". With a hint of mystery and a few come-hither signals, the external architecture entices the passer-by to come in and explore the interior. This has proved the more effective tactic; the building as puzzle acts as a challenge to solve it.

Inside the buildings, it is striking how much inventiveness shows in the treatment of the circulation areas, the foyers, stairs, ramps, landings, galleries, corridors. The stairs leading around the oblique interior tower of Helge Bofinger's German Film Museum and its cascade of steps down to the basement, the false facade in Richard Meier's Museum of Decorative Arts that affords a view from the ramps into the interior and vice versa, the cy-

Nationalgalerie, Berlin

lindrical hall of the Schirn, with its dialectic of public area on the ground floor and paying exhibition-zone on the inner perimeter of the rotunda above, the interior balcony on stilts in Kleihues's Museum for Prehistory and Early History – all these constitute stages on which the coming and going of the visitors is presented as an exhibit in its own right, more compelling even than the contents of the museum. "Everywhere one can at will relax one's concentration and take in the whole with its kaleidoscopically changing views, and every time the relationship of the architecture to its contents also changes," says Norbert Huse of Richard Meier's creation.[12] The silent confrontation of the individual with the art-work no longer seems to be the aim. The visitors are kept constantly circulating. The new museums thematize their own reception by showing not only what is to be contemplated, but the act of contemplation itself. The problems that Ante Josip von Kostelac had in establishing the vertical and horizontal perspectives inside the Jewish Museum show how important this aspect is for architects.

The need to produce something original to satisfy the client's, or the architect's own, expectations also involves the obligation to find for the various situations striking images, often images that can described verbally. Ungers' "house within the house" and his morphological sequence of architectural principles demonstrates, appropriately enough in an architectural museum, the possibilities of such a "logo" when used to effect by a philosopher-architect. Hollein's Museum of Modern Art, a great hulk with decorated prow that dramatizes the conflict between old town and the bulldozing for modernistic thoroughfares, is an equally suitable candidate for verbalization. The triggering impulse here was not the dialectic stimulation of the shell of an old building, as it was for Ungers, but the accident of the sharp-pointed triangular site-configuration.

In view of the status that cultural institutions have now attained in urban development programmes, it was evidently not enough simply to give each building a strikingly individualistic form. A neat motto had to be found for the whole sequence of new buildings, which would justify all the various projects as parts of an overall concept in municipal policy and would also come in handy for public relations. Thus, we now find "museum miles", "cultural forums", etc. all over the place. They have a propaganda function and are moreover the continuation of a tradition that goes back to long before PR was ever heard of in civic offices. In Berlin the Spree island was called the "Museum Island" back in kaiser times, although the name "Schlossinsel" (Palace Island) would have been more appropriate on historical and political grounds.[13] In Frankfurt they coined the term "Museumsufer" (Riverside Museum Strip), which was already current by about 1980. Within a few years the formula had engendered new foundations, among which fields were covered that do not immediately spring to mind as being suitable for museums – for example film, architecture.

The term was appropriate in view of the fact that even before the new museum wave a number of older institutions were already established on the left bank of the Main – first and foremost the Städel and the Liebieghaus, and also the postal, ethnological and prehistorical collections in their makeshift premises. Once it had been coined, the term was soon applied to the other side of the Main as well. The Historisches Museum, with its integrated historical components, was indeed on the riverbank; the Jewish Museum in the Rothschild Palais was a second focal point on the right bank of the Main, and the little Portikus gallery a third. Myths have a tendency to absorb nonconforming facts as well, and today the Museumsufer also includes buildings that are not on the river, like the Museum for Prehistory and Early History, the Goethe Museum, the Steinernes Haus of the Art Association, the Schirn Arts Gallery, the Leinwandhaus, and the Museum of Modern Art. Admittedly, seen from a helicopter, when the Frankfurt panorama extends to

the edges of the Taunus and Vogelsberg hills, virtually all of the old town is on the riverbank.

Chance had it that in this arrangement the local museums are on the right bank, i.e. in the centre of the city to which they relate, while the supra-regionally or internationally oriented museums are on the left bank. The "international" Museum of Modern Art on the "local" or north side of the Main is the single exception, a minor blemish in this logical pattern. It was not an accident but a deliberate planning decision – prompted by the historical premises – that Frankfurt did not build one of those hybrid museums that have been created in other cities in recent decades – the Centre Pompidou and the Musée d'Orsay in Paris, the Wallraf-Richartz and Ludwig museums in Cologne, or the museum complex of the Stiftung Preussischer Kulturbesitz now taking shape on the edge of the Tiergarten in Berlin. In Frankfurt it was thus possible to use the various smaller buildings and institutions as chessmen in the town-planning game, deploying them across the inner city in a network of foci of urban upgrading. The organizational advantage of this multiple, decentralized concept was that the projects could be realized gradually and independently of one other, as funds became available, and that priorities could be set without jeopardizing the whole. Moreover, opening the various institutions one after another over a number of years also had prestige value in that the public gained the impression of a busy cultural commitment, with new ideas constantly being promoted. The many small buildings, moreover, did not cost very much more than a single large complex would have done.

The establishment of the museum-zone as a chain of individual institutions permitted villas to be preserved on the Sachsenhausen side of the river that were essential for the city's image. For two hundred years the contrast of the tightly packed old town and the mansions set in their park-like gardens, lying like a suburban belt before you come to Sachsenhausen with its village character, was one of the most charming and typical features of Frankfurt. Here the wealthy merchant families could enjoy the pleasant side of country life and at the same time view the source of their prosperity, the city with its markets and counting-houses. What was left of this villa scene was rescued at the last minute by the passing of the Museumsufer resolution.

That the Museumsufer denoted not an agglomeration of different buildings but a holistic concept that would require major involvement of the urban planners was already evident when the first new museums were built. Till Behrens and Jochen Rahe used the Frankfurt Forum for Urban Development, a citizens' action-group for alternative town planning, to call attention to the destructive consequences of the widening of the embankment roads. They demanded that the interrelation of the two halves of the city be emphasized by new north–south links: "Frankfurt lies on the Main and not on two riverside clearways." This recalls an assertion made in 1886,

Städtisches Museum Abteiberg, Mönchengladbach

that the river and its banks was the city's finest and most important thoroughfare.[14] Such ideas were taken up in the report commissioned from the planners Speerplan in April 1980, which proposed a new pedestrian bridge downriver from Untermain Bridge as a counterpart to the Eiserner Steg; this has now been built. With the Museumsufer began a new awareness, which was also making itself felt in other cities that had hitherto neglected the potential of their rivers – Berlin, Cologne, Munich – though compared with Frankfurt they have so far relatively little to show for this process of reassessment.

The museum programme helped to polish up Frankfurt's tarnished image. It gave culture a footing once again in a city notorious for large-scale speculation, demolition, indiscriminate road building – anything for a quick profit. Where the city had been criticized for living entirely in the present, with its 380 banks and insurance-companies and the second-largest airport in Europe, the museums have given it a welcome stratum of historical depth, reintegrating the past with the present – all the more so as the extensions and conversions, from the Carmelite monastery to the nineteenth-century villas, have indeed helped to preserve historic monuments. Even if such a fine specimen as the neo-classical Villa Metzler had never been seriously at risk, the villa from the less esteemed Late Wilhelmine period, into which Ungers implanted his German Architecture Museum, had already been scheduled for demolition. "Only a contemplation of the past will enable us properly to appreciate the momentum and dynamic of the age we live in," wrote Jacob Burckhardt, a formulation that, even from the pen of this particular author, is not entirely without admiration for the irresistible force of progress.[15] Today we must rather say that the speed and uncertainty of change make it necessary to seek anchors in the past.

The city has improved its image considerably with its cultural investments. The museum projects have helped in no uncertain measure to mollify the critics, who did not return to the attack even when a new economic boom brought the prospect of more and more skyscrapers and multi-lane highways. The idyll is indissolubly bound up with the commercial activity that is both a prerequisite and a consequence. That the tourists who come to the museums and exhibitions spend much more than the price of admission while they are in town is but a minor item. The important thing is that a strong cultural policy promotes the continuing growth of the city as a service-centre. Investors, too, prefer to put their money in places that offer a cultural infrastructure and an attractive cityscape, besides favourable location on main traffic routes and a wealth of commercial contacts. All this is not exclusive to Frankfurt, but it certainly applies here. Seen in this light, the 11.5 per cent of the municipal budget that Frankfurt spends on culture every year (a greater proportion than any other city) is not

Museum Ludwig, Cologne

patronage, it is indirect financing which flows back into the civic coffers. From the windows of the new museums on the south bank, financiers and local politicians can, when they have satisfied their interest in Ming porcelain or Sepik sculptures, cast a satisfied glance at the tower-block silhouettes on the other side of the river. Yes sir, the cultural investment has paid off. The productive factor art salutes the productive factor capital.

Architecture in turn has profited from the Frankfurt programme inasmuch as here the architects were confronted with out-of-the-ordinary challenges, and challenges have never hurt architecture. The competitive element, with so many prominent members of the profession vying with each other, might have inspired particularly extravagant ideas, and some of the designs are indeed landmarks in the history of architecture. But despite the unwritten law requiring originality, an all too free rein was ruled out by the relatively modest dimensions of the sites, the height, depth and width restrictions, and the consideration of existing buildings and trees. There were always historical factors to be taken into account, and this was willingly accepted by almost all the architects. Richard Meier confounded the sceptics with his Museum of Decorative Arts, brilliantly striking that elusive balance between self-assertion and respect for the environment. Oswald Mathias Ungers could hardly have realized the idea of a house within a house so effectively in a completely new building as he does here, incorporating an astral inner body into a profane physical shell. Not every allusion is successful, particularly when it is more quotation than integral element of the composition. When Josef Paul Kleihues draws a parallel to, among other things, Friedrich August Stüler's stock-exchange building in the striped wallpaper of his "monastery wall" in the Museum for Prehistory and Early History, the transfer is not very illuminating. Why should the extension to a mediaeval monastery recall a lost commercial building, the design for which had anyway been imported from Berlin? On the other hand, this same Kleihues has shown in the Carmelite church, where he replaced the destroyed Gothic vault with a new steel roof-structure, how true the saying is – give or take six hundred years – that "great minds think alike".

The confrontation with what used to be has given the Frankfurt museum buildings a qualitative dimension that the new Italian museums had already acquired in the 1950s and 1960s, embedded as they are in the ample substrate of *centri storici*. Furthermore, new possibilities were opened up by the definition of the museum as a place of leisure and recreation. The art of *flânerie* has been nostalgically revived in recent years, and this has led architects to address themselves again to the idea of the "promenade". In Frankfurt, the *flâneur* now has a route where he can stroll pleasantly along beneath plane trees, pausing now here, now there, to regard with de-

tached curiosity the Melanesian men's house, to pay his respects to Myron's Athene, to study with vague interest the workings of the magic lantern. The dialectic of the place of learning and the temple of the Muses has long been superseded. Pleasure and edification have formed a coalition, just as a CDU mayor and an SPD culture-director once came to terms in Frankfurt. No longer uneasy bedfellows, there is peaceful coexistence between education and aesthetic pleasure, entertainment value and the purely economic factor, the residue of social commitment and the still conceivable "enlightening" moment, the slight shiver of awe and, under certain weather conditions, the occasional fresh breeze along the river.

1 *Zur heutigen Lage der deutschen Museen*, Memorandum des Deutschen Museumsbundes, typescript, Bonn 1967 – Resolution of Deutscher Museumsbund, Kempten 1990.

2 Heinrich Wagner, "Museen", in *Handbuch der Architektur*, ed. by Josef Durm, Part IV, Vol. 6, No. 4, Darmstadt 1893, p. 173.

3 *Zur heutigen Lage …*, as Note 1, p. 2.

4 Wendelin Leweke, "Geschichte der Paulskirche", in *Die Paulskirche in Frankfurt am Main*, Schriftenreihe des Hochbauamtes zu Bauaufgaben der Stadt Frankfurt am Main, Frankfurt 1988, p. 42.

5 Jean Fourastié, *Le grand espoir du XXIème siècle*, Paris 1949.

6 Presse- und Informationsamt der Stadt Frankfurt am Main, *Zur Diskussion: Was kommt zwischen Dom und Römer*, Frankfurt 1975, unpaginated.

7 Hans Joachim Klein, *Analyse von Besucherstrukturen an ausgewählten Museen in der Bundesrepublik und in Berlin (West)*, Materialien aus dem Institut für Museumskunde 9, Berlin 1984, p. 7 f.

8 Hilmar Hofmann, *Kultur für alle*, Frankfurt 1979.

9 Klein, as Note 7, *passim*.

10 Description of an anonymous design for the Kunsthalle in Hamburg, quoted in: Volker Plagemann, *Das deutsche Kunstmuseum 1790–1870*, Studien zur Kunst des neunzehnten Jahrhunderts 3, Munich 1967, p. 10.

11 Markus Lüpertz, "Kunst und Architektur", in: *Neue Museumsbauten in der Bundesrepublik Deutschland*, by Heinrich Klotz and Waltraud Krase, Stuttgart 1985, p. 32.

12 Norbert Huse, "'Öffentlicher Kontext' und 'urbane Struktur': Richard Meier in Frankfurt am Main", in *Richard Meier, Museum für Kunsthandwerk, Frankfurt am Main*, Berlin 1985, p. 12.

13 A competition for the development of the site contained the word "Museumsinsel" in its title as long ago as 1883.

14 Till Behrens, Jochen Rahe, "Die Frankfurter Mainufer: Museen – Grün – Verkehr, *Beiträge zur Frankfurter Stadtentwicklung 8*, January 1980, p. 9. – Architekten- und Ingenieurverein, *Frankfurt am Main und seine Bauten*, Frankfurt 1886.

15 Jacob Burckhardt, quoted in: Klaus Laermann, "Vom Sinn des Zitierens", *Merkur* 428, September 1984, p. 672 ff.

Roland Burgard

Towards New Architectural Dimensions

Frankfurt's new museum buildings are cornerstones and keystones in a programme of urban renewal that aims to bring to a conclusion the work of postwar reconstruction and to correct mistakes that have been made.

Urban development in the historical part of town has taken a different course in the four decades since the end of the war from that along the banks of the Main. Accordingly, the tasks faced by planners and architects were also different. A brief survey will show the significance of the 1980s in particular for the history of reconstruction after the ravages of war and speculation.

Postwar development of what had once been the mediaeval town centre proceeded in fits and starts but initially had no impact on the area around the cathedral (Dom) and town hall (Römer). The traffic-planners were the first to seize their chance, announcing a competition for a main artery in 1947; this established the present course of Berliner Strasse, Kurt-Schumacher-Strasse and Konrad-Adenauer-Strasse. The general streetline plan of 1948 fixed the building-areas and traffic-routes for the entire inner city.

Between 1949 and 1951 proposals were put forward for the reconstruction of the old town, and these led to the 1950/51 competition for the area between the cathedral and the town hall. The residential building along the north bank of the Main and around the cathedral dates from this period. Again in 1950/51, a restricted competition was held for the reconstruction of the town hall, and the adjacent site, the Römerberg, was the subject of a competition in 1951. The results caused heated discussion on the question of whether the houses should present their gables or their eaves ends to the street. The eaves party won the day but their victory was short-lived, for the only two houses to be built on the east side had to be pulled down again in 1969 when the trams were rerouted underground. In 1963 an international competition was held to find new ideas, under the motto "Frankfurt and the World". The programme for the area included a wide variety of uses, such as an exhibition-hall, a cabaret-theatre, a public library, a youth-centre, cafés, shops and a hotel; an extension was also to be built to the municipal offices. The final form of the winning project only remotely recalled the competition entry. The construction of the underground tram system, which passes under the Dom-Römerberg area and has a station there, induced the municipal assembly to decide in 1969 to build the extension to the municipal

offices, housing the Public Works Department, and an underground car park stretching from the cathedral to the Römer. After the completion of these two projects in 1972, the rest of the area was left to its own devices until 1979.

By the end of the 1970s, of the area between Berliner Strasse, Konrad-Adenauer-Strasse, Kurt-Schumacher-Strasse and the north bank of the Main only the Dom-Römerberg area, the Leinwandhaus, the triangular site between Domstrasse, Braubachstrasse and Berliner Strasse, the site Domstrasse 7, and the Carmelite church had not been rebuilt. All of these sites, with the exception of a few small pockets, were owned by the city of Frankfurt.

In 1972 the first new municipal museum of the postwar period, the Historisches Museum, was opened. It stands between the Burnitzbau and the south-west corner of the Römerberg. In 1978 the city council decided to erect a new building for the Museum for Prehistory and Early History adjacent to the Carmelite monastery. In the same year came the decision to rebuild the Leinwandhaus, the former Historisches Museum, as a gallery. For the rest of the Dom-Römerberg area, which was still awaiting development, an area programme was prepared in 1979 to include a hall for touring exhibitions, a youth music school, and a centre for old people and the handicapped. In 1982, after detailed study of various possible locations including the riverbank, it was decided to build the new Museum of Modern Art on the triangular site between Domstrasse, Braubachstrasse and Berliner Strasse.

Competitions were held for all the projects, whereby stress was laid on the observance of the structure of the historical city as far as was feasible, given the major changes in the urban plan that rebuilding had caused. Finally, in 1987, the concept for the new museum buildings in the Dom-Römerberg area was revised to include a Cathedral Museum.

The Römerberg, the focal point of the efforts to revive the historical core of the city through the creation of cultural facilities, lies between two traffic arteries, Mainkai to the south and Braubachstrasse to the north. Both tangents have been revitalized and given a new cultural image. While on the riverside it is the museums that attract the visitors, the northern interface with the modern city caters for art-lovers of all persuasions with a rich assortment of galleries. A large number of art-dealers have already set up shop along Braubachstrasse, between the new Museum of Modern Art in the east and the Carmelite monastery in the west. Efforts are being made to create a congenial environment for the museums: the Werkbundhaus in Weissadlergasse, in which the Federation of German Architects also has made its home, is one fruit thereof.

The whole idea, which is also designed to promote the local economy, was made possible by the close cooperation between Ernst Gerhardt, the city treasurer, Hilmar Hoffmann, director of the Department of Culture, and Hans-Erhard Haverkampf, the city architect.

The idea of a Museumsufer, a string of museums along the river embankment, developed from small beginnings in the early 1970s. The chief consideration was the conservation of the cityscape on the Sachsenhausen bank of the Main, with its abundant greenery. A first attempt was made to prevent the villas in their big gardens from falling into the hands of property speculators by placing them under preservation order. Then the city of Frankfurt acquired some of the buildings. The best way to keep their unique character as unchanged as possible was to adapt them to new uses in the cultural sector.

Thus was born the binding principle of distributing the art treasures among the existing buildings on the south bank, conservatively modernizing and extending

German Architecture Museum under construction

these buildings and avoiding demolition or new building on a monumental scale. It was widely felt at the time that the brash, self-assertive buildings of the International Style had had a detrimental effect on the city's image, and debate began on how to do justice to the historical context by adopting a more appropriate scale. It seemed meaningful to counteract the massing of commercial tower-blocks north of the river with a "monoculture" of buildings dedicated to culture on the south bank, between Friedensbrücke and Eiserner Steg bridges. Towards the end of the 1980s another factor was assuming more and more importance: the need to protect the existing green areas.

Preparations for the implementation of the Museumsufer project began in the summer of 1978, when the spatial programmes for the German Architecture Museum, the German Film Museum, the Museum of Decorative Arts and the Museum for Prehistory and Early History were drawn up. In 1982 discussion began on the concept for the Jewish Museum. The same year, the location for the Museum of Modern Art was decided and the competition held.

In the summer of 1980 the City Planning Department commissioned Albert Speer Architects and their project director Hanskarl Protzmann, later city architect of Frankfurt, to make an assessment of the projects that had just been launched and carry out an analysis of the need for extensions to existing museums. They were also to submit proposals for the location of projected institutions such as the Jewish Museum and the Museum of Modern Art. Of the three traffic-planning schemes envisaged in the "Speerplan" – the prolongation of the Theatre Tunnel along Berliner Strasse, the closure of Hofstrasse to motor traffic, and the new Holbeinsteg footbridge – this last was realized, and opened in 1990.

The decision of the Federal Post Office to build the new German Postal Museum on Schaumainkai provided a welcome addition to the riverside museum landscape; the competition was held in 1983.

The final phase of the Museumsufer programme began in 1986/87. With the competitions for the Museum of Ethnology and for the extension to the Städel Art Institute and the direct commissions for the Icon Museum and the Portikus, a relic of the old municipal library, four museums or exhibition-hall projects were started at once. The vision of a comprehensive museum landscape will soon become reality. The reconstruction of the Römerberg area, the filling of the last vacant lots, and the cultural upgrading of the embankments are of the very greatest importance for the development of Frankfurt. The River Main, always a magnet for the people of the city, has acquired a new appeal.

The end of the 1970s saw a climate in Frankfurt that was uniquely favourable to architecture. The many activities of the architecture-department of the Städel School, the preparations for the founding of the German Architecture Museum, and the constantly growing pub-

Schirn Art Gallery under construction

lic interest in questions of building were major contributory factors. With the wealth of new architectural projects the question necessarily arose as to how and by whom the planning and building should be carried out. The public authorities were aware of their responsibility for local architectural culture, and they wanted to raise it above the provincial level.

While the influence of the municipality on building in the private sector is basically limited to questions of planning permission and the enforcement of building codes (unless the investor and his architect are open to suggestions and willing to cooperate), it can exert a much greater influence on public projects. If a city is to possess private and public architecture that bears comparison by international standards, the role of the local authority is a crucial one: the standards it sets will often be emulated in the private sector; the people will identify with good public buildings; these usually occupy prime locations and therefore cannot fail to catch the eye; and the designer has a freer hand when there is no individual profit motive.

The target was defined in the concrete formulation of the specific projects: all building in Frankfurt has to stand comparison with Ernst May's "New Frankfurt", which is still the standard of quality in building today and for the foreseeable future. But elsewhere as well in the last five decades important examples of architectural concepts have been created by public and private entrepreneurs: even a small town like Columbus in the Mid-West of the United States has achieved great things with its schools and public buildings. For big international companies such as IBM, Olivetti and Siemens their buildings are part of the corporate image. All this needed to be borne in mind.

Directly after Hans-Erhard Haverkampf was appointed city architect in 1978, preparations began for the first series of museum competitions. The principle was adopted that architects representing widely divergent schools of thought should be invited to compete and articulate their standpoints in a Frankfurt museum project. The theoretical approach of the participants was more important than their actual experience in building; even firms that had no buildings to show as references were invited. To be sure of getting a really varied response, it was necessary to issue invitations internationally.

In the course of the open and the restricted competitions it became evident that certain key features of German competition practice discouraged foreign architects from participating. The anonymous procedure in the Federal Republic favours the design that seems best suited to the site in question; neither the personality of the architect nor the possibility of adapting and refining the project is taken into account. The obviously necessary dialogue between user and designer in evolving the concept does not take place. For architects who were not accustomed to the German competition system this factor, plus the difficulty of assessing specific local conditions, the relevance of preservation orders, etc., made it a risky venture. It also proved to be not always constructive to invite architects of a highly dogmatic turn of mind, for one could never be sure that any proposals they might submit could be realized in practice.

Museum of Modern Art under construction

Museum building was a central theme in architecture everywhere in the 1980s. Inevitably it became a battleground on which the conflict of doctrines and personalities was fought out. The essential discussion between user and architect over the balance between function and form was often obscured by the interests of those involved, who were all too well aware of the publicity value attaching to such projects. While for the architects museum building was for ten years and more a highly progressive field, in which the latest ideas and techniques could be tried out, the curators dreamed of four walls, a floor and a ceiling in which to display their collections. Their classical commitment as museums to "collecting, research and preservation" was in direct conflict with the architects' eagerness to experiment.

The inevitable bone of contention was: Does an exhibit need architecture? Or, does architecture need an exhibit? Does the one distract attention from the other? The debate was particularly controversial in the case of museums housing works of art. When architecture sees itself as art, two art forms collide. Does a work of art need art as a background? The question of priority is inescapable.

The architects found the question quite insoluble at first, for they felt called upon to create a total work of art. There were, however, from the outset, the exhibits to be borne in mind and certain quite categorical requirements to be observed. Since exhibits are first and foremost visually perceived, the illumination of the object determines the architecture. Some collections require side-lighting, others need to be top-lit; some require natural light, others artificial light. According to recent studies, storerooms can be used to present museum collections instructively, and even a workshop might be a suitable environment for some types of museum. The exhibits also require special atmospheric conditions if they are not to deteriorate. In the newly built Frankfurt museums it was easy enough to provide the lighting and air-conditioning needed for conservation purposes, but wherever museums were installed in old buildings that had hitherto been used for other purposes, compromises naturally had to be made, and these gave the curators some heartaches. The obligation to preserve the substance of the building impaired the conservational function of the museum.

Most of the Frankfurt museum projects found their architects through competitions. After the jury's decision it was a case of thrashing out an optimal version of the chosen project. It is worthy of note that all the municipal projects, even those of considerable size, were realized following the conservative "studio principle", that is, every stage in the work had to be approved by the chief architect or senior partner, and even minor decisions could be taken only at the top. Perhaps it is this rather old-fashioned way of working that guarantees a high quality of architecture; but the success of this leadership principle depends on how much time the head of the firm has available. A further common feature was the thoroughness with which the work was done, a thoroughness to which the scale of fees hardly did justice. Volumetric planning was handled in a variety of ways: while one spatial concept emerged simply from plan and elevation drawings, others were meticulously worked out with the help of many models, and constantly revised. Paradoxically, the advocates of both methods were generally equally surprised by the concrete results they saw on the building site.

The Frankfurt museums have acquired a new function in recent years, for the objectives of communal cultural policy have changed considerably since the 1970s. The city fathers used to see culture as a means of counteracting the growing commercialization of the urban scene; today they see it as a major factor in making the city an attractive place in which to live, work, and even holiday. In the competition between German and European metropoles a building policy oriented towards quality of design is a powerful ally. Frankfurt's museums play an important role in winning friends for the city, but their primary task will always be that of museums everywhere: to safeguard our cultural heritage even it it is sometimes difficult.

The Museums

Jüdisches Museum

Jewish Museum

Architect: ANTE JOSIP VON KOSTELAC

Built: 1985–1989

The objective was to incorporate all the functional space needed for the museum of Jewish history in the houses Untermainkai 14 and 15, with only very slight alterations.

The original division of the building into two units was not changed, it was utilized functionally. Number 15 houses the permanent collection, while No. 14 is used mainly for temporary events – touring exhibitions and lectures. Number 14 can therefore be closed to the public at times without causing any confusion.

The two houses were treated differently, in keeping with the differences in their substance. While No. 15 had many rooms with an interior decoration that was worth preserving, subsequent alterations had made the room divisions in No. 14 confused, too small, and not very suited to museum use. Hence the design provided for rearrangement here, although the statics were not changed.

The area enclosed is 14,200 cubic metres, the main area of use 2,250 square metres. The building costs were DM 28,000,000.

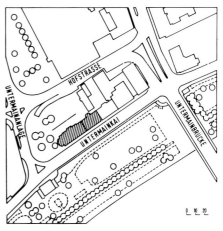

Untermainkai 14–15 (Rothschild Palace)

Isometric projection

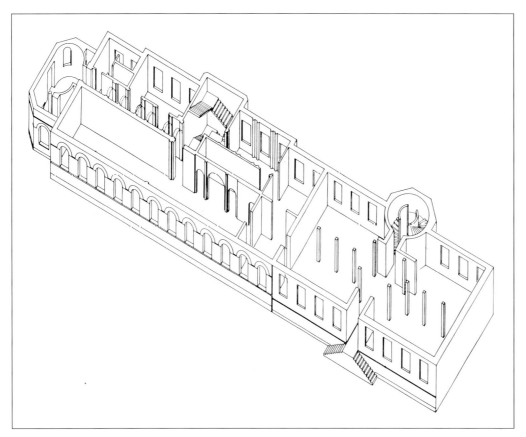

Isometric projection of ground floor

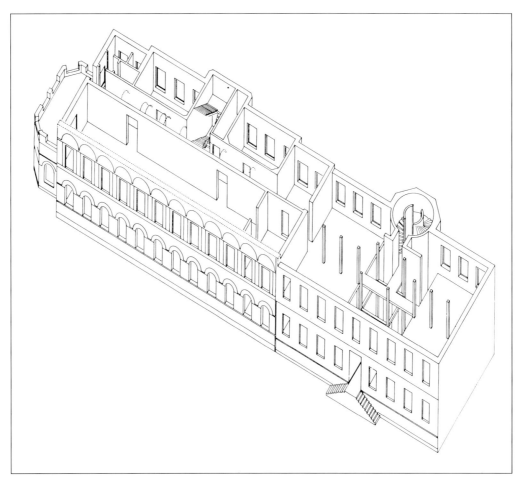

Isometric projection of first floor

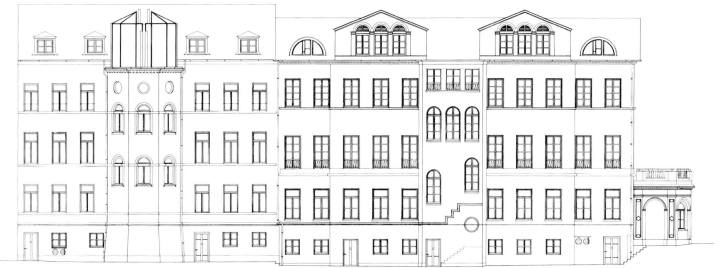

View from north

View from south

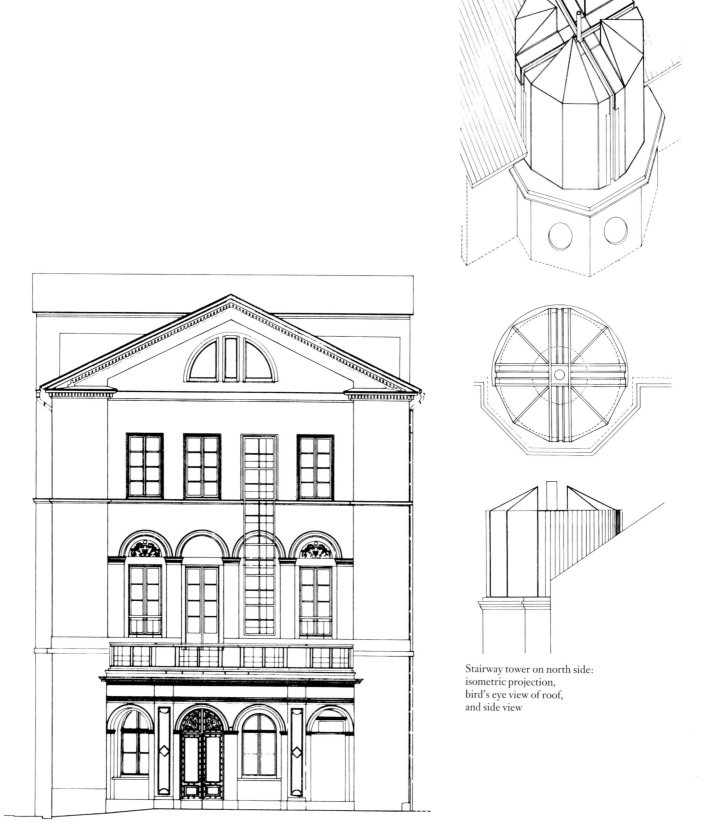

Stairway tower on north side:
isometric projection,
bird's eye view of roof,
and side view

View from west

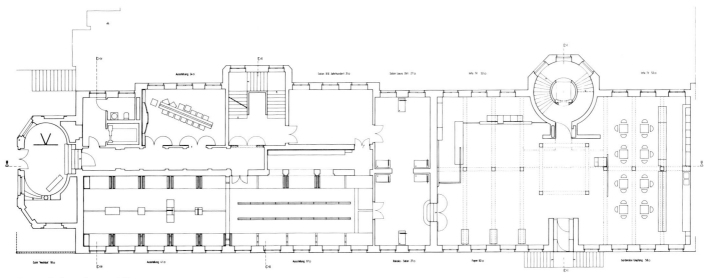

Ground-plan of ground floor

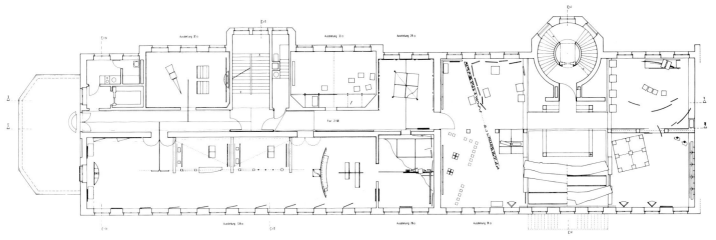

Ground-plan of first floor

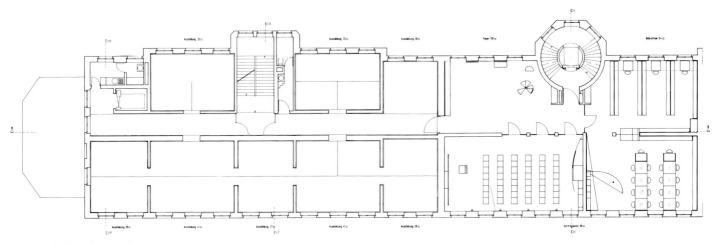

Ground-plan of second floor

Longitudinal section

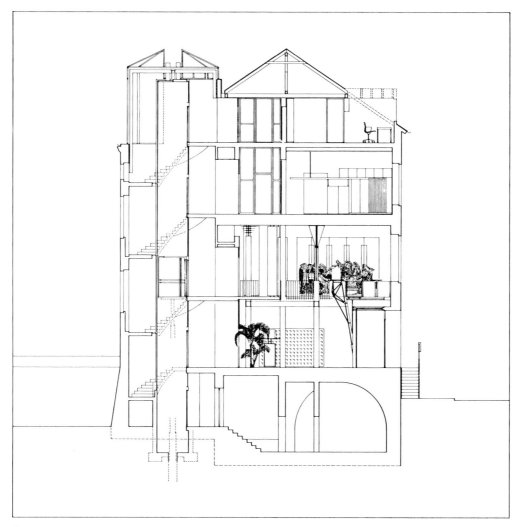

Cross-section

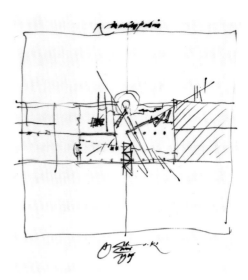

Plan-sketch of foyer

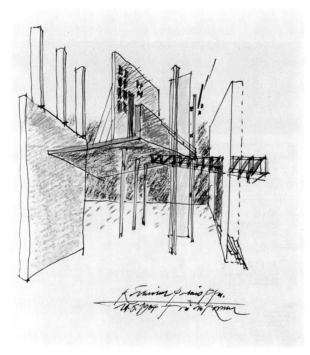

Isometric sketch of foyer

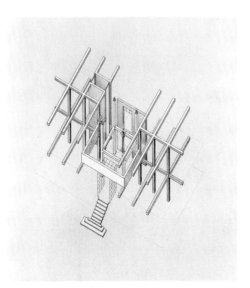

Isometric projection of foyer

Perspective section

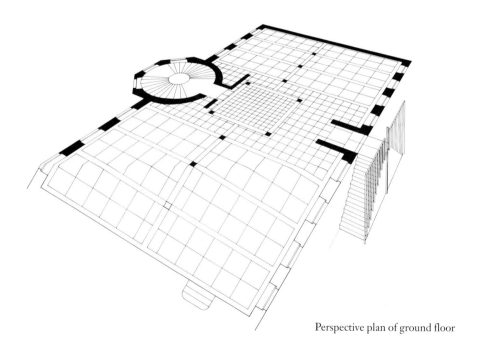

Perspective plan of ground floor

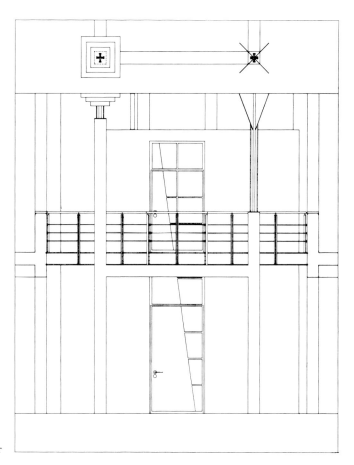

Elevation of foyer

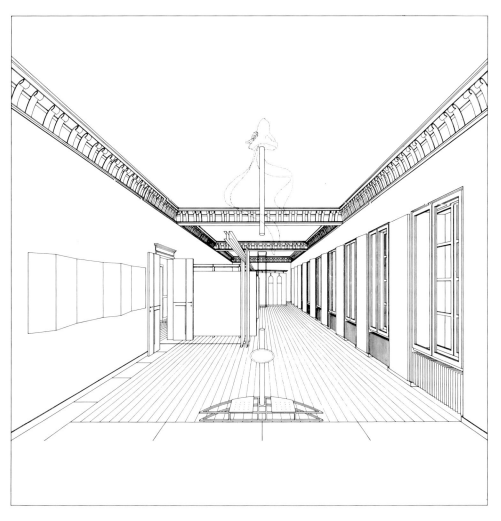

Perspective view of exhibition-room
for nineteenth century

Perspective view of the room for temporary exhibitions

Perspective view of the room for temporary exhibitions

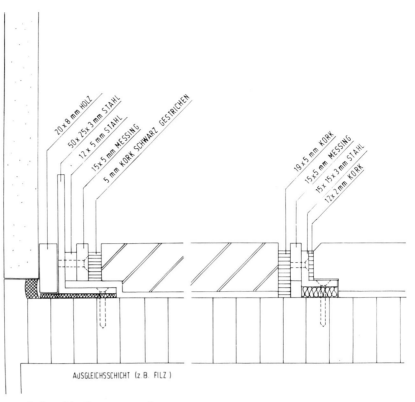

20 x 8 mm HOLZ
50 x 25 x 3 mm STAHL
12 x 5 mm STAHL
15 x 5 mm MESSING
5 mm KORK SCHWARZ GESTRICHEN

19 x 5 mm KORK
15 x 5 mm MESSING
15 x 15 x 3 mm STAHL
12 x 2 mm KORK

AUSGLEICHSSCHICHT (z.B. FILZ)

Detail-plan of the floor construction

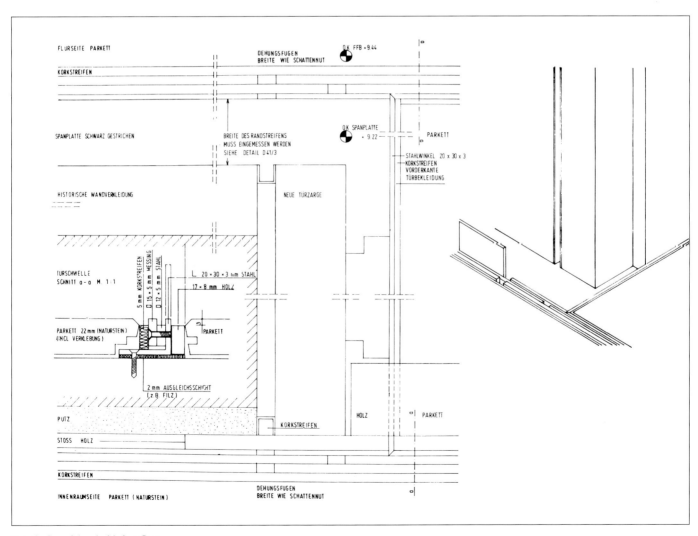

FLURSEITE PARKETT

KORKSTREIFEN

DEHUNGSFUGEN
BREITE WIE SCHATTENNUT

O.K FFB -9.44

SPANPLATTE SCHWARZ GESTRICHEN

BREITE DES RANDSTREIFENS
MUSS EINGEMESSEN WERDEN
SIEHE DETAIL D 41/3

O.K SPANPLATTE
- 9.22

PARKETT

STAHLWINKEL 20 x 30 x 3
KORKSTREIFEN
VORDERKANTE
TÜRBEKLEIDUNG

HISTORISCHE WANDVERKLEIDUNG

NEUE TÜRZARGE

TÜRSCHWELLE
SCHNITT a-a M. 1:1

KORKSTREIFEN
15 x 5 mm MESSING
12 x 5 mm STAHL
5 mm

L 20 x 30 x 3 mm STAHL

17 x 8 mm HOLZ

PARKETT

PARKETT 22 mm (NATURSTEIN)
(INCL VERKLEBUNG)

2 mm AUSGLEICHSSCHICHT
(z.B. FILZ)

PUTZ

HOLZ

PARKETT

STOSS HOLZ

KORKSTREIFEN

KORKSTREIFEN

INNENRAUMSEITE PARKETT (NATURSTEIN)

DEHUNGSFUGEN
BREITE WIE SCHATTENNUT

Detail-plan of threshold, first floor

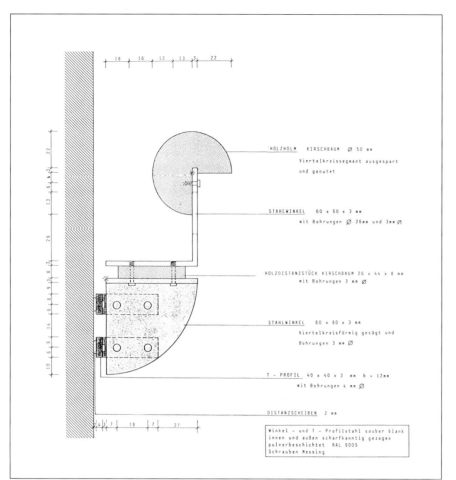

HOLZHOLM   KIRSCHBAUM   Ø 50 mm
Viertelkreissegment ausgespart
und genutet

STAHLWINKEL   60 x 60 x 3 mm
mit Bohrungen Ø 26mm und 3mm Ø

HOLZDISTANZSTÜCK KIRSCHBAUM 26 x 44 x 8 mm
mit Bohrungen 3 mm Ø

STAHLWINKEL   60 x 60 x 3 mm
Viertelkreisförmig gesägt und
Bohrungen 3 mm Ø

T – PROFIL   40 x 40 x 3   mm   b = 12mm
mit Bohrungen 4 mm Ø

DISTANZSCHEIBEN   2 mm

Winkel – und T – Profilstahl sauber blank
innen und außen scharfkanntig gezogen
pulverbeschichtet RAL 9005
Schrauben Messing

Detail-plans of banister

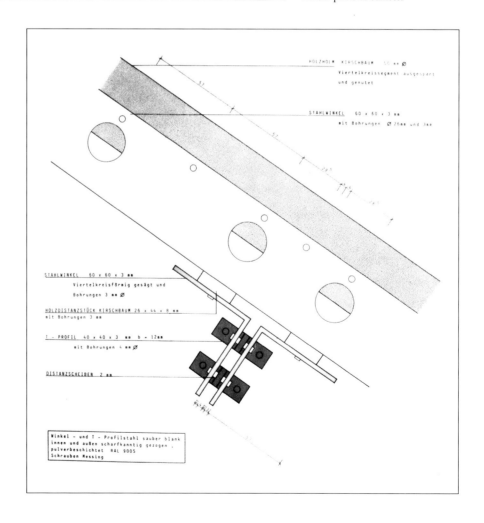

HOLZHOLM   KIRSCHBAUM   55 mm Ø
Viertelkreissegment ausgespart
und genutet

STAHLWINKEL   60 x 60 x 3 mm
mit Bohrungen Ø 26mm und 3mm

STAHLWINKEL   60 x 60 x 3 mm
Viertelkreisförmig gesägt und
Bohrungen 3 mm Ø

HOLZDISTANZSTÜCK KIRSCHBAUM 26 x 44 x 8 mm
mit Bohrungen 3 mm

T – PROFIL   40 x 40 x 3   mm   b = 12mm
mit Bohrungen 4 mm Ø

DISTANZSCHEIBEN   2 mm

Winkel – und T – Profilstahl sauber blank
innen und außen scharfkanntig gezogen .
pulverbeschichtet RAL 9005
Schrauben Messing

The Pain and the Precious

Dieter Bartetzko

The neo-classical buildings of the West End, along the old city walls and the bank of the Main, earned Frankfurt its reputation as one of the loveliest cities in Europe in the first third of the nineteenth century. They were buildings of noble simplicity. In the villas and country houses of the Frankfurt patrician families – and this was regarded as a specific feature of the upper classes here – luxurious interiors were hidden behind markedly sober exteriors.

Outward discretion contrasting with inward magnificence is also the first and most lasting impression the visitor to the Jewish Museum will retain. The two houses, Untermainkai 14 and 15, in which the museum is located are among the few examples of Frankfurt neo-classicism that have survived, and they are also two of the best. Both were built in 1819–21 by the city architect J.F.C. Hess as a terrace block for superior tenants. In 1846, when House No. 15 had come into the possession of the Rothschilds, it was extended by five bays by the celebrated architect Friedrich Rumpf.

Rumpf made the extension an exact copy of Hess's house. The interior, however, was entirely redesigned as a neo-renaissance mansion; later, rooms in neo-baroque and neo-rococo styles were added. The owners opened the palais, containing the Baron Rothschild library, to the public in 1894, and the neighbouring house, No. 14, in 1906. In 1928 the Rothschilds presented the buildings and the library to the city of Frankfurt. From 1967, the most essential repairs to war damage having been carried out, the buildings housed sections of the Historical Museum and a children's theatre. In 1980 came the decision to install the Jewish Museum therein.

That about two-thirds of the Main museum zone consists of historical buildings which have been more or less skilfully adapted to new requirements is easily forgotten, with the fame the new postmodern buildings have achieved. Like no other architect who has worked in Frankfurt so far, Ante Josip von Kostelac has respected historical traditions in converting these two neo-classical buildings. The strict conditions imposed by the Historic Buildings Commission may have had something to do with this: concerned at the lackadaisical, not to say reckless, way in which some architects treated historic monuments in realizing their concepts for the museum zone, the state conservation officer Gottfried Kiesow insisted not only on the restoration of all the facades but also on the preservation of the interior rooms in No. 15, the so-called "Rothschild Palais", even though some of these were only vestiges of their former selves.

Kostelac's original intention was to conserve these rooms in their damaged state as witnesses to their eventful history and use, and so counteract the modern mania for total restoration, for making historic monuments "as good as new". But major static faults and damage to the structure of the old buildings made it necessary to pull down and rebuild, and additions and restorations were unavoidable.

This is nevertheless a successful solution, which is far removed from the popular reconstructive fads of our postmodern era. All these historical interiors and decorations seem almost too good to be true in their ostentatiously careful restoration. The staircase, glittering in gold with brilliantly polished marble steps, the crystal mirrors, tiger-striped porphyry in black, pink and golden brown, the gilt or scintillating white stucco, the rosettes, portières and parquet, the neo-rococo of the old smoking-room, and the mannerist neo-baroque of the old salon seem deliberately artificial, almost like three-dimensional backdrops or full-scale models, recalling the history of the house without being part of that history. Intersected and surrounded by rooms that are obviously new, they have become carefully integrated exhibition pieces, testimonies to an unreproducible architectural history.

The newly designed installations and rooms appear consistent and appropriate in an architectural concept that is entirely pictorial. House No. 14, where nothing was left of the interior after the war damage and reconstruction, offered particular scope for new, creative thinking.

Kostelac has here placed a striking external sign of the change in use: the new glazed lift-shaft at the rear of the building breaks through the historical form like a sharp-edged crystal. Critics have accused the architect of arrogance and insensitivity for this, but compared with the camouflaging usual today, where under cover of post-

Model of the exhibition installation 'Emancipation and Isolation'

modern quotations lift-shafts appear as watchtowers and fire-escapes and chimneys are made to look like classical columns, Kostelac's intervention convinces by its courage and openness, the unveiled contrast it creates. This principle was obviously only half-heartedly followed in creating the new interiors. The foyer, for example, rises expansively through first-floor level and, despite its narrow dimensions, does not appear cramped; it wholly exemplifies the postmodern delight in quotation and decoration. The coffered metal portal echoes antiquity and neo-classicism, the black and white contrasts and ornamentation of the marble floor recall the distinguished brilliance of baroque churches and palaces, a tetragonal framework in gleaming chrome (which supports the large model of the Frankfurt ghetto that hangs above the foyer) projects from the porch and recalls the constructivism of the twenties, and the supports of the upper storey that are visible from below awaken vague associations of archaic steles, with their stepped or fin-shaped culminations.

The impression made by the room is dominated by an ensemble of four slender square pillars. Since Oswald Mathias Ungers' aula in the German Architecture Museum and the so-called "table/temple" in front of the Schirn cultural centre, this motif has generally been acknowledged to be the postmodern variant of the architectural archetype for festivity, celebration and cult. Kostelac sees his four-pillar model as a quotation of the foyer of the old Frankfurt municipal library – the building, that is, that marked the apogee of Frankfurt neo-classicism and in 1820 finally cemented the reputation of J.F.C. Hess, the architect of the houses on Untermainkai.

The exhibition-rooms are in keeping with the exquisite materials and the ostentatiously elegant form of the foyer: black marble stairs, glass cases, cupboards and stands of quality wood, computer and video equipment on altar-like plinths, lamps and candelabra in entrancingly elegant postmodern designs. The walls and hallways, all in a greyish blue, have an integrative and calming effect. They create the essentially neutral frame within which the postmodern and historical interiors stand out effectively and yet, embedded in an overall visual context, remain recognizable as individual parts of a superordinate whole.

Theatricality down to the smallest detail also dominates the exhibition concept of the Jewish Museum. In none of the many new Frankfurt museums has this style of presentation, popular for some years now, been realized so perfectly and so unconditionally. Each section presents itself as a striking environment. The tour of the rooms, arranged as a walk through the history of the Jews in Germany, takes the visitor through theatrical arrangements, lighting effects, stage-sets and living pictures. The message is not conveyed with pseudoneutrality but with involvement, with an appeal to the intellect and the emotions, provocatively and disturbingly.

Thus, the Jewish Museum has become an impressive *Gesamtkunstwerk*, a total work of art in which exhibits, presentation and architecture interact in a *mise en scène* that is a constant challenge to the visitor. But however convincingly the concept presents itself, and it *is* convincing for the most part, it does contain elements that could jeopardize the intentions and the *raison d'être* of the museum. The magnificence of the interior architecture and decoration, the costly materials and the lustre of the precious exhibits, underlined by the theatrical presentation, combine to convey a kind of subliminal message that we do not consciously register. The history of the Jews appears not as a cycle of oppression, hatred and persecution with interludes – generally short – of tranquillity, but as the history of a community that offered mutual security in relative prosperity. Anti-Semitism and pogroms seem strangely unreal; the Third Reich and the holocaust appear to be an isolated and unforeseeable catastrophe.

One example: in an enclosed room the celebration of the Sabbath is shown as the weekly festal day of Jewish families. We see a table with a white cloth, costly china, silver candelabra. Elegant display-cases in the style of postmodern furniture by designers such as Aldo Rossi or Oswald Mathias Ungers, in expensive woods with shimmering brass trim, surround the central arrangement. Atmosphere outweighs information; festive luxury outshines the actual message. How many families were in a position to celebrate the Sabbath like this, and when?

True, the environments that attempt to show the persecution and mass murder in the Third Reich do hold us in thrall and disturb us with their sinister constructions of wire netting and metal posts that look sharp as knives; they fence us in with barriers and narrow openings. And on leaving the bare room in which the horror of the concentration camps is documented, the magnificence of the period staircase that immediately follows seems like a slap in the face. All the more easily, however, as experience shows, will our subconscious allow the memory of better times to push the horror of the pogroms into the background, and – though we know better – we allow ourselves

Foyer

to be reassured by the seemingly golden aura of the good life. It is no accident that in the Federal Republic of Germany people love Toyve, the milkman from *Fiddler on the Roof*, while many of these same people moan that it really is time to stop stirring up the past, to put the lid on the distressing documentation of the holocaust, Nazism and its consequences.

"If no voice is to be raised on our behalf," said Eugen Meyer, president of the Israelite Community in March 1933, "let the stones of this city be our witness." These stone witnesses to Jewish life certainly include the magnificent Rothschild Palais, the Old Opera House, built in the nineteenth century largely with donations from rich Jewish families, and the university, the libraries and so on that they helped to establish. But they also include the pathetic stone remnants of the old ghetto, the rubble of the destroyed synagogues and the gravestones that were smashed or smeared with Nazi slogans (not only in the 1930s). With these, with their disruptive presence, the suggestion of refined taste and luxury could be countered.

The Fassbinder scandal proved, among other things, the continuing power of anti-Semitic stereotypes fuelled by thoughtless-

Model

ness. The cliché of the "wealthy Jew" comes from the sort of people who, eager to wash their hands of the matter by pointing out that they "weren't even born then", see the Palestine problem as a mitigating factor for their own guilt. They may well now see in the Jewish Museum nothing but the opulence of the "wealthy Jew".

In all his architecture, however, Kostelac seeks the decisive contrast, not the general affability of postmodernism. Even if the contrast he and the others involved were aiming for in the Jewish Museum has frequently eluded their grasp and degenerated into a mannered display of fine craftsmanship and a penetrating preciosity, their ability to set a scene, to create striking images, is undeniable. Some corrections could be made: a few disruptive elements in the exhibition architecture and the overly brilliant would become a realistic depiction of Jewish life in Germany. The stones are there ready.

Museum für Vor- und Frühgeschichte

Museum for Prehistory and Early History

Architect: JOSEF PAUL KLEIHUES

Built: 1985–1989

The organizational structure of the Museum for Prehistory and Early History emphasizes the following spatial arrangements:
– the main storey (entrance and church level) is reserved for the exhibition areas;
– storerooms, archives and restoration workshops are in the basement, and further depositories are located in the cellar beneath;
– administration and scientific direction are on the upper floor.

The stairs and lift serving the separate administration entrance on Karmelitergasse connect all the functional levels, linking the storage and restoration areas with the exhibition areas and the administration offices.

The primary factor affecting urban integration was the spatial and architectural ensemble of the Carmelite monastery, and particularly the church with the chapel of St. Anne. The existing layout does not permit extensive overbuilding, and for that reason the storerooms and restoration workshops had to be relegated to the basement and cellar. A further problem was how to do justice to the Carmelite church and the chapel, which were basically intact but

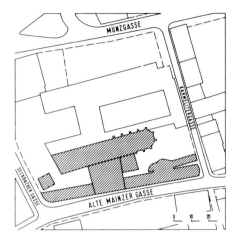

Karmelitergasse 3

needed to be restored. The chancel would suffer if its breathing-space were encroached upon; building along Karmelitergasse (as suggested by the competition programme of 1979/80) would have cramped its surroundings, and was therefore out of the question. I therefore put forward a different concept with the following features:
– emphasizing the morphological site-plan (longitudinal tendencies in an east-west direction) with a parallel building on Alte Mainzer Gasse;
– creating an open frontage on Karmelitergasse and so enhancing the chancel of the old Carmelite church;
– emphasizing the transept of the church by framing it on both sides on Alte Mainzer Gasse.

The elaboration of this concept was designed to introvert the entire complex. The exhibition areas open to the north with a view of the Carmelite church and monastery. On the Alte Mainzer Gasse side, however, the character of a closed ensemble is emphasized in that the wall surfaces here have only functional openings.

The enclosed space is 32,700 cubic metres, the main usable area 2,600 square metres. The building costs amounted to DM 30,438,000.

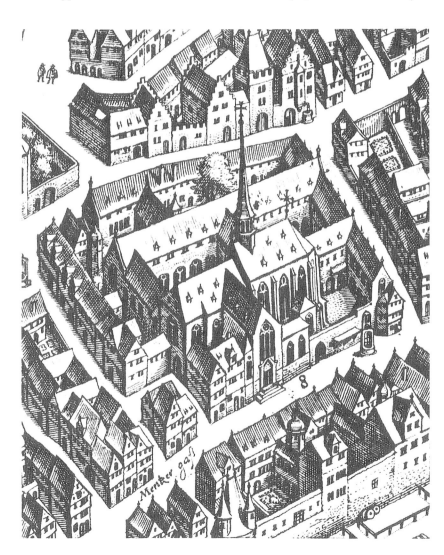

Historical plan of Frankfurt,
Merian, 1628

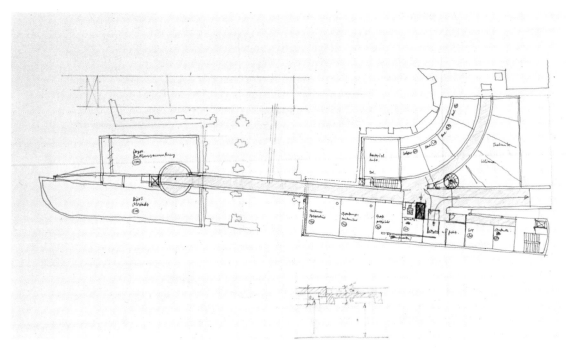

Plan-sketch of first basement

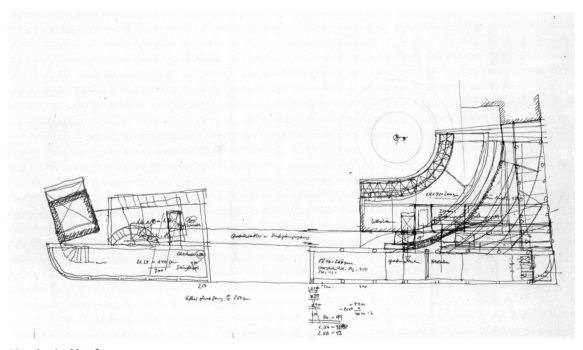

Plan-sketch of first floor

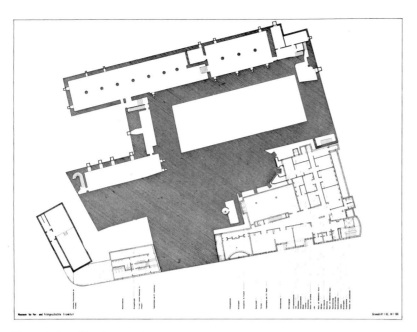

Ground-plan of first basement

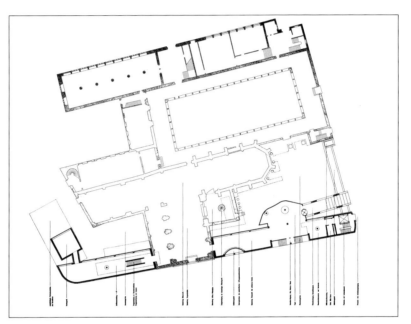

Ground-plan of ground floor

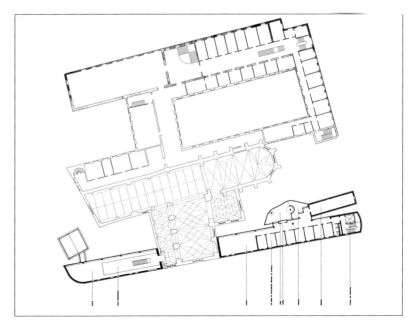

Ground-plan of first floor

Museum für Vor- und Frühgeschichte 53

Isometric projection, bird's eye view

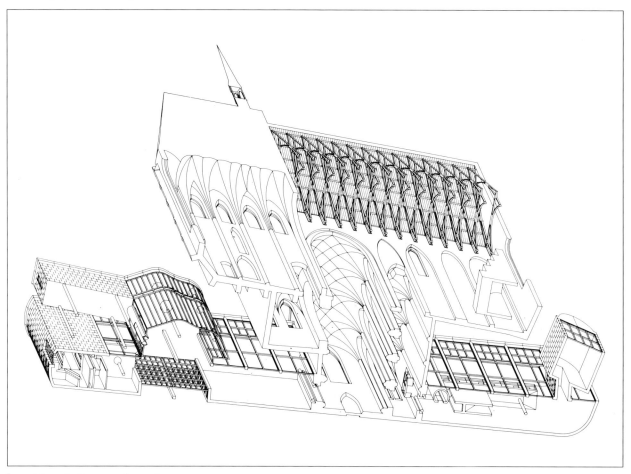

Isometric projection, worm's eye view

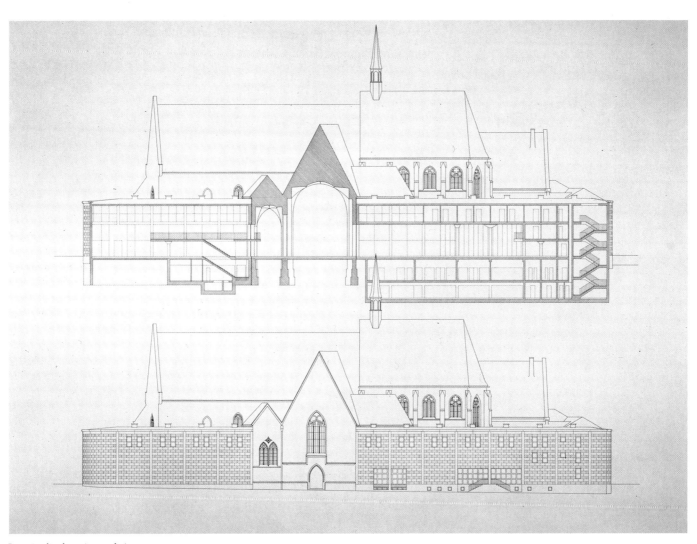

Longitudinal section and view

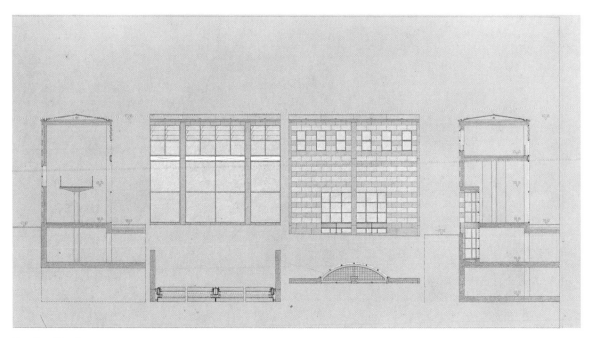

Details of facade, sections

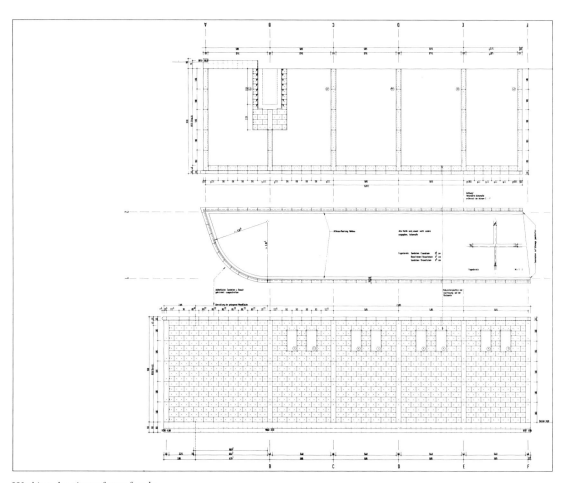

Working-drawings of west facade

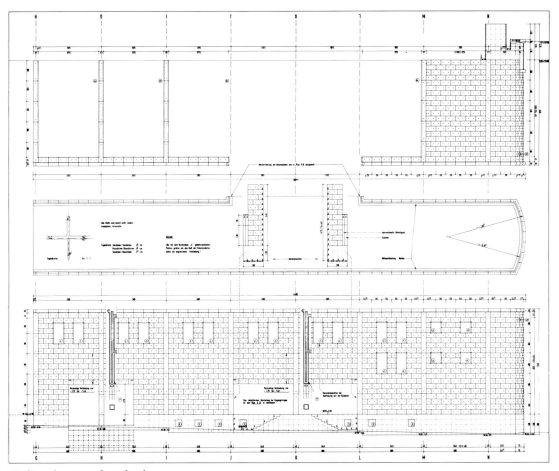

Working-drawings of east facade

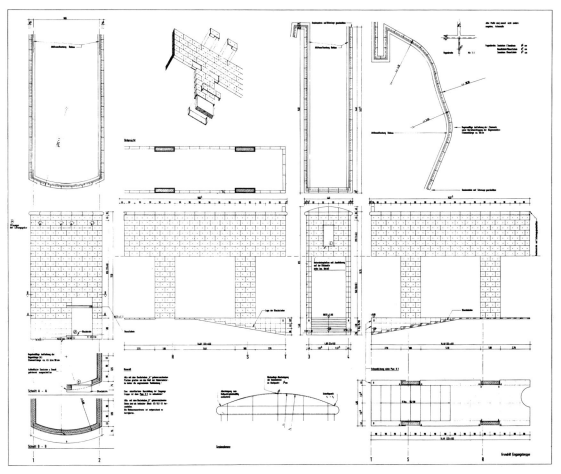

Working-drawings of details of east facade

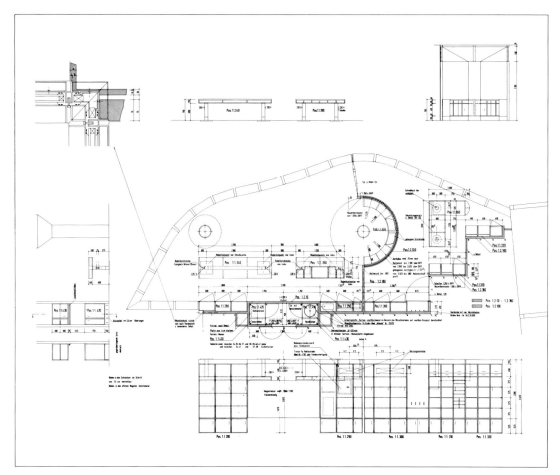

Ground-plan of first floor, details

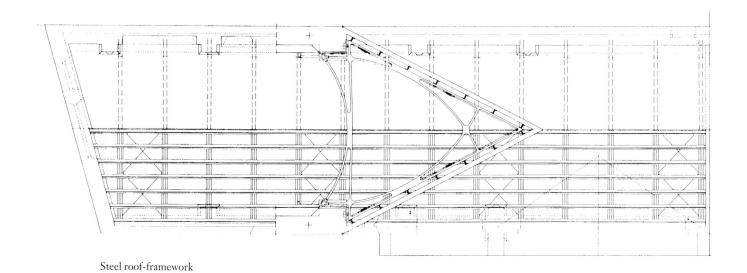

Steel roof-framework

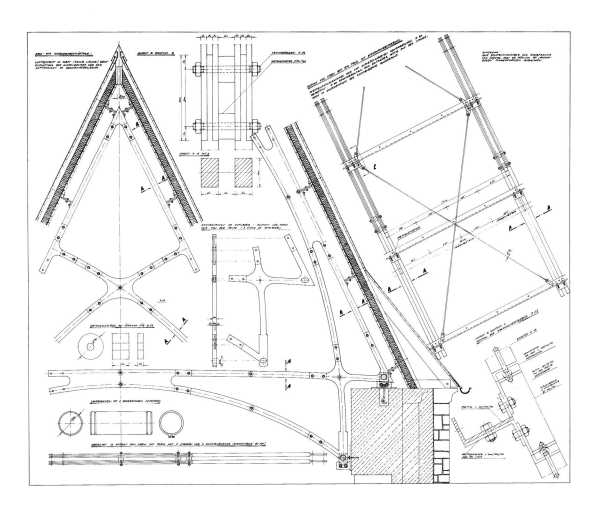

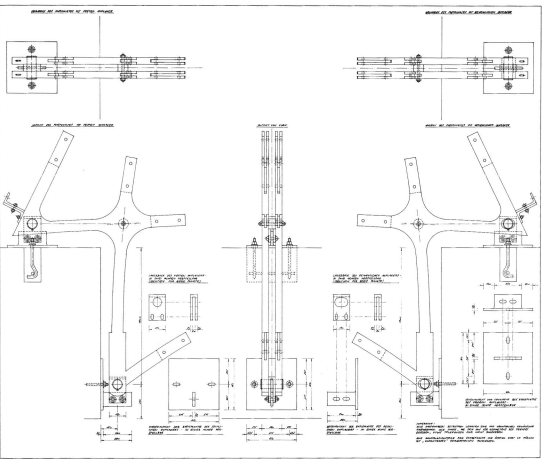

Technical drawings of steel roof-framework

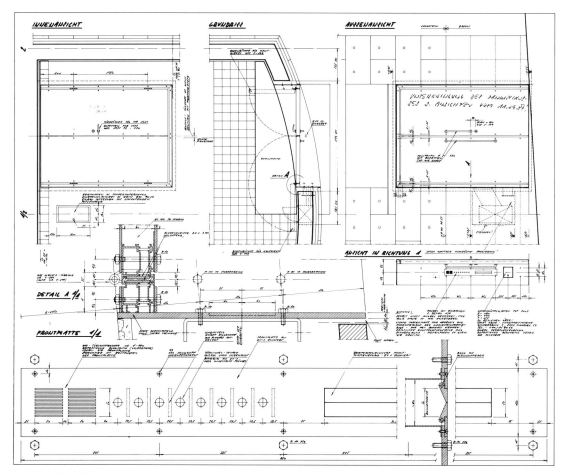

Entrance for staff and the disabled, technical details

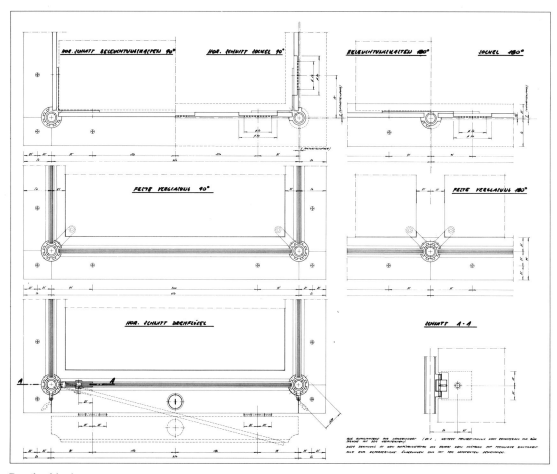

Details of display-cases

The Romantic Rationalist

Manfred Sack

Jury members who have reservations about his architecture do not find it easy to accept his better arguments and vote for him. And jury members who have a weakness for his architecture find it hard to set aside their personal inclinations and offer a credible defence of their objective verdict. For the rule of strict anonymity in such competitions is useless in his case. His design would be recognizable immediately, even among hundreds of entries, and it certainly was among the sixty that were presented in 1980 for the Frankfurt Museum for Prehistory and Early History. The brown packing-paper, the precise delineation, the white highlighting, the grey, silver and gold – all are as unmistakably cool and individual as

the architecture the drawing depicts. Anyway, whatever the scandalmongers might say, the jury under the chairmanship of Oswald Mathias Ungers chose the design by Josef Paul Kleihues and unanimously awarded him first prize.

The museum is, as one would except, perfect down to the last detail, a beautiful museum that delights in presentation, a practical building that comes to terms pretty well with the fashions of the day, and a successful example of the new that had to adapt to a dignified old building. The architect does not make a circus of history, nor does he kowtow to it obsequiously, timidly or coquettishly; he reflects the old in an ambitious artistic achievement.

This museum is not in the museum zone on the far bank of the Main, where Sachsenhausen starts; it is in the centre of the old part of Frankfurt, on the Carmelite hill. This is where the "Brethren of Our Lady of Mount Carmel" settled in the thirteenth century, gradually building their monastery and their church, which became a Late Gothic structure two hundred years later. The church was restored in 1933–34, but suffered a direct hit in 1944 and was burnt out, with all the furniture deposited there by bombed-out Frankfurt families. After the war the refectory was used for temporary exhibitions and the monastery rooms housed archives, a restaurant and the "worst theatre in the world", as it called itself, Die

Schmiere. At the end of the 1970s the city council decided to restore the ruined church, which had been further ravaged by the elements, and add a building to house the Museum for Prehistory and Early History, which, with the 28,000 items in its collection, had been squashed for thirty years into the little Holzhausen Palais on the edge of the city.

The museum can now spread itself out in the Late Gothic nave of the Carmelite church and in the south transept, which has been widened with the addition of an aisle, the small chapel of St. Anne in the southeast angle of nave and transept, and the reddish-brown and yellow-ochre striped new building. The latter extends along Alte Mainzer Gasse, high and forbidding like a monastery wall. The nave and transept roughly form an H with the extension, so that the idyll is open to view at the sides.

In the four decades after the war the church had been in a ruinous state. But precise data of the 1930s restoration were available, and the opportunity was taken to make excavations and studies of the building and the terrain. It soon became clear that the ideal of a conservative restoration of the church was unattainable. The substance of the building permitted only a few documentary signs of its checquered history to be preserved, and so the end result was a complex interweaving of original, reconstructed and radically new elements. For the church, Kleihues designed a fine new roof framework of steel and wood, a delicate construction of convincing modernity, a contemporary variant of the cathedral roof – it is the best part of the whole complex.

Not only the cloisters with the frescoes by Jörg Rathgeb from 1514, but the entire collection of monastery buildings is still a secluded idyll today, even if the narrow streets that surround it are misused by motorists as short cuts. It would have been a fairly pointless exercise to indulge in formal whimsy in so confined a space, and it would have gone against the architect's temperament. We may take it that this part of the old town, though less "glamorous" than the Römerberg with its relics of the Staufen era, caught Kleihues's fancy; in this museum he has certainly produced one of his most pleasing creations – perhaps a little theatrical on the outside, but internally of convincing clarity. The attractive new building fits in with the fine old church without presumptuousness, and without excessive deference.

The long tract of the new building integrates smoothly with the transept and nave of the church. The space flows: the height,

character and mood of the rooms change, daylight playing the determinant role. The collections are set out on the ground floor, arranged meaningfully by type of exhibit. The curators have obviously made the most of a floor-area more extensive than anything they had known before. The transept in particular is crammed with glass cases – less would have been more.

Only in the western part of the new building is the upper storey also used for exhibits. In the forked eastern section the upper storey is reserved for administration and library. Below, the beautifully designed foyer with the pillar, the two mushroom columns and the idiosyncratically curved wall of windows expands into the green side court. It also provides a view of the St. Anne chapel and the chancel, which with its white plastered walls and red sandstone edgings is not at all pretentious.

Sandstone is also utilized by the architect in the design of the long facade of the extension, which has horizontal bands of reddish-brown and yellow-ochre sandstone panels. These are interrupted by a few vertical bands, a large window and the entrance, and of course by the tall white double-gable of the Carmelite transept, which is fairly tightly ensconced but bears it all with mediaeval sang-froid.

The first thing that strikes the eye on the banded facade is the profusion of glistening screws, two to each sandstone slab. They are not just ornaments, as in Otto Wagner's Post Office Savings building in Vienna; they are really needed to anchor the slabs and thus permit the extremely narrow joints on which the architect insisted. The contractors, who objected to this specification with an eye to "tolerances", had to give in the end. The uncompromising stance of Kleihues and his assistant in charge of the

Frankfurt project, Mirko Baum, resulted in fact in an unusually high standard of craftsmanship; but they did have a patient and very liberal client in the shape of the City Architect's Office and its experienced director, Roland Burgard.

There is virtually nothing that Kleihues did not design expressly for this building: all the screws, of whatever diameter, the cute little ceiling-lamps that dazzle the eye, the sophisticated angular lanterns that cast light on to the ceiling from pyramid-shaped reflectors, even the cast aluminium rods of the tip windows, and of course the wonderful display-cases in natural aluminium, complicated constructions with plinth, canopy and round pillars.

He also designed the mighty double-T supports with their superstructures that bear the heavy gravestones on the none-too-solid church floor. Sometimes, admittedly, the architect's imagination has run away with him in his mania for originality, particularly in some of the special display-cases, one of which would be more at home on the ocean waves with its sharply pointed prow and stern. This capricious individuality has also found expression in the east end of the extension, which is divided into two prongs; here a freer articulation seems to have been striven for, with columns, sharp edges and curved surfaces, but the result is somewhat contrived – it is the only bizarre part of the whole complex. And the only superfluous addition is the so-called lecture-hall, which the client needed for school classes of thirty people or so: it is small post-modern temple with a vaulted ceiling, but it will hardly be much used since it has an echo.

The whole museum is designed to one unit of scale, like the hospital that Kleihues built in Berlin-Neukölln. The module is 15

Model

centimetres, with fractions and multiples. Every screw, every window, every display-case, every column and every pillar is derived from this module, so precisely that the tiles, for instance, are 14.8 centimetres square because the joints are two millimetres thick. An architect of such precise mentality is naturally annoyed when a column does not fit into the tiling scheme because the plumbers who installed the toilets ignored the scale; and he only grudingly agrees to the longer window requested by the museum staff, for whom better lighting is understandably more important than a system of ordered proportions.

This is true Josef Paul Kleihues, ruthless in his pursuit of order.

Exhibition-room,
view east into chancel

Kunsthalle Schirn

Schirn Art Gallery

Architects: BANGERT, JANSEN,
SCHOLZ & SCHULTES

Built: 1983–1985

The unusual quality of the location, between the cathedral and the Römer (town hall), is due to the architectural relics of historical heritage. Roman and Carolingian foundations, material elements of the mediaeval core of the city, and fragments of various concepts for rebuilding stand as signs of their times – objects in an imaginary museum.

With the programme of public facilities such as art-gallery, music-school for young people, and workshops, as well as living accommodation and commercial premises, the Cathedral-Römerberg project unifies the heterogeneous area between the two poles of cathedral and old town hall through careful planning of space. The urban environment as a recognizable product of historical development, destruction and renovation is the keynote of the concept.

Three constituent parts, significant in theme and type of building, help to formulate the urban composition: a block of rowhouses on a historical ground-plan, with reconstruction of the frontage on the Römerberg square; townhouses of mediaeval dimensions on Saalgasse; and a public building in the shape of a cross parallel to the east-west/north-south street intersection, reaching out into all the marginal areas.

The enclosed space is 65,450 cubic metres, the main area of use 10,850 square metres. The building costs were DM 57,100,000.

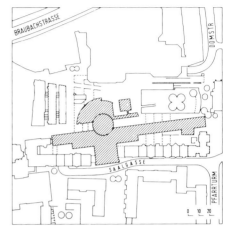

Am Römerberg 6a

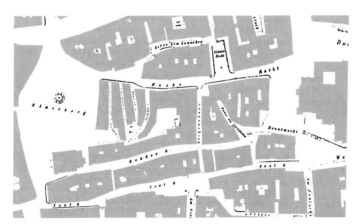

Layout of Römerberg area before World War II bombing and today

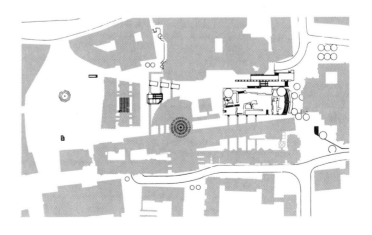

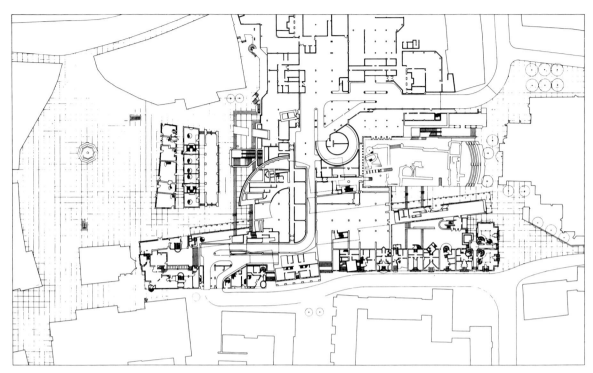

Ground-plan of ground floor E 1

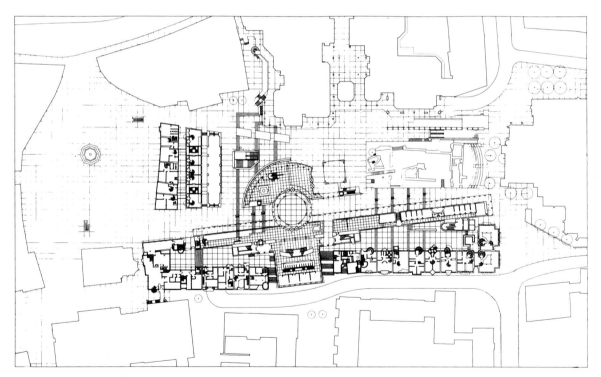

Ground-plan of ground floor E 2

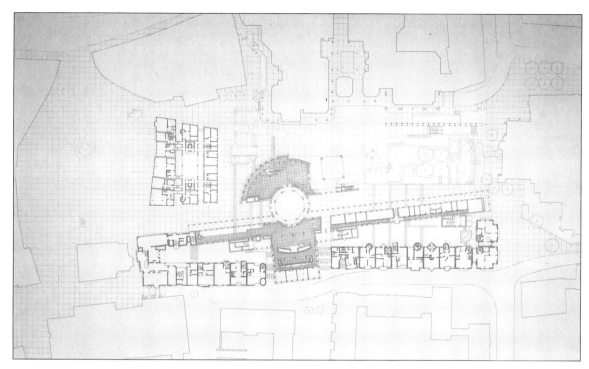

Ground-plan of ground floor, residential building E 2

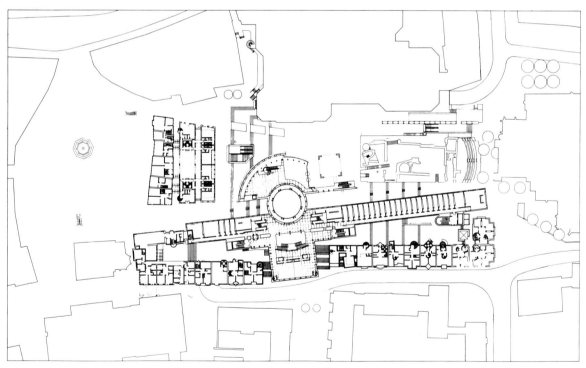

Ground-plan of first floor

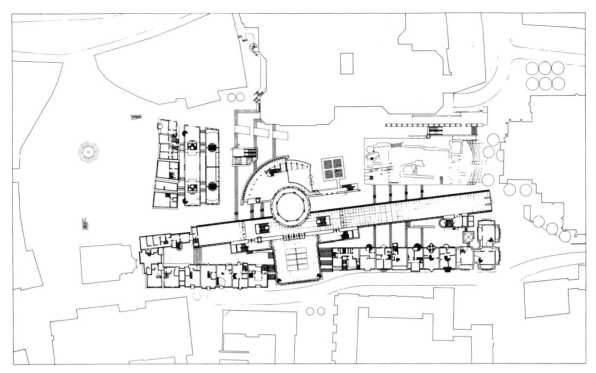

Ground-plan of second floor

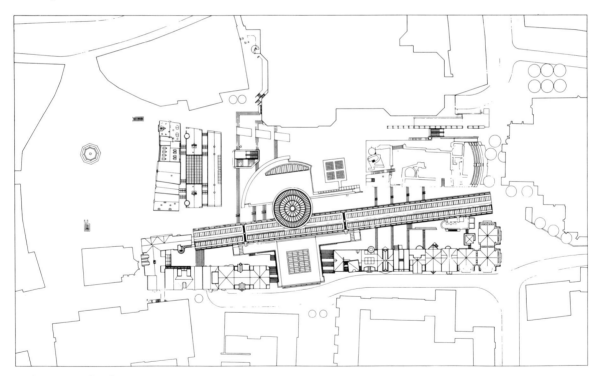

Bird's eye view of roof

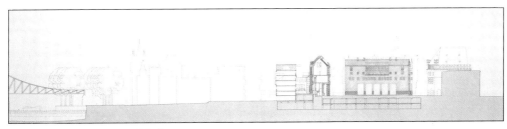

Section with view of historical block

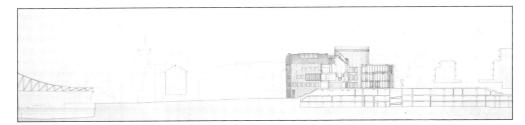

Longitudinal section of main building

View from east

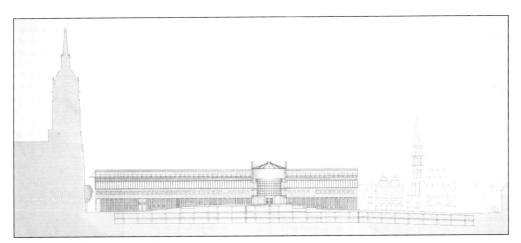

View from north with section of rotunda

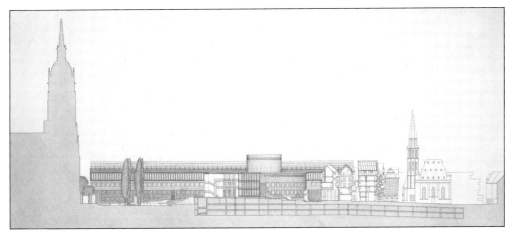

View from north with section of historical block

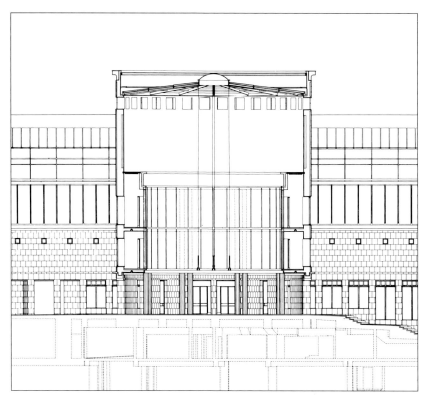

Section of rotunda

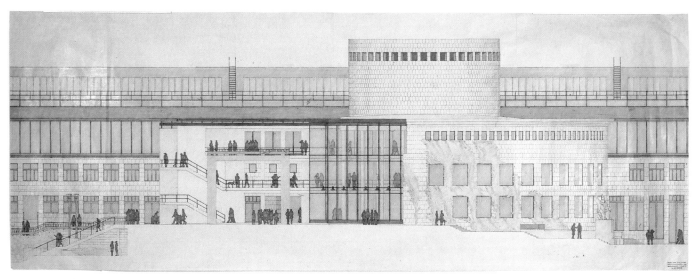

Detail of facade

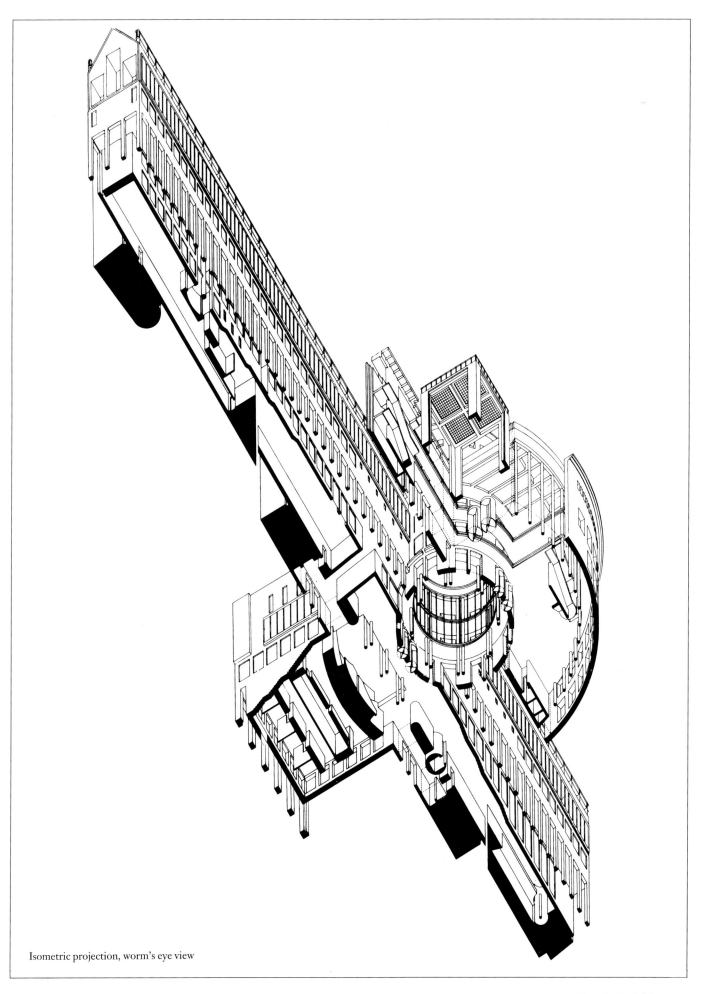

Isometric projection, worm's eye view

A Usable Patchwork of Quotations

Mathias Schreiber

The Schirn as Uzi – from a bird's-eye view the new Frankfurt culture-centre, whose name recalls the mediaeval market-stalls, particularly the sausage-vendors, does look like an Uzi sub machine gun. The long barrel is pointed directly at the cathedral, the circular cut-out section for the cultural meeting-place on the north side is the sights, while the theatre below, on the south side, is the butt and the magazine in one. A purely polemical association? The huge bolt of the Schirn does indeed look as if an invisible person were about to shoot down the Gothic cathedral for its annoyingly delicate elegance. A short-sighted attacker, presumably, for the stone murder weapon almost touches its intended victim.

Those immediately responsible, apart from the politicians and the Historical Preservation Office, are the three managers of the Römerberg Project-Group, who under the direction of the City Building Department "had to coordinate" twenty departments and twenty-four architects and special engineers, as Roland Burgard, one of the three, tells us. The Project-Group had instructed the 103 entrants in the architectural competition to design a three-storey building with an elaborate "spatial programme", in order to provide the "enlivenment" that was clearly felt to be necessary and fill the "vacuum" between the cathedral and the old town hall. So an airy one-storey building was ruled out from the start. The jury, headed by Max Bächer, decided unanimously in 1980 in favour of the Berlin team of Bangert, Jansen, Scholz & Schultes.

The architects themselves now speak euphorically of "experience through images", of "ordering components" that compensate for the contradictions that persist, such as that between the Department of Works building and the Leinwandhaus, the clothmakers' guildhall, and of an ensemble of "meaningful types of building" that "defines the area between the cathedral and the Römer with clearly delineated spaces and routes of circulation". The official documentation goes far back into history, recalling stoa and basilica, the Roman forum and a mediaeval castle, and enthusing boldly about portals, arcades and rotundas. His-

toricizing rhetoric does not console us, however, where the creative and protective force of architecture in the environment has failed. The gallery tract, which is pretty banal even if it is nobly clad in yellow-ochre slabs of natural stone and greets us cheerily with its pitched roof, is actually compared with Vasari's Uffizi in Florence. Italian Renaissance on the banks of the Main? The *genius loci* appears to have erred by several degrees of latitude.

However, the different "types of building" are in fact evident. The basic idea of the ground-plan is the "penetration of the circle". If the circle, the symbol of the sun, of infinity, of the harmony of man and the cosmos, is impinged upon, attacked or fragmented by another figure, a straight line or a rectangle – incidentally a favourite motif of the Russian avant-garde painter El Lissitzky – tension is created, an intriguing disturbance of balance, a tumultuous meeting and clashing of forms. This is evident even where the circle, as in the case of the Schirn, remains the determinant pivot of the composition.

The most striking part of the building, which will define the cathedral square from

now on, is the long "arcade-house"; the tall "arches" are however not arches at all – the term "colonnade" would be more appropriate. Where the terrain slopes downwards, the classic concrete colonnade, which found more elegant expression in fascist Italy than in Germany, reduces the casual stroller to the role of a petty bourgeois – oh, if only there were a goal, an open cathedral door for instance, at the east end of the overpowering structure! Above this construction, which is far too high and far too long, float many bare chambers for music-making and administration and a very straight and narrow exhibition-room which gets a lot of side light and even more top light. (Admittedly, the orgy of light can be softened at will with blinds and mobile wall-elements – indeed, the hall can be completely blacked out.) The monumental art corridor, interrupted by an irritating circular bulge, is basically intended to be a revival of the shopping arcade of the nineteenth century, as is the spectacular round building itself, with its skilfully depressed glass cupola that is hardly visible from the outside. With the ring of square mini-windows below the cornice it also cites the "Herr de Witt House", a

Model

round colonnaded building designed around 1781 by the French revolutionary architect Ledoux, but never built.

This so-called rotunda interrupts the pedestrian route from the Römer to the cathedral both festively and brutally, and certainly without sense or practical value. The paved inner court affords a view of the ambulatories on the upper storeys, but no access to them. In the main part of the building there are more than enough stairs to climb, and some were already boarded up before the building was opened, to give more floor space in the gallery. The circular area offers protection from rain and bird droppings, but it hardly invites "communication", if only because it is terribly draughty.

The building's superfluous, gimmicky silhouette blocks the view from the Römer to the cathedral tower, and the despoliation of the external space has not even been compensated for by the gain of a serviceable or beautiful interior – it is the height of postmodern idiocy. Nor are echoes of Ledoux, the Pantheon, or the rotunda in Schinkel's Altes Museum any justification. Nevertheless, at least the cupola can be wonderfully photographed from the inside.

The rotunda, which might have looked well in the middle of a field, has a massive lower quarter-rotunda placed before it. The principle appears to be core and shell, house within a house. The three, sometimes four storeys, that under the excessively long spine of the art-gallery are indeed of adequate height, are here, under the flat roof, squashed together into three unprepossessing "communication levels".

This confusing and tortured complex, with its asymmetrical ground-plans, pointed angles, bizarre railings and crooked walls, is a hybrid structure; intended for graphics exhibitions, performances and chatting over coffee or wine, it opens on to the cathedral and the archaeological garden. A pretentious foyer surges against a three-storey glass wall. The only problem is that it does not serve as a foyer at all.

This frankly superfluous area is reached first and foremost from the round interior court. The two big revolving doors, on the cathedral side, are usually kept locked. The reception-hall proper, which is really entrancing with its symmetrical flights of stairs, reddish marble floor and white columns, lies to the south of the rotunda. The pseudo-foyer to the north is part of the "cultural meeting place", where it serves mainly as a great source of light, a pointedly transparent end-element. May the culture-seekers, denied the view of the silo-like

cathedral as they came from the Römer, hope to admire the church from here? No. Through the huge glass window that encloses the manneristically pointed corner one has a clear view of the pillars of a monstrous concrete table, which the euphemists in the Faculty of Architectural History have christened the "portico" and the "temple motif".

The auditorium to the south, which can also be used for exhibitions, combines formal refinement with extreme attention to practical needs. Almost everything here is variable: the stage and its technical equipment, the lighting, the arrangement of the black chairs. Towards Saalgasse, where the new townhouses stand in a truly colourful

row, the shallow tunnel-vault, which is largely articulated by huge mullioned windows, culminates in the glazed arch of a light, clear facade. The arch recalls the fine portal of Eggert's Frankfurt Central Station. This frontispiece is as attractive as the main reception-hall. The paradoxical combination of formal exuberance and extreme practicality here evident is the yardstick against which the rest of the complex, which cost around sixty million marks, fails miserably.

The "grand gesture of rationalist architecture", with which – according to the builders – the nave of the Schirn marks the east-west axis, disintegrates in all too many places into a patchwork of quotations.

View from the cathedral

Museum für Moderne Kunst

Museum of Modern Art

Architect: HANS HOLLEIN

Built: 1987–1991

The design of the museum, as regards both internal structure and outward appearance, is based on the one hand on considerations of urban planning and the city image, with reference to the particular triangular shape of the site, and on the other hand on the requirements of a building for the display of works of visual art.

The striking corpus of the building, a stepped unit conceived as a solitaire, is an important element at the gateway to the historical part of the city. With the use of tra-ditional materials, like red sandstone and plaster, a further harmonization with the existing buildings has been created.

The main entrance is on the corner facing the historical centre of Frankfurt, the cathedral and the Römer.

The access to the three main floors inside is up a flight of stairs set diagonally through the building, offering an interesting encounter with the collections and clever use of light and space.

A specially designed roof landscape permits both maximum entry of daylight and integration of the air-conditioning plant.

The area enclosed is 45,875 cubic metres, the main area of use 4,050 square metres. The building costs were DM 48,000,000.

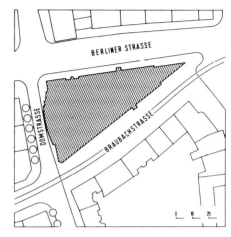

Domstrasse 10

Perspective sketch

Design sketches

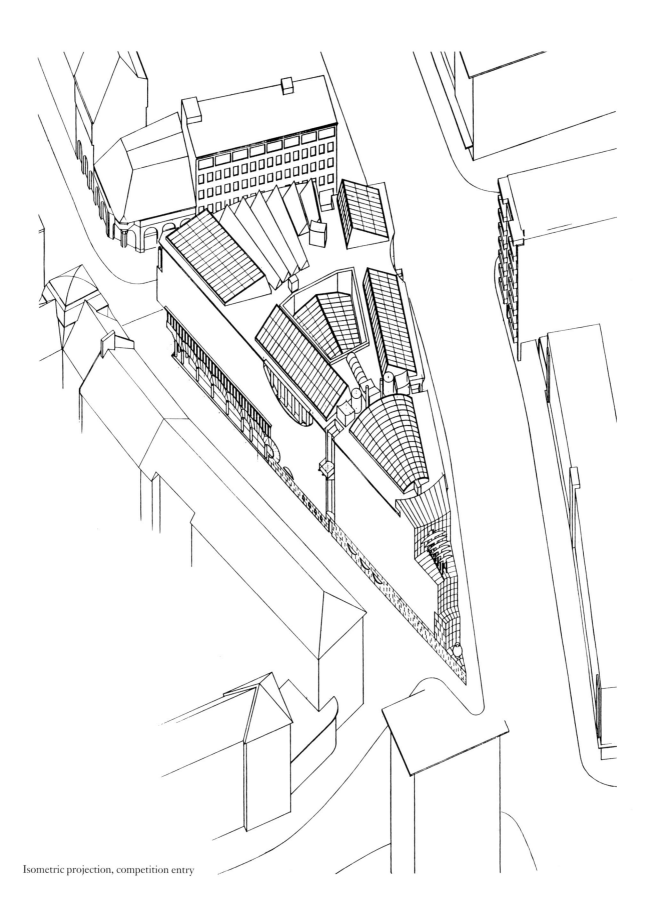

Isometric projection, competition entry

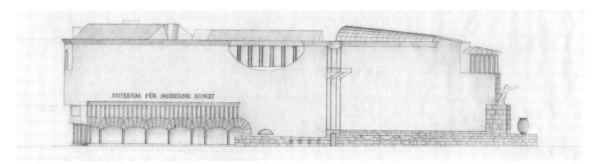

View of Braubachstrasse facade

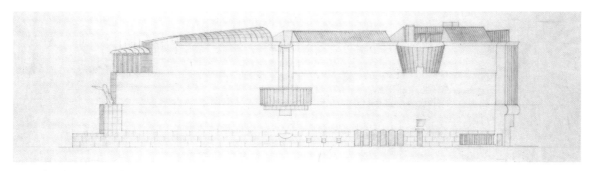

View of Berliner Strasse facade

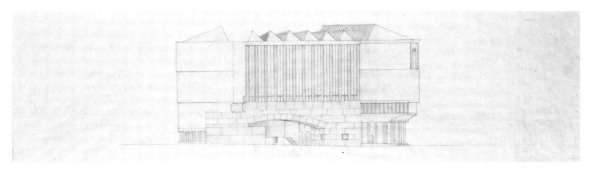

View of Domstrasse facade

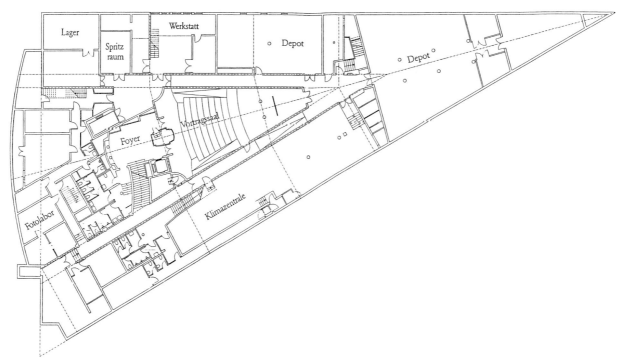

Ground-plan of first basement

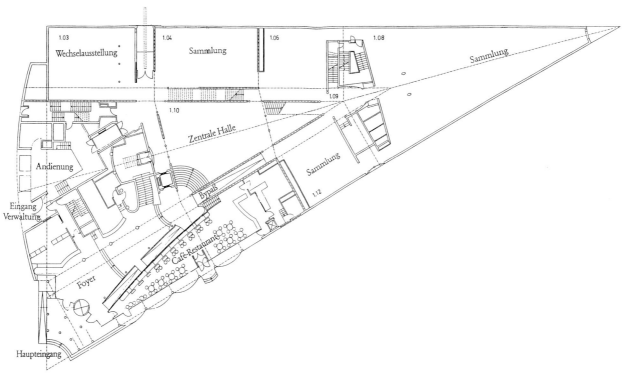

Ground-plan of ground floor

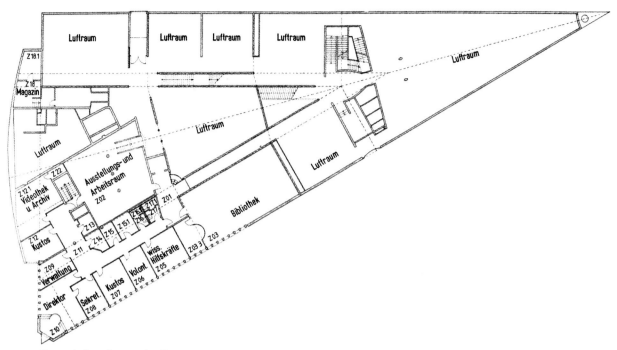

Ground-plan of mezzanine floor

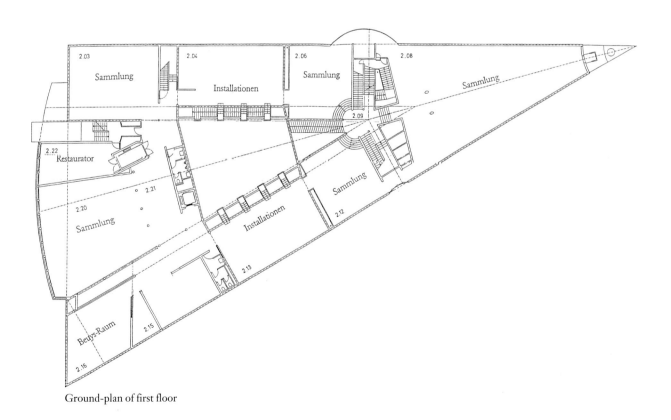

Ground-plan of first floor

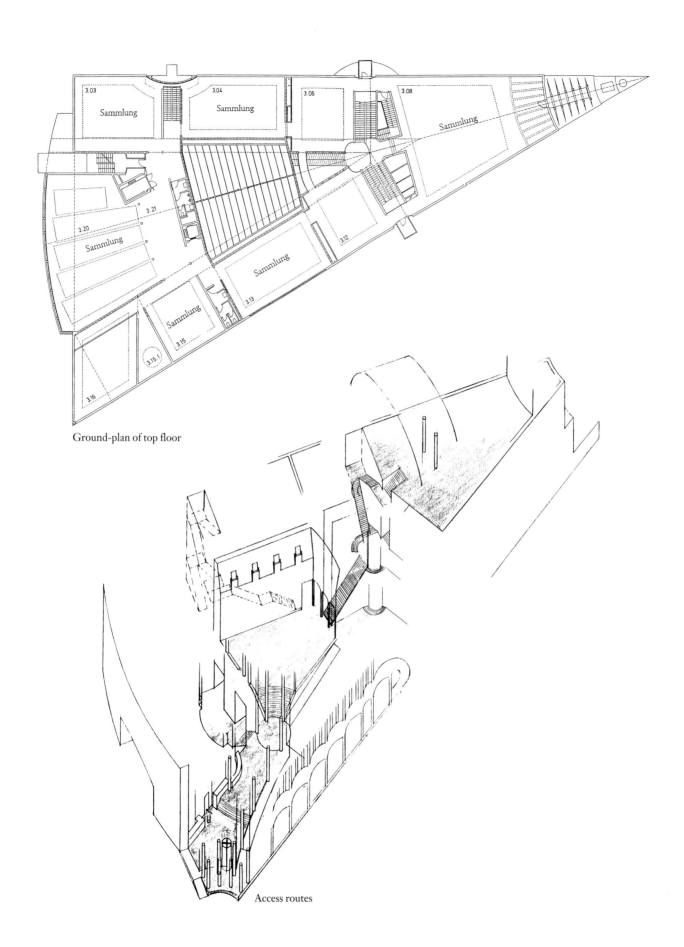

Ground-plan of top floor

Access routes

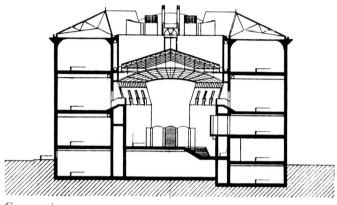

Cross-section

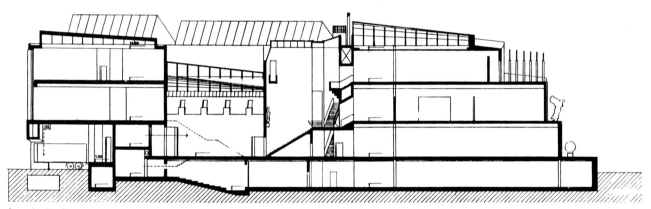

Longitudinal section

Perspective view of exhibition-hall

The Squaring of the Triangle

Michael Mönninger

In an essay that appeared in 1947, 'The Imaginary Museum', André Malraux describes the intellectualization of the perception of art. Disjunct from the work of art itself and from reality, Malraux argues, a new sphere evolves, a sphere in which masterpieces of all times and places are assembled before the mind's eye. Thanks to photography, and the limitless stock of pictures in the head of the viewer, any image can suddenly be put into context with all others. Instead of serving a religious or practical purpose, the work of art becomes increasingly abstract and autonomous. Above and beyond its material substratum, Malraux concludes, the virtual totality of all works culminates in a world of modern art with its own standards and ideals.

Even if, in describing the intellectualization of art, Malraux has also described the dissolution of the classical museum, his analysis can certainly be applied to one of the most spectacular buildings of the 1980s. Hans Hollein's Museum of Modern Art in Frankfurt is the arche type of the "musée imaginaire" in several respects. For the building was an intellectual departure that challenged comparison with other buildings long before construction even commenced. A brief, casual glimpse of Hollein's model photos and sketches, and it was impossible to forget the extraordinary triangular form. The wedge-shaped building differed so sharply from all the other designs of the 1980s that one could well believe this was a type of building that was either so ancient as to have been forgotten or completely new and unimaginable.

The characteristic configuration of Hollein's sharp-ended triangle does in fact suggest archetypes. The imaginary architecture museum unfolds in the viewer's head as he searches for the model, and it presents material for comparison, such as the ground-plans of the Berlin Science Centre, where James Stirling went to work with his biscuit-cutter to produce a conglomerate of classical types such as church nave, stoa, amphitheatre and bell-tower. But the model for Hollein's Frankfurt design cannot be traced in history, however long we may look. If we seek a more modern derivation

for the wedge shape we might think of the prototypes of the modern lecture hall or auditorium, e.g. Melnikov's clubhouse for the Moscow tram workers. But such modern parallels do not fit the bill, not even in functional terms. Nor is the citation of I.M. Pei's extension to the National Gallery in Washington formally relevant, because there two triangle shapes are wedged into each other to produce a blunt trapezoidal shape.

The secret of Hollein's imaginary architecture is that it challenges comparison with buildings of various times and places, but has in fact no equivalent. The building is, to use a linguistic term, distinctive, but not on the face of it significative. Just as in language single distinct letters are sharply delimited from other letters without being semantically significant in themselves, Hollein's museum, with its distinctive contours, occupies an isolated place in the history of form, without revealing its significance through analogies to related building types. In the building-watcher's mental picture library it appears as a simple *difference* with-

out point of reference. As a solitaire, the building admits of very disparate associations which sound attractive but have no semantic content: a cream-coloured piece of cake that could just as easily be interpreted as the foaming bow of a ship, a wedge or an iron.

To pursue the linguistic parallel: just as in language the meaning emerges only when letters are combined to make words, the Frankfurt museum reveals the meaning of its form only in combination with other urban elements. The configuration of Hollein's museum derives, at first glance, from a banal cause: it was only a piece of architectural tidying up of a barren bombed site, which was so unattractive that since the Second World War it had been used only for Nissen huts.

The triangular piece of land lies in the old part of town, as once delineated by the Staufer city wall. The historical area includes the Dominican monastery in the east, the cathedral-Römer area in the centre, and the Carmelite monastery to the west. Wedged into the intersection of two streets

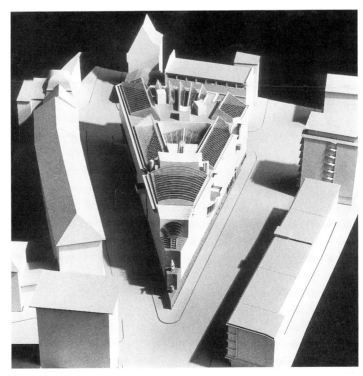

Competition model

– Braubachstrasse, laid out in 1904, and Berliner Strasse, dating from the late 1940s – the ground-plan of the new building entirely follows the logic of this constraint. Hans-Erhard Haverkampf, erstwhile head of the city building-department, waxed enthusiastic about this "powerfully expressive location for expressive architecture", and even assigned it a compass function: "The volume is compressed into an arrow that points east, the direction the development of the city of Frankfurt will take in coming years."

Likewise seeking to discover external significances, the entrants to the competition did not think to take the purely negatively defined site for what it was, a waste product. The zeal with which the 98 entrants in the 1982 open competition battled against the arbitrary site boundaries was tremendous. The winners of the second prize, Schultze & Schulze (Kassel), presented a ground-plan that recalled the piston of a petrol engine. Heinz Tesar of Vienna gave his design, which won third prize, a screw-like twist, just to show his independence of site dictates. O.M. Ungers, who won fourth prize, went so far as to resolve the triangle into a right angle with bar-element across the ends. Only Hans Hollein of Vienna was self-confident enough to adapt himself totally to the topographical situation. His ground-plan is not an autonomous artistic entity; it results from nothing else than the maximum utilization of the space available. The museum advances right to the edge of the road and practically oversteps the existing street lines to provide as much useful area as possible. Despite this extrinsic determination of architectural form, the strange and wonderful happens here in that an isolated element suddenly acquires within a context a significant meaning that is more compelling than any autonomous semiotic gesture.

Nevertheless, the expressive qualities of this building are not translatable. Despite the meticulous observance of contextual factors, the museum remains an alien body, in its abstraction and coldness almost recalling the geometric figurations of the early Russian constructivists. One is almost tempted to call it "absolute architecture", that attitude to design that Hollein and other "progressives" propounded in the 1960s. That was when, to escape the dictates of functionality and serial aesthetics, a generation of young architects preached the way forward into the universe of limitless emotions. Sensualism and psychologism, mega-machines and mobile cities, pneumatic architectures and psychedelic spatial ef-

fects – all these concepts were to make architecture an extension of the sense organs. "Architecture is the most human of the arts," Hans Hollein said in a lecture in 1962. "It is elementary, sensuous, primitive, brutal and archaic, and at the same time the expression of the most subtle feelings of man, the materialization of his spirit. It is flesh and spirit at once, and in the truest sense erotic."

From here to the broader concept summed up in the maxim "All is architecture" was only a small step. In 1963 Hans Hollein and Walter Pichler showed in their small but very consequential exhibition in the Galerie St. Stephan in Vienna the Austrian variant of what Archigram in England and the Metabolists in Japan had been working on: a shaping of the environment that in its extreme precision and totality devoted as much attention to man as the NASA engineers in building the first manned spacecraft – a vision that was utopian and tempting, and also frightening, a vision that, if one carefully studies the ground-plan of the Frankfurt museum, is distantly reflected in its spacecraft-like silhouette. Interestingly enough, this is also the approach of the expressive Viennese avant-garde of today, first and foremost of the celebrated duo Coop Himmelblau, even though in their case it manifests itself in a completely different formal idiom.

In Frankfurt, these exalted ideas have borne fruit above all in the interpenetration of volumes and the dynamics of the access concept, in amplification of which even the columns have been transmuted into streamlined elipses.

Right at the outset, the visitor finds that there is no "front door" – he is admitted diagonally, from the corner of Domstrasse

and Braubachstrasse; with this stratagem Hollein emphasizes on a functional level the connection with the historical core of the city and the cathedral. But this use of a corner entrance also disturbs the sense of balance of a rigidly symmetrical perception of space. After a slight, hardly noticeable bend in the entrance area, an immensely long vista opens from the foyer through the central hall and the stairwell to the apex, sharp as a knife-point, of the ground-floor exhibition-room; this vista of over sixty metres is the greatest linear distance between two points in the whole building.

The other entries also had a top-lit hall in the centre of the museum for meetings and events, but mostly in the form of a rotunda. This was a subconscious expression of the planner's antipathy to the fragmentary site, because the proposed cylindrical hall would act as a sort of joint, softening the impact of what from the outside seemed an unmotivated angularity. The trapezoidal shape Hollein has given his central area not only creates a greater visual dynamic, it also has the practical advantage of providing additional hanging space for large-sized works, which would have been lost in a round building. One only has to compare it with the rotunda of the Schirn Art Gallery, which can at best be used as a "sculpture environment" but hardly as a display room.

In his Municipal Museum on the Abteiberg in Mönchengladbach (1972–82) Hollein had already followed the principle of "letting the visitor wander around" by linking the rooms at their corners. In Frankfurt, too, he designed a kind of cloverleaf system, a forking of the ways, so that at least three rooms at once open up from a single point. Here the access is not from the side but

Model

centrally from the stairwell, which runs through the building vertically and supports it like a hollowed-out spinal column. The sequence of the exhibition-rooms, which are 5 metres high, follows the triangle of the outside walls, with the reference to the central atrium always being preserved.

Hollein has designed this central hall as a house within a house, with little internal balconies on the upper storey. Where the walls of the hall widen like a funnel to the glass roof – the glass vault is reminiscent of the Milan gallery Hollein is so fond of – the visitor can look down into the trapezoidal hall through openings in the wall and reinterpret the interior as an outdoor space. That these openings recall mediaeval defence structures, the machicolations of fortresses, may be interpreted as a playful historical element, like the hint of a Palladian motif in the flush-columned arcades around the central hall.

Each room in the museum can be entered in at least two different ways, either from the central staircase or via a system of "bypass" routes that provide secondary access. Hollein has also given a tangible demonstration of this idea on the Berliner Strasse facade, where a round oriel suddenly leads the visitor outside the building, restoring his orientation in the cryptic darkness of the exhibition-rooms.

Annoyingly, however, the building throws away this gain on the opposite side, where the entrance area, with its undulating sandstone arcade, panders to the base zone of the neighbouring buildings in such a banal way that the whole structure becomes eclectically bogged down. The entrance is like the hole in the side of the Titanic, and the building bleeds to death. The glazed frontage around the corner is somewhat more detached from its surroundings; it shimmers with the glossy tastefulness of the "Kurhaus Renaissance" of the 1950s, probably with the intention of rehabilitating the rebuilt postwar houses round about, some of which have been unjustly criticized. But the vertically articulated panorama window and the delivery entrance call to mind not so much an ice-cream parlour as the stern of a car ferry.

The alternation of top light, side light and artificial light is one of the big surprises in the museum, which from the outside resembles a bunker-like fortification. Hollein has set oblique studio skylights on the roof like solar reflectors, flooding the place with light. Only the rooms in the acute-angled eastern corner of the museum are pitch dark, ideal for installations; the rest can be lit flexibly. Since all good things come from above, including light, Hollein has lavished particular attention on the roof. Instead of an amorphous tar-and-stone wasteland with transformers and air-conditioning plant he has made of the technical superstructures a little landscape of houses and huts in copper and turquoise. However, this microarchitecture is not a garden the public can walk around in, so unfortunately only the staff of the neighbouring Works Department building can enjoy the view of Hollein's lonely, enchanted roof-forest.

With very little facade modelling Hollein has nevertheless endowed his huge art galleon with lightness and grace, as can be seen in the stepped eastern apex. He has softened the sharp corner not by adding things but by leaving things out, so that now, at once fragile and agile, it points the way for the museum. The sparse decoration on the building, quite free of redundant kitsch, also awakens associations that are the very quintessence of the fleeting: the lemon segments of the window incisions, the petits-fours of the roof treatment, the cream-coloured faces of the walls, the gâteau-slab of the all-round sandstone base are all appetizing gourmet elements that bear witness to nothing so much as the desire to absorb this imaginary museum not only intellectually but also sensuously. Almost aggressively, the building renounces the ascetic connotations of the museum and shows a wealth of invention that is so painfully absent in innumerable everyday buildings like cinemas, theatres and shopping-centres. This happy non-conformism only goes to show how tardily the few exemplary architectural works of our day have reacted to more general needs.

Hollein's architecture is much more than simply the result of a commission to build a museum, and one can criticize only one thing: that it lacks that element of irritation that has long been obligatory for contemporary art – the jagged interface where imaginary art (or architecture) impinges on the banality of life.

Ausstellungspavillon am Portikus

Portikus Exhibition Hall

Architects: MARIE-THERES DEUTSCH
KLAUS DREISSIGACKER

Built: 1987

An exhibition-hall for small and special exhibitions has been created on a prominent site in Frankfurt. This lies at the beginning (or the end) of the old city wall, which is now a green-belt area. The main feature of the site is the ruin of the old municipal library, built in 1848, of which only part of the south facade with the portico facing the River Main remains.

Without fear of mixing old and new, the architects pushed a box directly behind the facade, wedging it in between the postwar support-walls. They used corrugated metal facing to suggest an industrial shed, a building that is anonymous and gives no clue to its contents.

With the incorporation of the old portal, the exhibition-hall has become a landmark, and a site that was lying unused has been given a function, while the remains of the original structure have been preserved.

Four standard units serve subsidiary functions such as office-space, storerooms, technical facilities and toilets, two each being deployed in the angles formed by the long sides of the hall and the old facade, but not contiguous with either.

The interior is not anonymous, but it stresses its neutrality as an exhibition-hall in that functional requirements are not allowed to impinge on the simplicity and clarity of the space.

To create even illumination in a windowless interior, the hall is lit from above through an opal glass roof.

The area enclosed is 1,140 cubic metres, the main area of use 140 square metres. The building costs were DM 330,000.

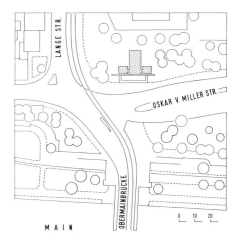

Schöne Aussicht 2

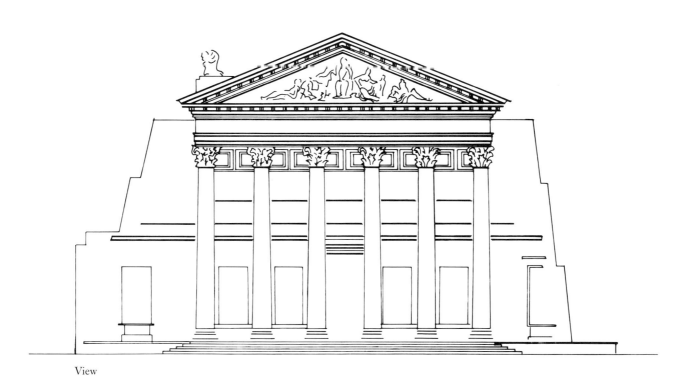

View

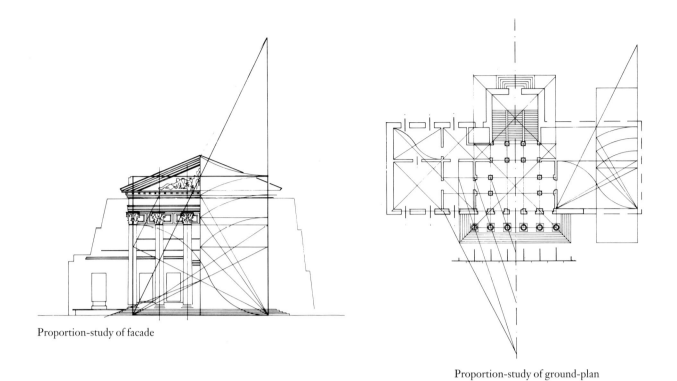

Proportion-study of facade

Proportion-study of ground-plan

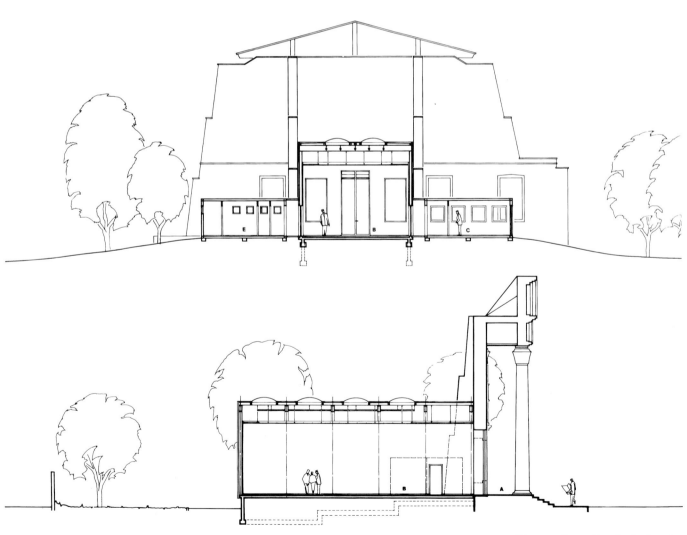

Cross-section and longitudinal section

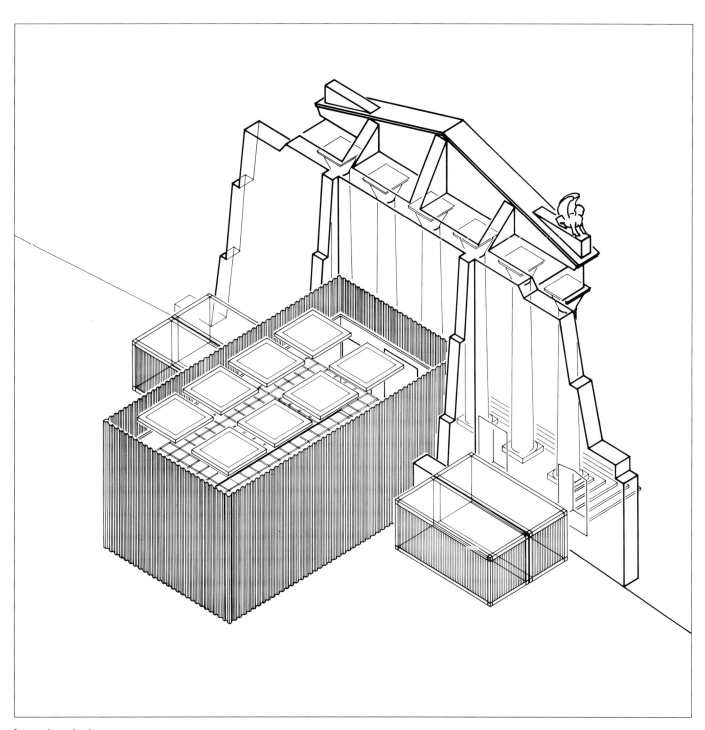

Isometric projection

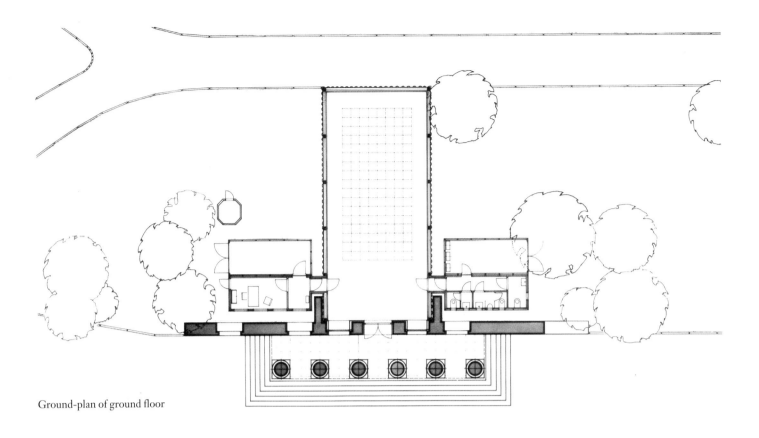

Ground-plan of ground floor

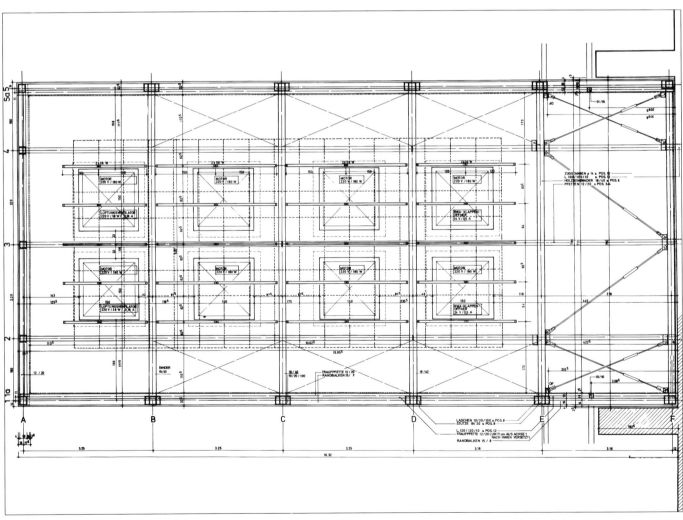

Worm's eye view of roof and plan of electrical installations

92   Ausstellungspavillon am Portikus

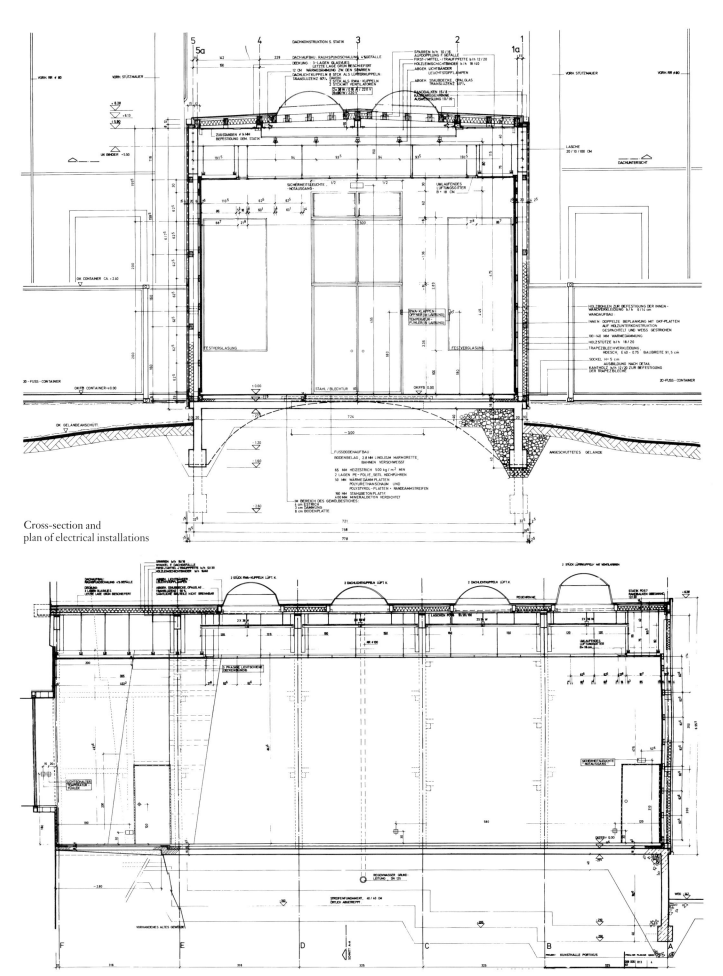

Cross-section and
plan of electrical installations

Longitudinal section and plan of electrical installations

The Colonnaded Box: A Radical Antithesis
to the Elegance of the Museum Landscape

Dieter Bartetzko

The Municipal Library on Schöne Aussicht, on the bank of the Main, was the noblest neo-classical building in Frankfurt. Built in 1820–25 to plans by the city architect, Johann Friedrich Hess, it was a temple of enlightenment and knowledge, well-proportioned and simple. Only the portico, with its six Corinthian columns, set that festive, almost triumphal architectural note in which the citizens of Frankfurt recognized the manifestation of the freedom their imperially privileged city had regained after the French occupation.

This freedom had also found expression in the thirty years of arguing (from 1788 to 1818) about whether and at what cost a municipal library should be built. It is one of the strange features of the history of Frankfurt that here, compared with other commercially prosperous cities, there was much more wrangling about the erection, the appearance, the equipment and the cost of public buildings. This is, if not the only, certainly the most banal explanation for the simple elegance, so greatly prized today, of many of Frankfurt's historic buildings. For – though this is no excuse for petty-mindedness – the penny-pinching of their clients led well-established architects like Salins de Montfort or Hess to produce masterly achievements. Making a virtue of necessity, they initiated "Frankfurt Neo-classicism", the only creative contribution the city ever made to the architectural history of Germany (before Ernst May's "New Frankfurt").

As far as the Municipal Library was concerned, Hess had to do without the relief-decoration he wanted on the gable and an extensive figural programme. He had his way only with the metal inscription above the columns, "Studiis libertati reddita civitas" ("The city, restored to freedom, [dedicates this] to studies"). In 1837 Arthur Schopenhauer, who lived a few doors down, objected to the sentence as "home-made Latin", but it was decided not to correct it for reasons of cost.

In 1840 a life-size statue of the seated Goethe in Carrara marble was placed in the foyer of the library. It had been made by Pompeo Marchesi in 1834 and commissioned privately by the Frankfurt scholar E. Rüppel, the merchant H. Mylius and the silk dealer M. Seufferheld. Annoyed that after endless debate the Frankfurt senate had shelved plans for a monumental (national) Goethe memorial on the Main island, they acted on their own initiative. Marchesi's work of art was soon regarded as the most successful portrait-sculpture of the poet, and the citizens were rightly proud of being able to show it in their no less famous library.

In 1896, when Frankfurt – now a major Wilhelmine city – was belatedly endeavouring to win architectural prestige, the library was extended to plans by Carl Wolff, acquiring two temple-like extensions, to east and west. The gable was given the relief Hess had planned, and the building was embellished with figural sculpture. Finally, after the end of the First World War, the new city administration corrected the inscription as Schopenhauer had wished: "Litteris recuperata libertate civitas" it has read since then ("The city, its freedom recovered, [dedicates this] to letters").

The building suffered severe bomb damage in 1944, valuable books were burned and Marchesi's sculpture was completely destroyed. During the early 1950s the facade walls, which were still standing, were pulled down and the fate of the surviving portico hung in the balance for nearly forty years. Again and again plans were proposed

to demolish it because it was a traffic obstruction; some said that the relic should be preserved as an anti-war memorial, while others argued that the remains were a nuisance and should be removed and re-erected in the gardens that marked the course of the old city wall, as a romantic ruin.

The fragment survived. When the opera house ruin was finally rebuilt as a congress and concert hall, the macabre title of "the most beautiful war ruin in Germany" passed to the now freshly whitewashed portico.

So much for the history of the building whose relic has now been given a new lease of life. It is a history that may seem scarcely credible in this modern metropolis, which now has the biggest cultural budget in the Federal Republic of Germany, with its postmodern urban renaissance that culminates in the riverside museum park. Yet it is characteristic of the architectural (and not just the architectural) tradition of Frankfurt, linked in a curious way with both the good and the not so good aspects of the local architectural scene.

Let us go back to our starting-point. The portico was last a subject of debate in 1986 when Christoph Mäckler, the young Frankfurt architect, in his much-discussed "Frankfurt Project", proposed incorporating it as emblem and reminiscence in a neo-classical block of flats. Things turned out differently. This gallery container has not become a

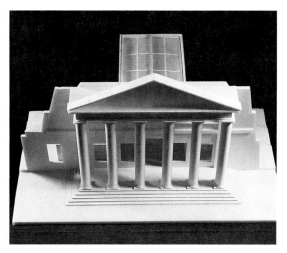

Model

"flying building", as Kasper König opined. Possibly the intention with so light a touch was to counter the bombast of the museum promenade opposite. It is also possible that Robert Venturi's architectural sleight-of-hand with the "decorated box" was what König and Deutsch/Dreissigacker had in mind, and inspired the idea of the colonnaded box. But the fact of the matter is – to be polemical – that the portico camouflages an architectural man-of-war, a bastion of art, from which broadsides are fired at the actual and suspected superficiality of the other museums.

Or is it fairer to the building to take it for what it really is – an art object, an environment that also serves exhibition purposes, a utilitarian, walk-round sculpture that inveighs against the magnificence of the postmodern? From this point of view, the deferential gesture to the neo-classical relic seems more like a side-effect; it is, in the literal and the metaphorical sense, limited to the "facade".

Nevertheless, the portico is again serving the people, it is once more what it was originally intended to be – the decorative entrance to an interior devoted to study and the enjoyment of art. And, as architecture of antithesis, a crude testimony to economy and restriction to the bare essentials, the colonnaded box unwittingly becomes a part of that complex tradition of building in Frankfurt already mentioned, which nobody seems to remember any more.

On the initiative of Kasper König, a new arrival at the Städel School, an exhibition pavilion has been erected that the architects, Marie-Theres Deutsch and Klaus Dreissigacker, conceived as a radical antithesis to the familiar elegance of the riverside museum zone. The main building, sited on the axis of the historical portal, is a longitudinal rectangle, a windowless cube. It is clad with corrugated iron, such as is used for fencing in building sites. Above the roof-line the saucers of eight small glass cupolas are visible. The whole is like a rather too large building-workers' hut. And the offices and

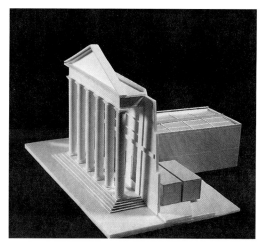

Model

administration rooms to the left and right are in fact housed in metal containers of the sort that are also seen on building-sites.

The provocatively bare exterior is in utter contrast to the interior, which is striking in its restrained festive air. After passing through the old library portal the visitor finds himself directly in a moderately large exhibition hall (6.00 × 7.20 × 15.70 m.). The room is unpartitioned, its proportions are harmonious, the walls a neutral white, and the floor is covered with unpretentious grey-marbled linoleum. The only decorative element is the grid pattern of the top light: opal glass softens the natural light during the day and the artificial light in the evening. The whole is a convincing exemplar of the exhibition-rooms of modern architecture: simple, serving the exhibits, a welcome contrast to the often exaggerated showiness of the theatrical postmodern museum interiors.

The real test of the new building is its relation to the historical architecture of the portico. At first sight every effort seems to have been made not to detract from its effect. The new buildings literally hide behind the colonnade, and seen from the back or the side their neutral facades avoid all competition with the decorations of the historic monument. But on a closer look one notices

a feature that has a devastating effect on the picture: the portal and two adjoining windows have frosted glazing. This transforms the facade, which used to be transparent, into an optically inaccessible sham, which alternately recalls the shabbiness of abandoned, bricked-up buildings and the containers of the 1970s whose shapeless exteriors ignored the surrounding urban landscape. It robs the portico, which used to be both a stark ruin and a representative temple frontage, of a good part of its effect; but it is a mistake that can of course easily be rectified.

But a metal cube (or, as the architects themselves say, a "box") will in all probability meet with little understanding on the part of the public. The provocative exterior virtually predestines it for derisory appellations like "metal shoebox" or "builders' hut gone astray".

Nevertheless, the building has a lot in its favour: it shows that people were prepared to dissociate themselves from the formal extravagance of the postmodern riverside museums, had the courage to put up an exhibition building outside the established cultural scene, were ready to take the risk of opening a gallery on the edge of the east end, which is in danger of degenerating into a slum, and were determined to respect the historical fragment.

Ikonenmuseum

Icon Museum

Architect: Oswald Mathias Ungers

Built: 1988–1990

After the reconstruction of the complex of the Teutonic Order prebend from 1963 to 1965, a separate museum was planned in the old refectory to house the icon collection of the Schmidt-Voigt Foundation (administered by the Museum of Decorative Arts), with exhibition-rooms, an administration block, depositories, and staff rooms, all within a small area.

A modern, non-derivative interior decor was effected, creating a synthesis with the existing building without bowing to the exigencies of fashion. Renouncing all ornamental embellishments, the architect used accentuated lighting to allow the glowing colours of the icons, most of which are small, to speak for themselves.

By incorporating a gallery in the high hall Ungers was able to enlarge the exhibition-space whilst guarding against the dwarfing of the actual exhibits.

The area enclosed is 3,320 cubic metres, the main area of use 422 square metres. The building costs were DM 3,900,000.

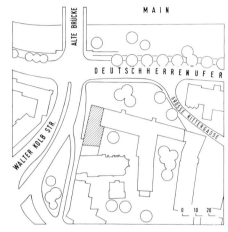

Brückenstrasse 3–7 (Deutschordenshaus)

Perspective view of hall

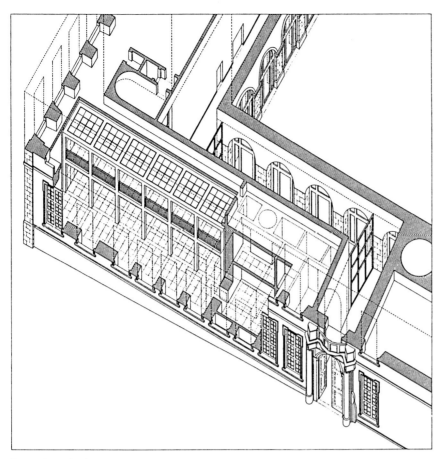

Isometric projection

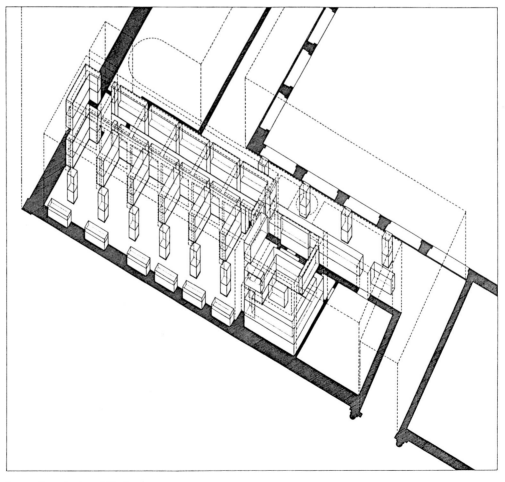

Isometric projection of display-case concept

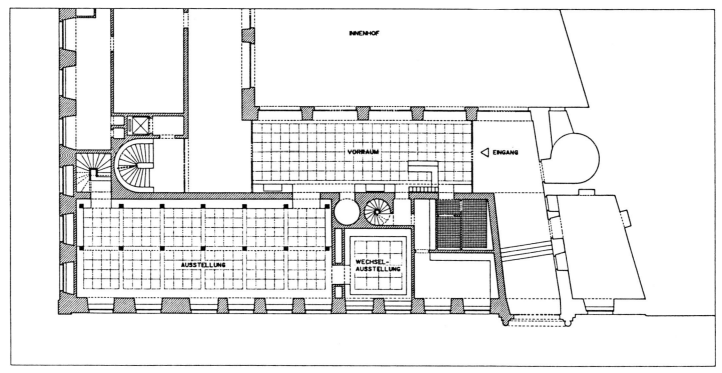

Ground-plan of ground floor

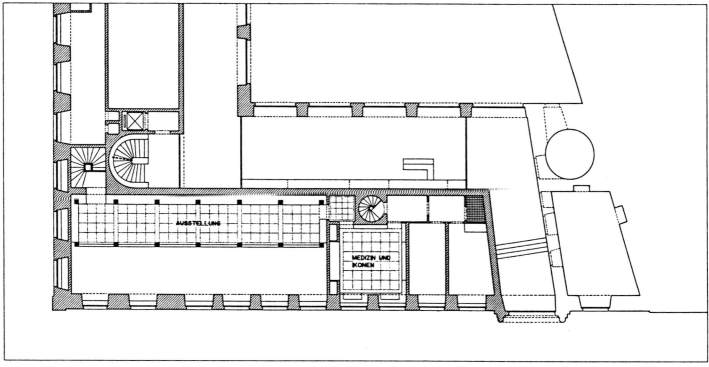

Ground-plan of mezzanine floor

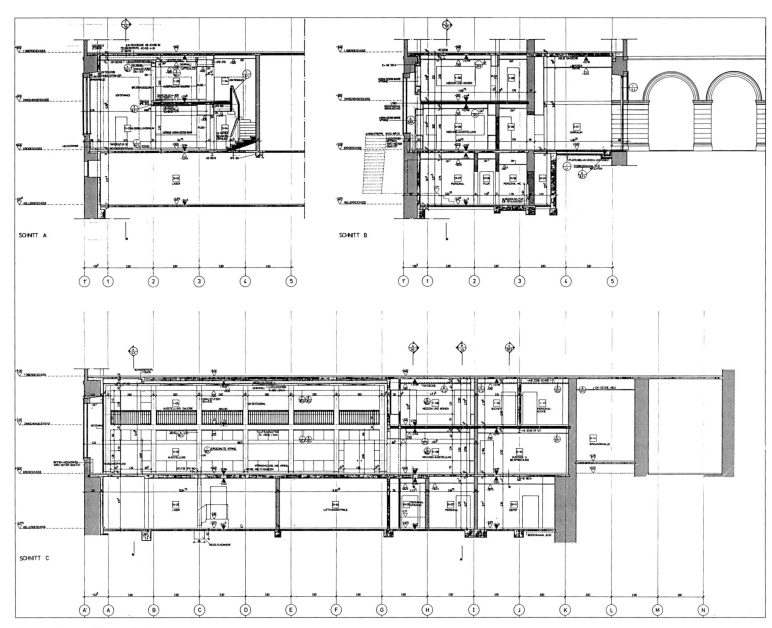

SCHNITT A

SCHNITT B

SCHNITT C

Cross-sections and longitudinal section

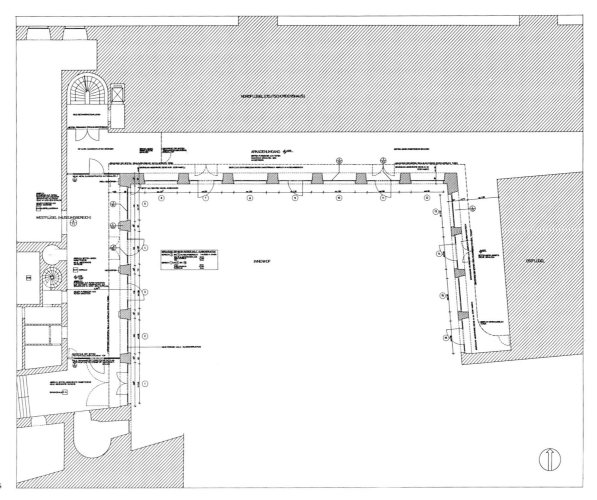

View of arcades

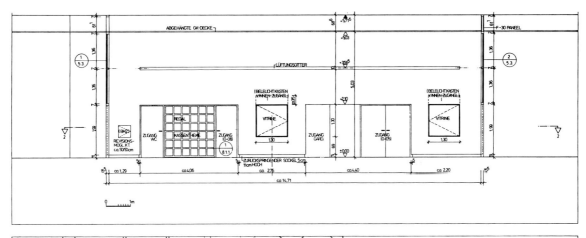

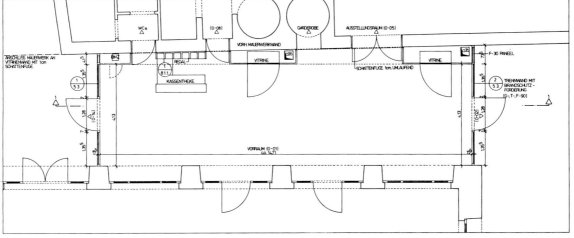

Elevation of inner foyer wall
Ground-plan of foyer

Ikonenmuseum 101

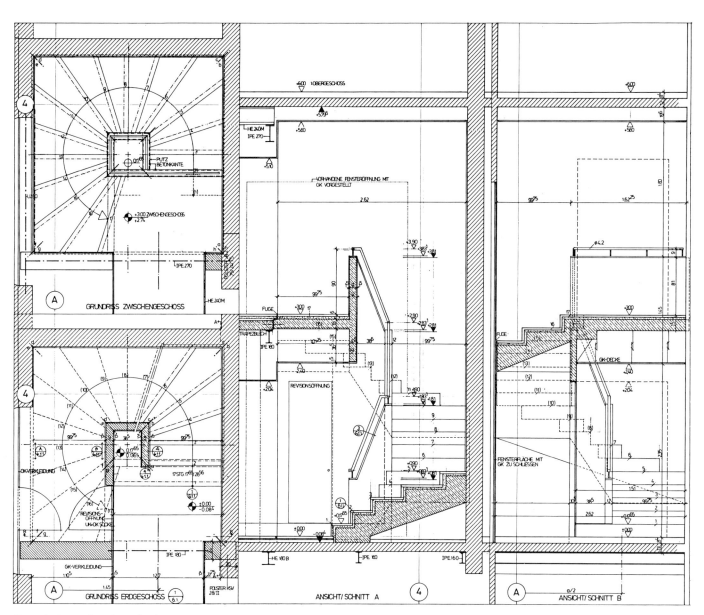

Ground-plans and sections of staircase

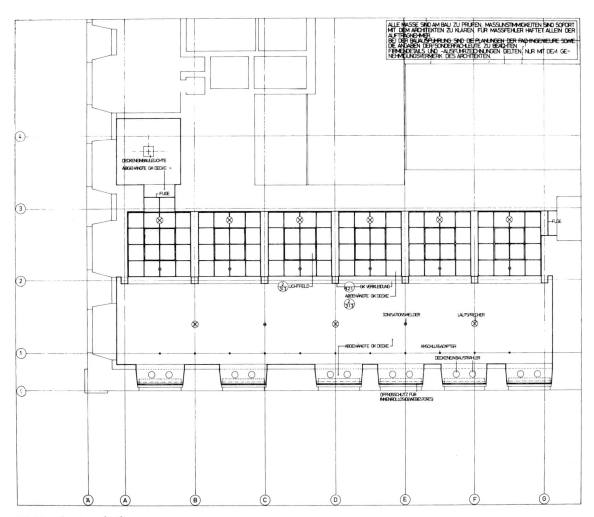

Working-drawing of ceiling

Stereometry without Aura

Falk Jaeger

Municipalities nowadays are glad when they can acquire major art collections through bequest or foundation, the purchasing budgets of their museums being little more than petty cash when we look at the horrendous prices being fetched in the auction-houses. Often, however, such donations are made on condition that an appropriate home be provided exclusively for the collection. Frankfurt has also acquired a museum in this way, housed in the Deutschordenshaus, where once the Teutonic Knights held sway, and now the easternmost pearl in the string of museums along the south bank of the Main. The foundation comes from the heart specialist Dr Jörgen Schmidt-Voigt, who has parted with his collection of 800 icons from Eastern churches.

Orthodox icons in the former house of the Teutonic Knights may well sound strange. But the building has long been secularized, and now houses among other things the city's science and art administration. The old refectory once held the Nidda Heddernheim archaeological collection. The baroque complex actually dates from the twelfth century; it was given its present form between 1709 and 1715 by Daniel Kayser, who erected it on Gothic foundations, and by Oswald Mathias Ungers, who rebuilt it between 1963 and 1965 in a slightly modified form after war damage.

The new Icon Museum is certainly not one of those whose visitors leave the building exhausted. An area of only 422 square metres was available for the complete museum, with display rooms, offices, depository and staff facilities. There was little possibility of expanding the space available, though some was created by adapting part of the inner arcade for a foyer.

The foyer is entered through the baroque portal, a short corridor, and a simple steel and glass partition. It gives a first indication of the architectural vocabulary employed. The ticket-counter and the shelving behind, the door openings and the display-cases have the square grid as their formative idea, and so does the floor. Where the old building does not fit into this scheme, peripheral strips ease the transition, both here and in the exhibition rooms. Opposite the paydesk

one looks through an arcade into the inner court of the three-wing ensemble; large white windows fill the arches. A recessed, filigree steel and glass wall would have left the arcade open, as it was after rebuilding, but unfortunately the slight gain in space was preferred to the more elegant solution.

The striking feature of the main exhibition-room is the gallery. This is an independent construction, placed in the room like a two-storey, six-bay loggia and marked off from its surrounds by indirectly lit interstices – not a new device but one used here to great effect. Otherwise, the architecture is visually unobtrusive; there is no narcissistic posing. The design and positioning of the display-cases is also markedly reticent, so that the icons can be shown to best effect. A small room on the left is used for temporary exhibitions, and a spiral staircase at the rear end leads to the gallery and another small display room.

The relatively modest scale of the museum induces us to take a closer look, to pay greater attention to details, and now we may be excused for feeling somewhat irritated.

Perhaps the glass cases could be pushed into line, but other shortcomings will be harder to remedy. The stone steps of the spiral staircase to the mezzanine floor have fine sedimentary strata, but nobody bothered to study the orientation of these strata, they just run haphazardly. The steel banister looks as if it were the work of an apprentice. The finish of the gallery also leaves much to be desired; for static reasons it is a steel construction, and its cladding is of plasterboard. The use of such a finish for piers and ceiling soffits requires great precision if it is not to look amateurish and diminish the whole effect. Unfortunately, the craftsmanship is not all that precise, and the meticulousness and subtlety of the design are not adequately reflected in the execution.

"Windows on eternity" Schmidt-Voigt calls his icons, "imbued with a spiritual religious significance". In the semi-darkness of Orthodox churches, with the scent of incense and the sound of liturgical chants, one can hardly escape the fascination of these devotional images, glittering and shimmering mystically in the candlelight. There they

are part of a greater architectural and iconographical context, arrayed on the richly decorated screen, the iconostasis, and only through their aura do they acquire their spiritual meaning. In the Icon Museum they are torn out of this context, classified in typological categories and presented simply as works of art. The architect Oswald Mathias Ungers and his assistant Hikaru Hane chose this clinical presentation in agreement with the museum managers. But the coolly rationalist inventorization robs the icons of their soul. To present them as objects of scientific research and so alienate them from their mythical world appears to be the purpose of the museum, but this is bound to cause some uneasiness in the visitor. Only the scale and form of the objects exhibited were taken as the guidelines for this white, stereometric architecture, whose axes, alignments and surfaces relate reflexively whichever way one looks; yet the architecture fills not only the existing space, as if it had always been there, but also the historical frame that had been created for it.

Exhibition-room

106 Museum für Kunsthandwerk

Museum für Kunsthandwerk

Museum of Decorative Arts

Architect: RICHARD MEIER

Built: 1982–1985

The design for the new museum is part of a general concept that includes the existing Villa Metzler, the leafy park and the bank of the River Main.

The purpose of the building is to display the art-treasures that were formerly housed in the villa.

The new building, with its facade of metal panels enamelled porcelain white lending it lightness and elegance, is also intended to give the museum its own specific identity. It accentuates its ground-plan and superstructure by taking up, repeating and multiplying the scale and dimensions of the original Villa Metzler. The basic quadrangular form that thus emerges, and whose main axes also determine the design of the park and the pedestrian routes and passageways, is penetrated asymmetrically by the extension of existing perspective lines and site boundaries.

The enclosed space is 55,860 cubic metres, the main area of use 8,000 square metres. The building costs were DM 48,700,000.

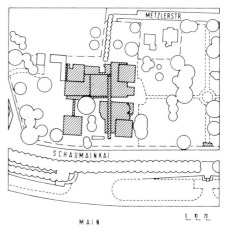

Schaumainkai 17

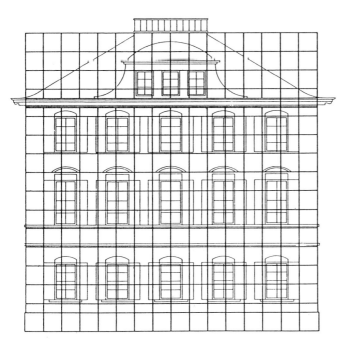

Proportion-study of old and new buildings

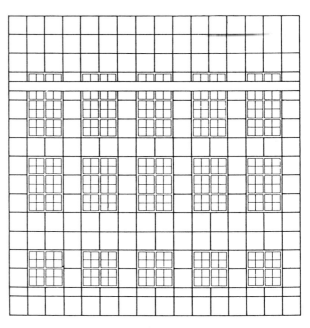

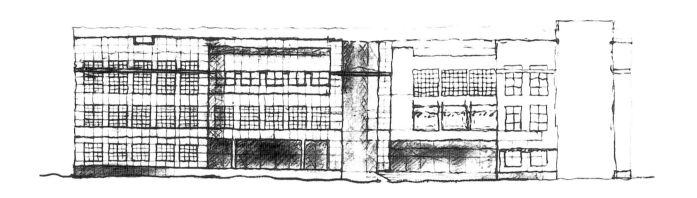

Facade sketches

Elevations and sections

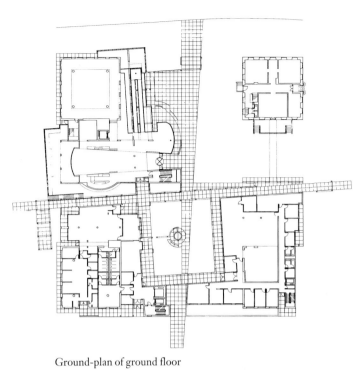

Ground-plan of ground floor

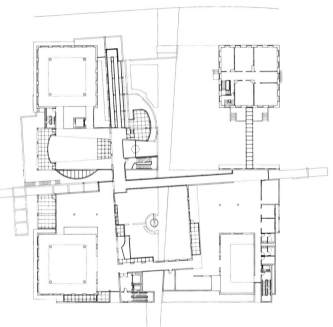

Ground-plan of first floor

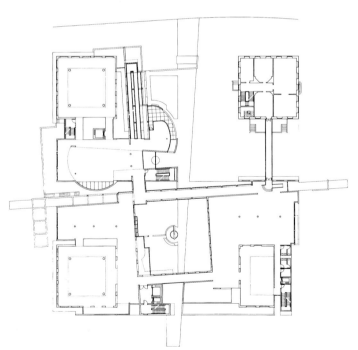

Ground-plan of second floor

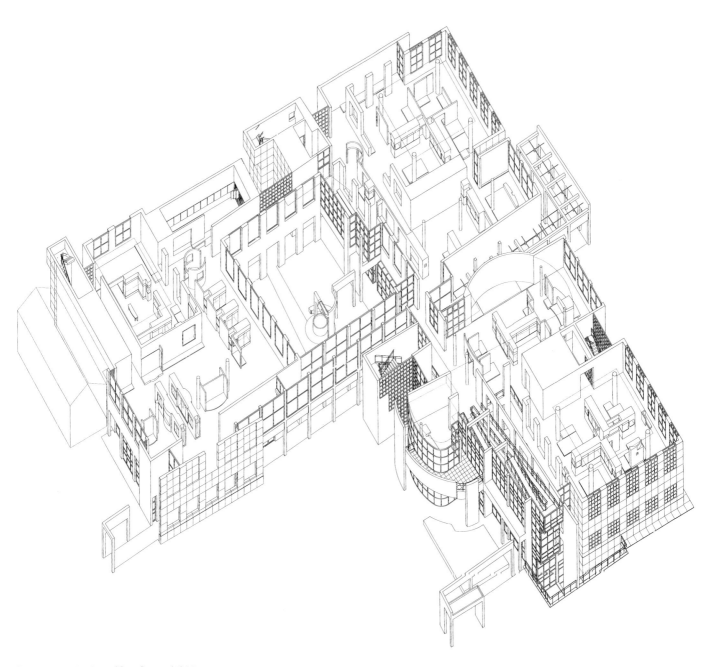

Isometric projection of first floor exhibition-rooms

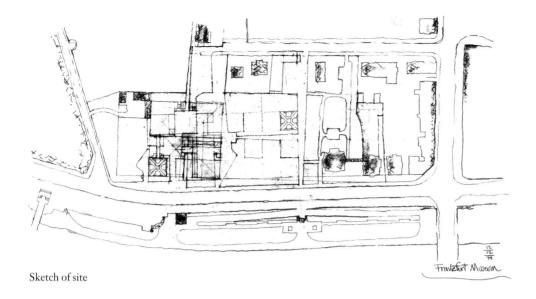

Sketch of site

Sectional perspective view

The Grand Chaos

Kenneth Frampton

"I go outside .... The magnificent chaos of the museum follows me and mingles with the bustle of the street .... We are and we move in the same vortex of the mélange that we inflict on the art of the past."
Paul Valéry

Richard Meier was fortunate enough to receive this important commission as the result of a limited international and national competition staged in Frankfurt in 1979.

Altogether, Meier was to engage in a more brilliant and subtle contextual game than his competitors, immediately exploiting the existing urban fabric and the history of the site for all its worth, while still implanting a rigorously abstract architecture on the four corners of the available territory. Meier's design integrates the building with the park as a hierarchically modulated composition of cubes, courtyards and intersecting cross-axes, with each formal element playing a precise role in relating the architecture to the essential attributes of the landscape and the pre-existing urban structure.

The first move in this syntactical game was to integrate the Villa Metzler into the composition, by echoing its 17.6 metre cubic envelope in the form of a gridded cube which not only assumed the same basic dimensions but also replicated in its elevational harmonies the size, scale and rhythm of its windows. In the competition design this abstract allusion was made more referential by a continuous non-projecting "cornice" which interrupted the top tier of windows at exactly the cornice height of the Villa Metzler. It is surprising to discover that this cube, conceived as a representational whole, appears only twice and on both occasions it assumes the form of an outriding corner pavilion which serves to establish the western limits of the composition. The positioning and appointment of these cubes is such as to define and accent the presence of the larger, three-corner, L-shaped complex lying behind. This complex embraces the Villa Metzler as though it were the fourth "corner" of the pavilion system. It is significant that these outriding cubes acquire their volumetric identity by being rotated off the main grid of the complex, the latter remaining parallel to the original grid of the Schaumainkai subdivision.

Appropriately enough, giving their identification, these corner pavilions align themselves with the inclination of the Villa Metzler as it accommodates its front facade to the beginning of a bend in the river.

The L-shaped complex brings into play the other primary generic elements of the scheme, namely the courtyard and the intersecting axes, the former centring the body of the building as a whole, the latter relating the orthogonal grid of the Schaumainkai to the principal system of vertical circulation, namely the pedestrian ramp, in contradistinction to the main approach to the building from the Schaumainkai. This normative cross axis bisects the L-plan and is extended along one coordinate to form the broad walk or "park" axis which will culminate eventually in another diminutive courtyard structure – the proposed extension wing for the adjacent museums of anthropology.

The intersection established by this primary cross axis is modulated throughout the site at different scales, first appearing in the longitudinal and vertical axes of the park itself and then reappearing as symbolic cruciforms "denoting" the ghostly centroids of bourgeois villas long since demolished. One of these Neo-Suprematist crosses assumes the three-dimensional form of a low box-hedge, a provision which is presumably intended to provide a certain intimacy for the café terrace which occurs on that side while serving, at the same time, to mediate between the exfoliation of the building mass along this edge and the general landscaping of the park.

Before turning to the genesis of the building in the evolution of Meier's work and to its subsequent development in the detailed design stage, it is necessary to remark on the spatial tension engendered, at the point of entry, by the conjunctive overlapping of two shifted axes, that is to say, the $3\frac{1}{2}$ degree misalignment of the main park axis and the ramp, with the rotated orientation of the entry approach and the corner pavilions. The deliberate rotational and volumetric disjunction ricochets throughout the scheme at every level. The result is a schismatic planar composition which has been heightened rather than lessened as the

building has developed, so that the three corner pavilions are even more in evidence as volumes in the final scheme. As a result, the realized building generates a great deal of "irregular" (i.e., non-parallel) corridor space on every floor. It is a well-known fact that architects tend to work in series and that irrespective of variations in the specific program, something of the same imagery and even, on occasion, a similar *parti* emerges in one building after another, although in this metamorphosis, the initial idea is gradually transformed until it becomes exhausted and played out – an architectonic hypothesis to which the architect has nothing more to add. Richard Meier is no exception to this rule and his Museum of Decorative Arts takes its place within his work as yet another version of a continuously evolving *idée fixe*. It belongs to a series of "cultural" complexes, which begins with the Atheneum Visitors Center, designed for New Harmony, Indiana in 1975, passes through the Hartford Seminary, Hartford, Connecticut, dating from 1978, to assume a more culturally decisive form in the Museum of Decorative Arts, under construction on the Schaumainkai from 1981 to 1985. It may be claimed that this idea attains its most condensed formulation in the High Museum of Art, designed for Atlanta one year after the Frankfurt museum but in fact finished one year before. Contingent site conditions and specific planning strategies aside, one may claim that where the literal and symbolic core in Frankfurt is the punched out, "degree-zero" facade which lines the central open-air courtyard of the scheme, in Atlanta, it is the internal, top-lit quadrant court, together with its circumferential access ramp. Where the former alludes to the "negative" tradition of modern European architecture, that is to say, to the critical legacy of Adolf Loos,

Model

the latter pays homage to the transcendental romanticism of the American Dream; that is to say, primacy is given to the romantic idealism of Frank Lloyd Wright rather than to the scepticism of Loos. Unlike Frankfurt, the synthesizing paradigm in the High Museum is the spiralling ramp and void of Wright's Guggenheim Museum, New York, of 1943, in which Meier himself was to work thirty-five years later when he created the Aye Simon reading room, to one side of Wright's original ramp.

In addition to the volumetric strengthening of the corner pavilions, a number of subtle transformations have occurred in the translation of the original design for Frankfurt into the realized work. Apart from the displacement of the original lecture hall into the basement of the north-western corner pavilion, most of the changes have occurred in the details of the buildings, that is to say,

in the internal articulation of the structure and in the simplification of the fenestration. The former now appears in the consistency of the square-planned, four-columned structural logic of the corner pavilions; the latter occurs in the correspondence which is finally established between the glazing-bar grid and the joints of the modular porcelain cladding panels. Thus where the large fenestration of the corner pavilions originally consisted of 24 pane windows, they now appear as windows of the same size only divided into 6 large panes. Whether this scalar transformation has been beneficial to the composition as a whole is hard to say without the benefit of seeing the building finally complete and occupied. It is significant, however, that this simplification was to be due as much to technical as to aesthetic considerations. The triple glazing involved in the thermal wall system of perimeter heat-

Model

ing adopted for the lower floors led to the decision to reduce the number of glazing bars in each window plane, so as to avoid an unduly fussy or crowded effect. Evidently it was something of a challenge to develop the original design in accordance with the severe restrictions imposed by local thermal standards and energy conservation regulations and it is at this juncture where most of the difficulties of cross-cultural translation seem to have arisen. For while there is little to choose between the climatic severity obtaining from time to time in certain parts of both northern Europe and the United States, the normative engineering techniques and standards employed for dealing with these extremes vary considerably between the two continents. In addition, one may remark in passing on the more intangible cross-cultural differences which are revealed through the impact of natural light – that is to say, of the different experience one may have of Meier's work depending on whether one views it under the invariably grey opalescent light of Frankfurt or the iridescent, almost Mediterranean blue skies which obtain, most of the time, in much of the American continent. The brilliance and precision of the exterior obtain in both cases, but it is the ambient light interior which is, as one might expect, more nuanced in Europe than in the United States.

There is one other dramatic change which merits comment before turning to evaluate the building as a museum, and that is the omission of the glass brick fenestration which in the initial design served to separate the pedestrian ramp from the corridor circulation of the north-western wing. During construction it was decided to leave out these glass blocks solely because of the unexpected spatial drama which was revealed in the interpenetration of the adjacent volumes; a spatial interplay which extended into the courtyard itself. This omission has had the effect of strengthening rather than weakening the initial concept where, as is indicated in the cutaway axonometric of the competition design, a continuous U-shaped wall with pierced windows divides the gallery space from both the fountain courtyard and the system of general circulation. This last, comprising the pedestrian ramp and its attendant connecting corridors, lines the inner perimeter of the L-shaped complex and links via a glazed bridge into the Villa Metzler.

In marked opposition to James Stirling's Neue Staatsgalerie in Stuttgart, which is devoted mostly to painting, Meier's Museum of Decorative Arts keeps its faith with the open-plan traditions of the modern movement, so that the problem of housing the exhibits themselves is resolved through the creation of aedicular structures inside the volumetric space; the erection, that is, of diminutive free-standing space dividers within the main body of the building. In contradistinction to similar structures built in The High Museum, Atlanta, these "thick-wall" partitions remain permeable to the cross light which fully penetrates the corner pavilions from two adjacent sides. Moreover the Frankfurt museum's free-standing cabinets are internally illuminated by planes of diffused artificial light and this imparts an iridescent quality to the general ambience of the interior. Once again, unlike Stuttgart's Neue Staatsgalerie, the effect here, as in Atlanta, is literally to "in-lay" the exhibits into the fabric of the building, so that the implicit concept of the institution comes closer to the feeling of intimacy embodied in Sir John Soane's museum in London, rather than to the didactic, open-ended galleries which were the normative form of the comprehensive collections established in the nineteenth century.

Unconsciously or not, Meier's labyrinthine approach to that which by definition has to be monumental, or at the very least systematically mnemonic, contains within itself a critical dimension in as much as it inhibits and resists the taxonomic dedication of the museum as an institution. And

Window front and access ramps

while one can indeed decipher the various classes of exhibits to which these cabinets are dedicated, there is a sense in which the appearance of the appointed objects on their respective shelves or platforms has been rendered accidental; that is to say it has been given an aura of an intimate, haphazard and highly personal delectation, as though this were the rambling house or ruined tomb of some cosmopolitan, melancholic prince.

Exhibition-room

Museum für Völkerkunde

Museum of Ethnology

Architect: RICHARD MEIER

Building starts: 1991

In contrast to the somewhat haphazard and labyrinthine nature of a typical nineteenth-century museum of ethnology, the new building presents itself rather as a string of galleries, lit from the side and above, harbouring a continuously unfolding sequence of ethnological exhibits. The galleries are linked by a glazed hall that looks on to the park on the north side.

Besides offering a well-arranged setting for the exhibits, the design was also determined by the attempt to encompass in a unifying format the various facets of an ethnology museum, from display to research and didactic functions. The variety is expressed in two ways: firstly in the cubic shape of the pavilions, which are integrated by the continuity of the glazed hall and by bridges over the entire length of the gallery area, and secondly by the various routes that can be taken within the galleries. This provides different ways of approaching the collection: the visitor can obtain a quick overview or embark on an extensive journey of discovery.

The glazed main hall offers delightful views of the park and so affords relaxation from the strain of continuously looking at heterogeneous objects.

The area enclosed will be 48,260 cubic metres, the main area of use 7,332 square metres. The building costs are estimated at DM 87,000,000

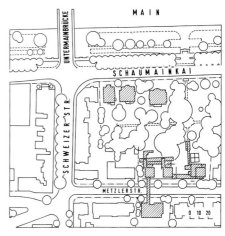

Schaumainkai 29

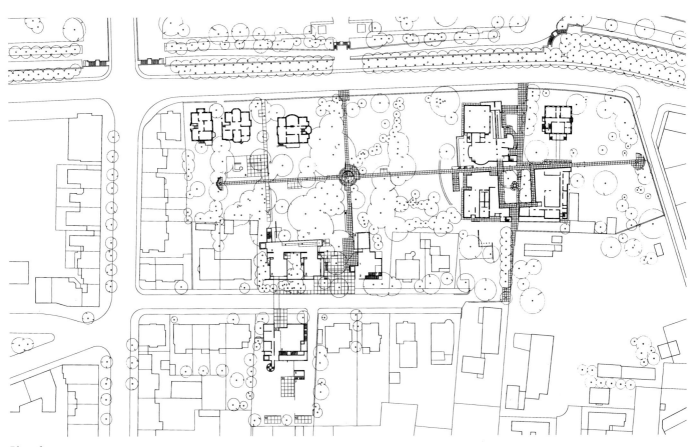

Plan of open spaces

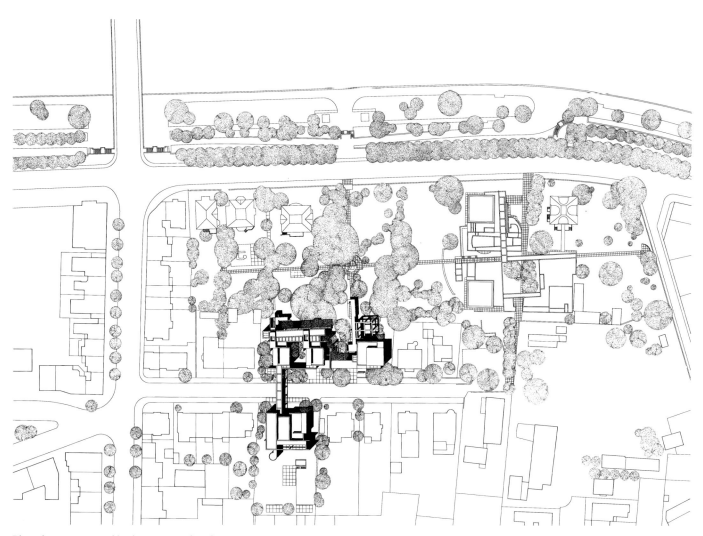

Plan of open spaces and bird's eye view of roof

Perspective view from park

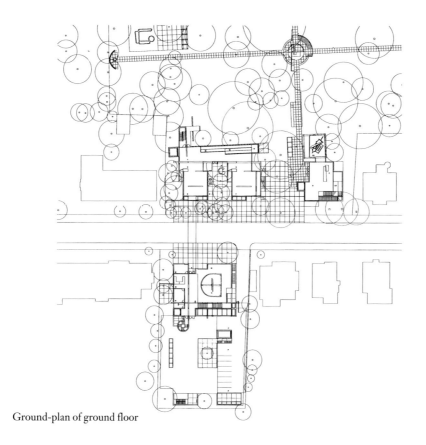

Ground-plan of ground floor

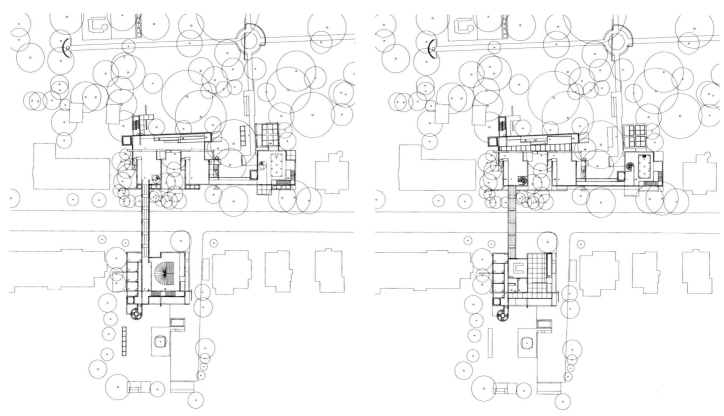

Ground-plan of first floor

Ground-plan of second floor

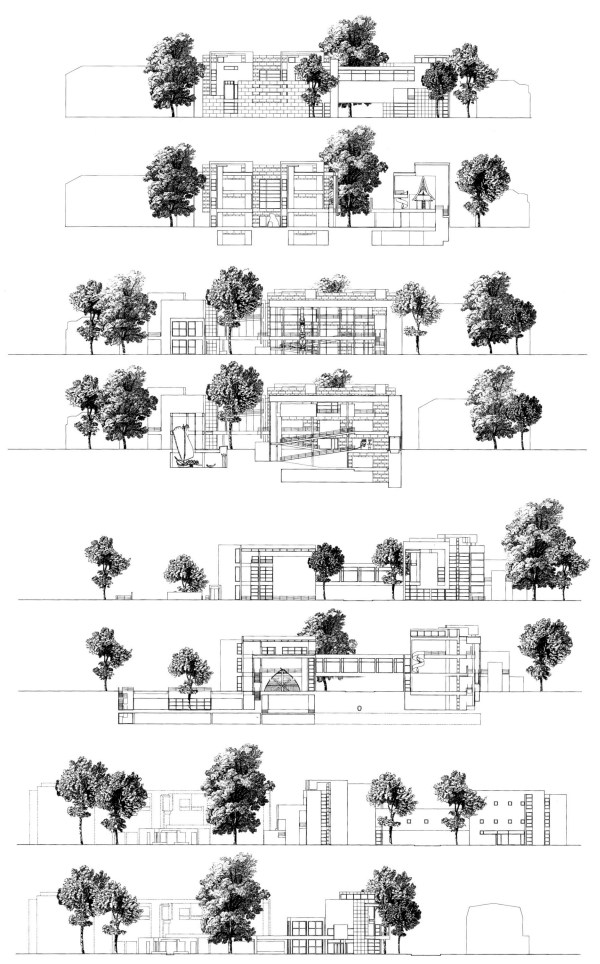

Elevations and sections

Unity in Variety

Dieter Bartetzko

There is no doubt that among the new post-modern buildings on Frankfurt's museum promenade Richard Meier's Museum of Decorative Arts is the absolute favourite with the public. Nor is there any doubt that the new city council took a very popular decision in choosing Meier's design for the extension to the neighbouring Museum of Ethnology. Most important, however, this design dispelled the doubts as to whether one could build at all in the midst of the lush greenery of the museum park, work on which had only just finished. One can, with the loss of only 33 instead of, as feared, 69

trees. And the city gained an architecture that, despite its evident consideration for the park, is of captivating individuality and elegance. This seems to be the exceptional case of a compromise that has succeeded in every way.

The design has three main components. A large glazed main hall provides urgently needed space for monumental exhibits; axial galleries and a bridge over Metzlerstrasse form a structural spine; and along this spine are deployed flexible ensembles of pavilions and cubes, reaching as it were out into the park.

As in the Museum of Decorative Arts, basic elements of the classical modernist movement determine the large cuboid elements of the building: obliques, cylindrical and grid formations, plain walls and broad areas of glass. White plaster, interrupted by white enamelled metal panels, will determine the external appearance, again as with the Museum of Decorative Arts.

All in all, we may expect the combination that has already proved its worth and is so greatly appreciated: the pleasing neutrality of Meier's un-severe late modernism, which leaves intact the surrounding historical

Model

buildings, with their wealth of ornamentation and variety of styles, coupled with the unobtrusive but effective versatility of the intricate medley of new buildings, which constitutes an independent formal counterpart to the older ones.

The mistake made in the Museum of Decorative Arts, where the overabundance of light proved detrimental to the exhibits, will be avoided here: Meier and his assistants have expressly pointed out that the upper galleries will have top lighting with blinds.

The interior architecture combines sequences of rooms that alternate between straight galleries of clarity and simplicity and smaller rooms that are interlinking and varied. Whether this will succeed in unifying the diverse aspects of an ethnology museum, as Richard Meier claims, or the result will be a confusing labyrinth, will be apparent only when the building is finished.

But the change in the function and symbolism of the neo-baroque villa built in 1904 seems inevitable. It is the embryo of the Museum of Ethnology, but – as with the neo-classical Villa Metzler at the Museum of Decorative Arts – it will no doubt be relegated from the main building to become the quaint, old-fashioned vestibule of the new.

The site may have been somewhat degraded as a historical monument, but it has at least been saved. One should not forget that this was one of the buildings on the bank of the Main that were threatened with demolition fifteen years ago. To be part of a museum ensemble and not the centre seems, under the circumstances, to be the inevitable price of survival.

Model

The commentary to the design states that visitors will, on looking out of the windows of the extension, feel as if they were floating in a sea of trees. The effusive language is superfluous: the architect has made the best of a difficult situation, siting his museum at the rear of a park that is eminently worth preserving, and transferring a good third of the mass of the building into the neighbouring Metzlerstrasse.

Informally grouped elements of the complex have their proper place in the park, while the cubic tract of the extension is fitted into the scale of the buildings lining Metzlerstrasse. Even the bridge unit linking the two ensembles and spanning the street is visually acceptable here (unlike at the Villa Metzler, where a similar construction virtually impales the neo-classical monument). Exuberant formulations are not needed; the quality of the design speaks for itself.

Deutsches Filmmuseum

German Film Museum

Architects: HELGE BOFINGER
& PARTNER

Built: 1981–1984

A historic villa dating from 1912 was gutted (its street facade was preserved) and transformed into a museum.

The central section of the facade on Schaumainkai was used as the scale for the organization of the interior, in that its dimensions were projected through the body of the building. This resulted in a cuboid space in which a tower was constructed that rises through all as a space-constituting element; it is twisted diagonally out of the central axis like a rotating component.

The tower is bordered on three sides by floor-to-roof open space. The horizontal exhibition circuits and the vertical transit routes via stairs are arranged around it.

Unfortunately, the exhibition concept was not coordinated with the architect's spatial plan, so that the envisaged unity of architectural space and exhibition has to some extent been destroyed.

The area enclosed is 17,550 cubic metres, the main area of use 4,890 square metres. The total cost was DM 16,400,000, of which DM 9,600,000 went on the actual construction work.

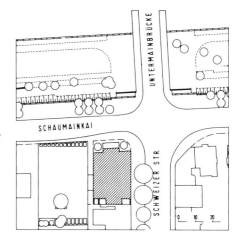

Schaumainkai 41

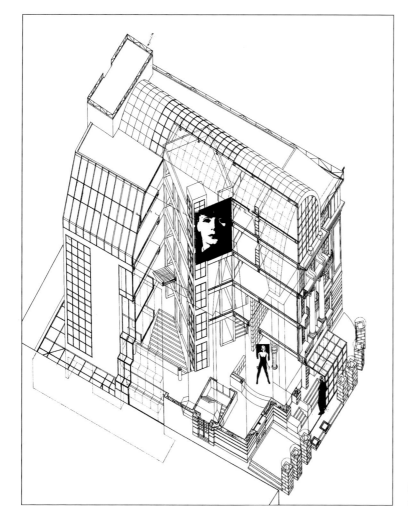

Isometric projection
of original design

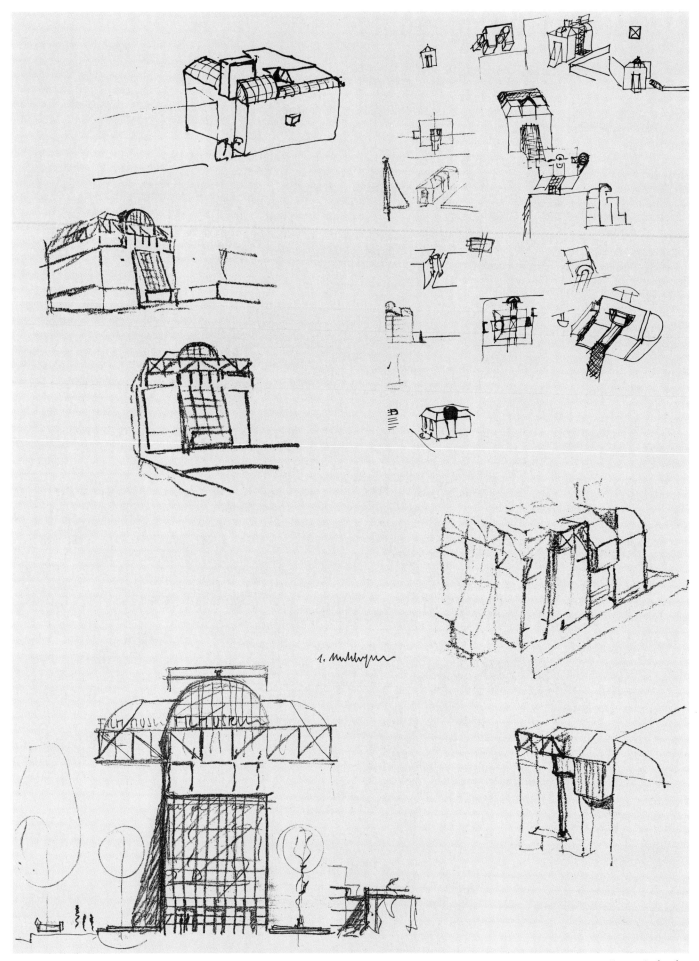

Isometric sketches

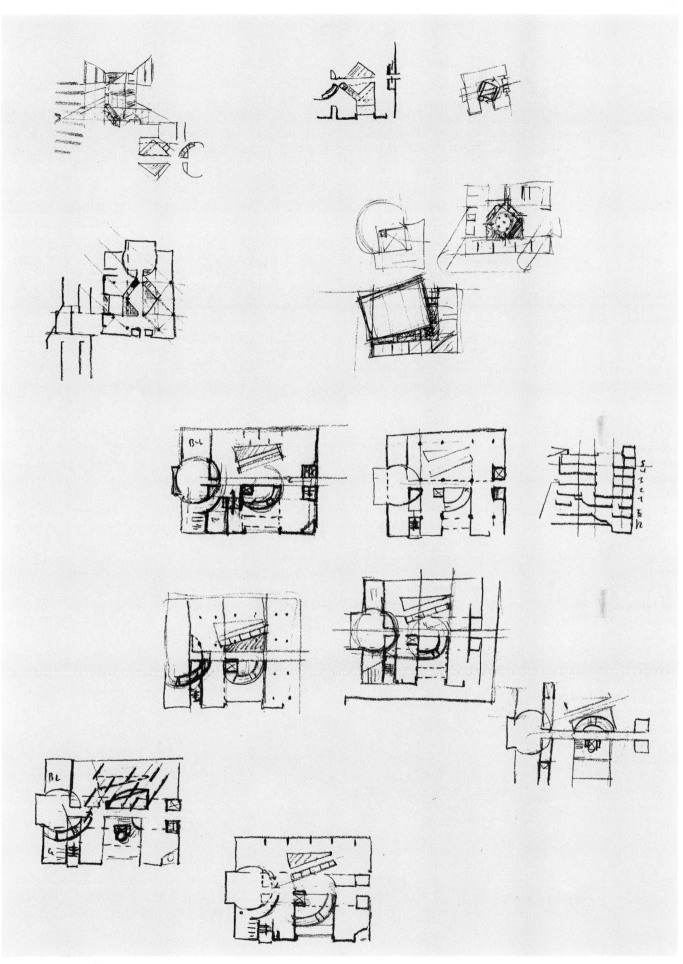

Plan-sketches

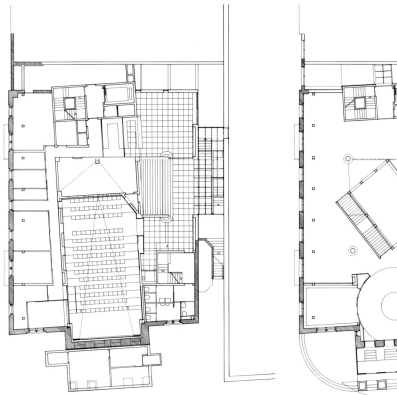

Ground-plan of first basement

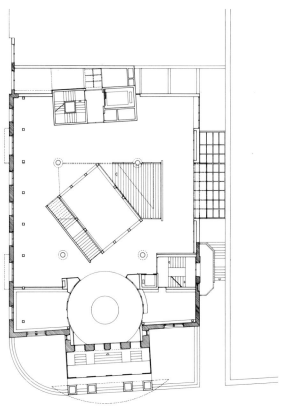

Ground-plan of ground floor

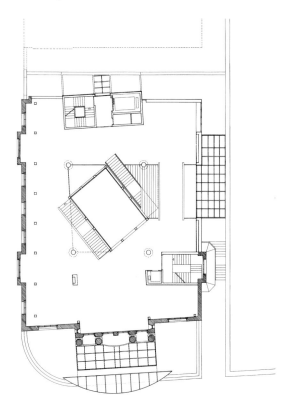

Ground-plan of first floor

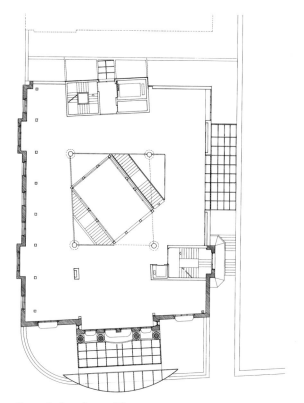

Ground-plan of second floor

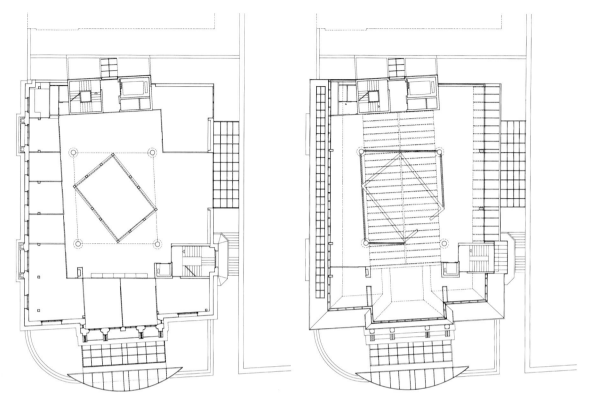

Ground-plan of third floor

Ground-plan of fifth floor

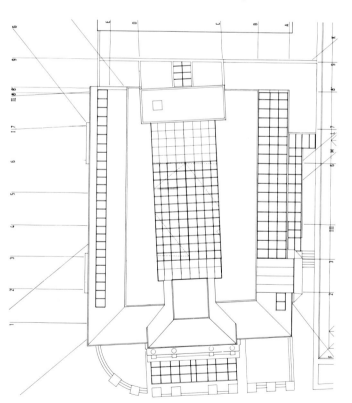

Bird's eye view of roof

View from north with German Architecture Museum

View from east

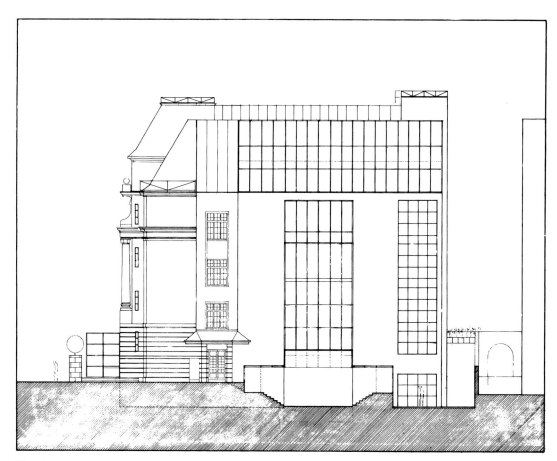

View from west

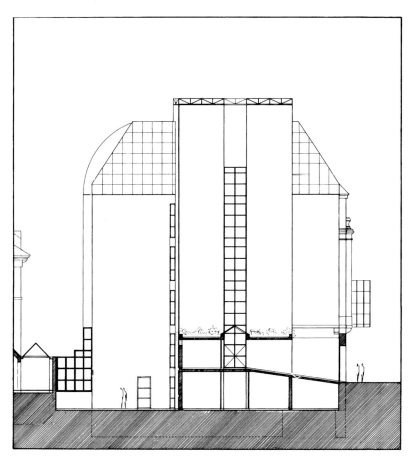

View from south

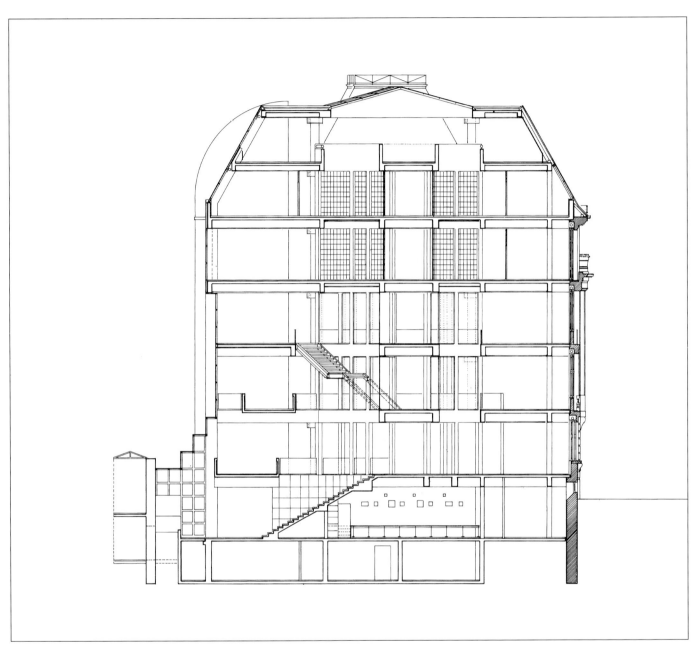

Section

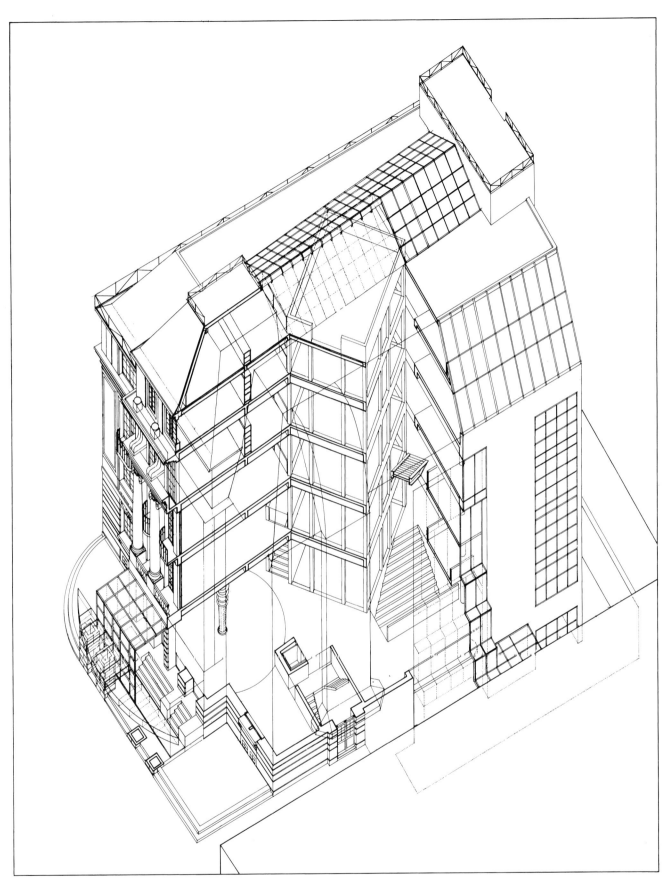

Isometric projection

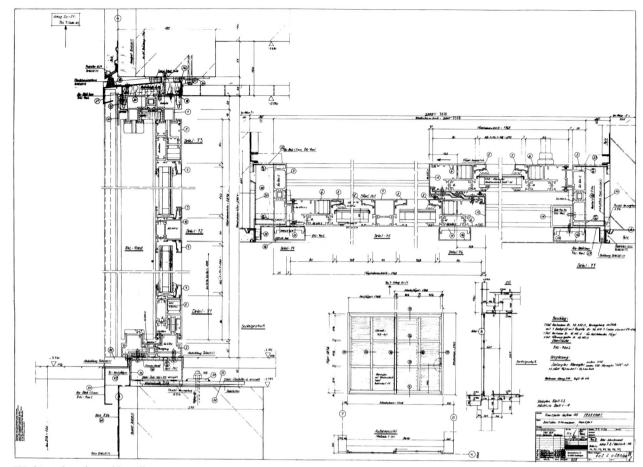

Working-plan of movable wall

Working-plan of porch

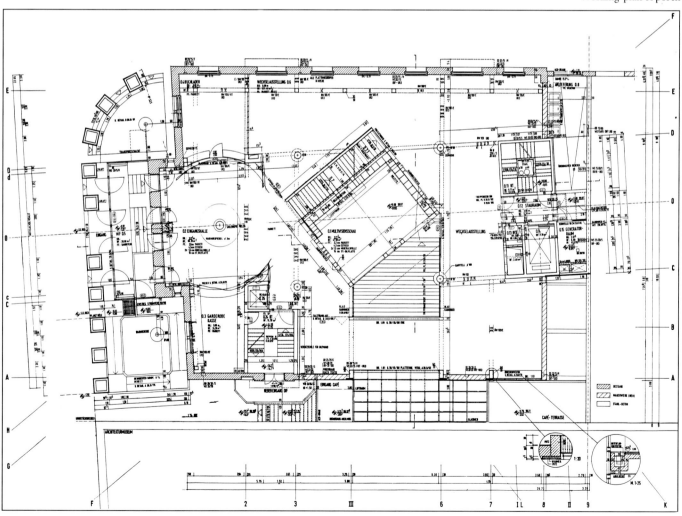

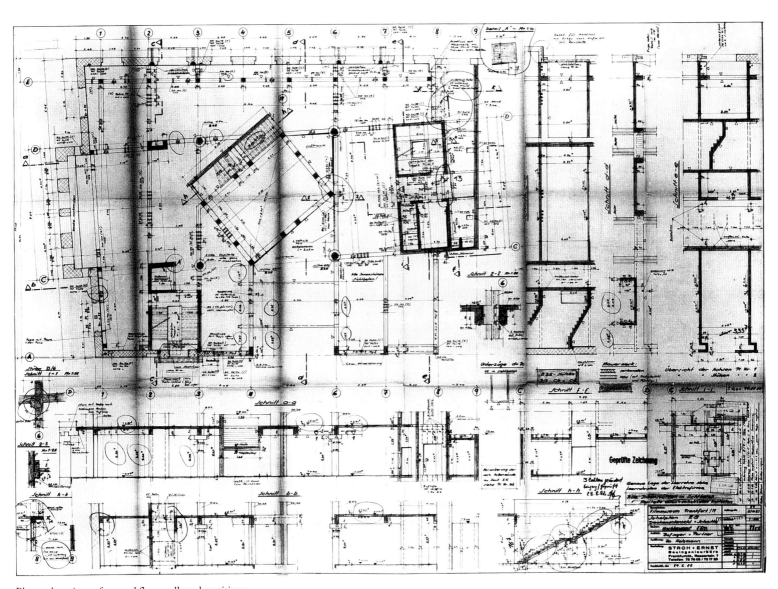

Plan and sections of ground floor walls and partitions

Staging of Accidents

Monika Zimmermann

The tasks were very similar: two Frankfurt patrician villas were to be turned into museums. Nevertheless, they are different tasks; specific factors determine each, although neither architecture nor film is really an ideal subject for a museum. An architecture museum can find a solution (and has done so in Frankfurt) by becoming an exhibition of itself, but a film-museum building will be expected to provide services, it will have to function. So it is not really fair to compare one with the other. However, as things are in Frankfurt, and in view of the proximity of the two buildings, Helge Bofinger does have to stand comparison with Oswald Mathias Ungers. That is his misfortune, although it is a misfortune he himself provokes with a multitude of references.

Unlike Ungers (who pursued his plan stubbornly down to the last detail), the Wiesbaden architect Bofinger rapidly found himself caught in a mesh of relatively banal conflicts of interests. Admittedly, the constellation had been difficult right from the start, for an architect was being commissioned to build a film museum who had so far aroused attention with the openness and transparency of his buildings. Where there is much light, there is little darkness – but film, as a medium, needs darkness to be seen. Bofinger, as might have been expected, designed a building that is open to all sides and admits much of the natural environment. And, as might have been expected, this is in contrast to a museum concept that is based on things not being what they seem, operates behind the scenes, and needs the artificial projection of reality. So the clash was pre-programmed, and the result is not a compromise, it is more of a parataxis.

Thus, the Film Museum (and in this it involuntarily resembles the Architecture Museum) has become a house within a house. Behind Bofinger's structural shell an independent inner life unfolds, although it was not the architect but the film and stage designer Jan Schlubach who was mainly responsible for this. As further evidence of how Bofinger's style was cramped, his building has a negligible outward presence; it retreats (at least on the two street fronts) behind the facade of the late-nineteenth-century villa. The latter's historizising, colonnaded formal idiom seems, moreover, to lead directly over to Schlubach's lavish land of make-believe, so that the solid new building within is left with hardly more than the task of supporting the flimsy backdrops without and within. (The fragile state of the old structure was the reason why the building costs soared from the original estimate of six million to sixteen million marks.)

Bofinger's hidden and in many ways disguised architecture can best be seen from the uppermost of the seven floors. Here, where the library is located and the daylight can pour in unhindered through a big glass roof, the basic principle of the whole building is immediately apparent: a rectangle is set obliquely in the centre of the interior space, which is also rectangular – the situation is the same at both top and bottom of the building. On each floor four columns are the load-bearing elements, and they are positioned opposite the sides of the smaller rectangle so that they also mark off a rectangle. The so defined triangular cutoffs would have constituted light-wells running the whole height of the building if the architect had had his way, but fire-regulations foiled the plan, which in any case failed to impress the museum managers, for it would have brought a lot of what they did not want at any price: light.

An intermediate ceiling, which now also fills the triangular cutoffs, is a rudimentary vestige of the original idea, with its reflective surface. Where clarity and transparency had been the aim, a veil now seems to have descended. One wonders at corners and edges that seems meaningless, at huge columns with outsize capitals; four thousand square metres of museum space are swallowed up in an impenetrable network of the apparent and the real. Effective spaciousness, at any rate, is not the main characteris-

Model with vaulted roof (not executed)

tic of this museum; it is more like a labyrinth or a hall of mirrors, at least on the
three main floors. And where the staff work
and the offices are located, again the architect's ideas do not seem to have found
favour. To take just one example: the semi-
nar room, which is in the centre of the
building, has walls of glass bricks, in order
not be completely cut off from the outside
world, but now it has been lined with
shelves, inside and out, and turned into a
sort of darkroom or boxroom.

So Bofinger's design has remained little
more than a promise. The promise is given
right at the start. At the main entrance the
new building is in the foreground, breaking
boldly through the old facade and also push-
ing the inner superstructures to one side.
The glazed porch, which is crowned by a
flat semi-circular roof, is an anthology of
quotations. It is intended to be a reference
to "classical" film architecture and to evoke
an aura of glamour and glitter. A neon in-
formation-strip is borne by a cluster of
polished brass columns.

But this whimsicality contradicts another
allusion: Bofinger quotes Ungers by placing
the slender columns on massive pillars.
They are cut from the same Main sandstone
that mantles the base of the neighbouring
building, and this suggests a community of
spirit where in fact the opposite is the case.
The Architecture Museum is the fruit of
logic, of deliberation – the Film Museum is
a showpiece of more or less happy accidents.

Model

The only thing really common to the two
museums is the cafeteria in the basement of
the Film Museum, but this, with its Viennese coffee-house clichés, has more in common with any other cafe than with either of
the two museums.

On entering the Film Museum one suddenly finds oneself on a kind of circular revolving stage. Here one can choose from a
number of entertainment programmes that
either present or conceal themselves in the
segments behind glass and mirrored walls.
One can also create one's own small sensa-
tion – by proceeding confidently down the
stairs. The fine marble staircase, which at
first looks just like any other flight of steps,
gradually reveals itself to be an illusionistic
construction of truly theatrical scale. De-
scending it, anyone would feel like a film
star in the spotlight.

Who cares that it is actually a descent
into the cellar? Stars always come down to
earth eventually; and the stairway leads in
fact to the cinema, the crucial element in a
film museum. Moreover, it is an element
that is completely cut off from the outside
world and lets in reality only by way of artificial light. This at least Bofinger has respected: his cinema is as dark as the night.

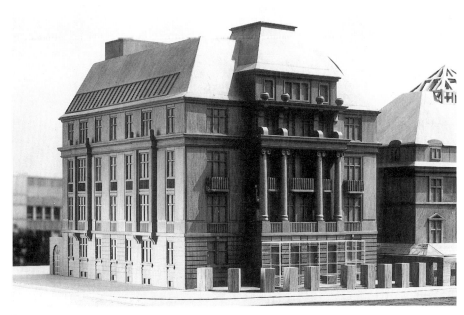

Foyer

Deutsches Architekturmuseum

German Architecture Museum

Architect: OSWALD MATHIAS UNGERS

Built: 1981–1984

A double villa on a relatively small site on the corner of Schaumainkai and Schweizer Strasse was available for the museum. The villa itself is hardly of architectural merit; even if it purports to evoke the architecture of the Bibliotheca Laurentiana, one can only say that it is with some irony that it resembles its famous model. But that is neither here nor there: only the nostalgic value of the house is important. It is part of a collective memory that the site on which it stands and local history have engendered, and it is that which makes it worth preserving.

The entire site was transformed into a house, or an interior by being enclosed within a wall. This made the old villa itself an object in an exhibition area, so that it is both an item in an exhibition and a place where exhibitions are held. This gives it a significance that goes far beyond the actual and original purpose of the house. As an object it is alienated.

The area enclosed is 12,850 cubic metres, the main area of use 1,735 square metres. The building costs were DM 12,400,000.

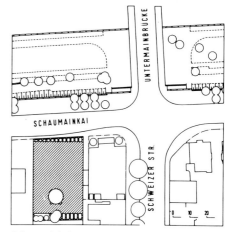

Schaumainkai 43

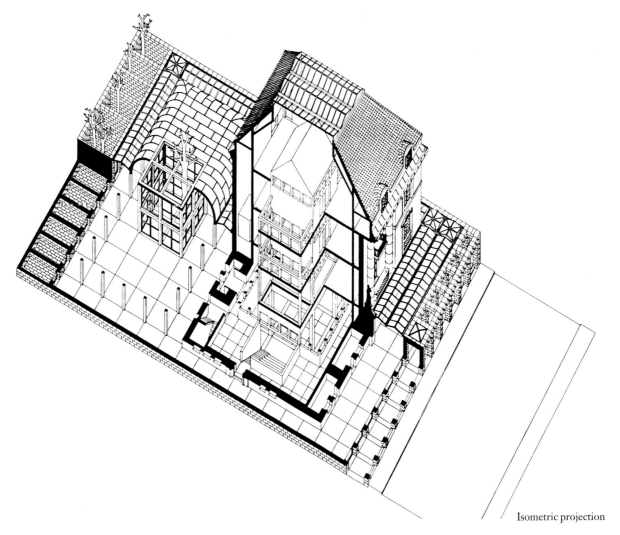

Isometric projection

Design sketches

Views from north, south, west and east

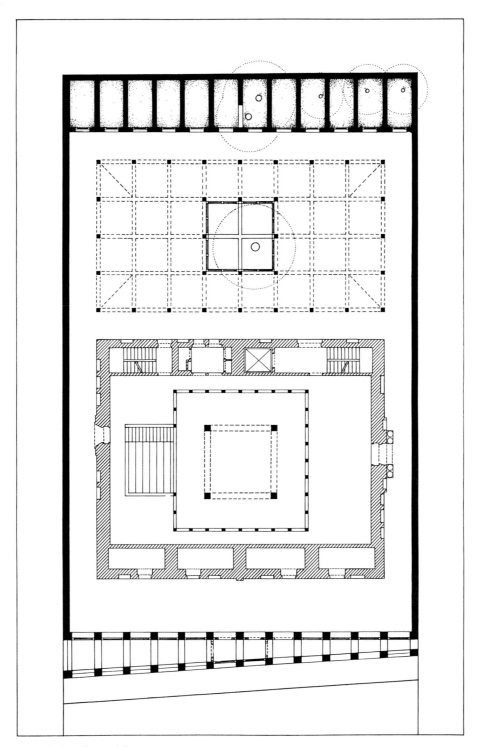

Ground-plan of ground floor

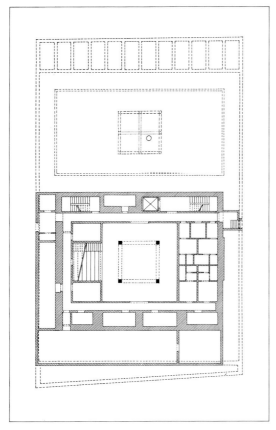

Ground-plan of first basement

Ground-plan of first floor

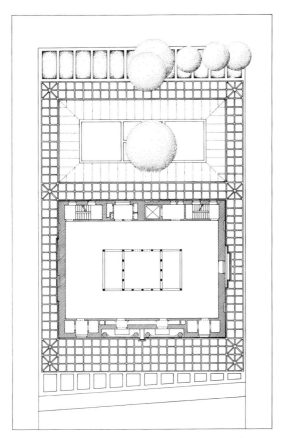

Ground-plan of second floor

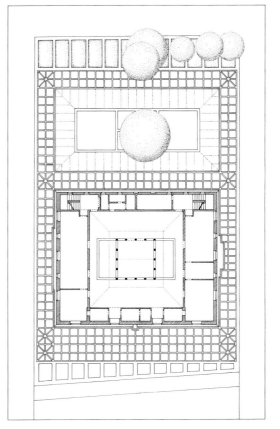

Ground-plan of third floor

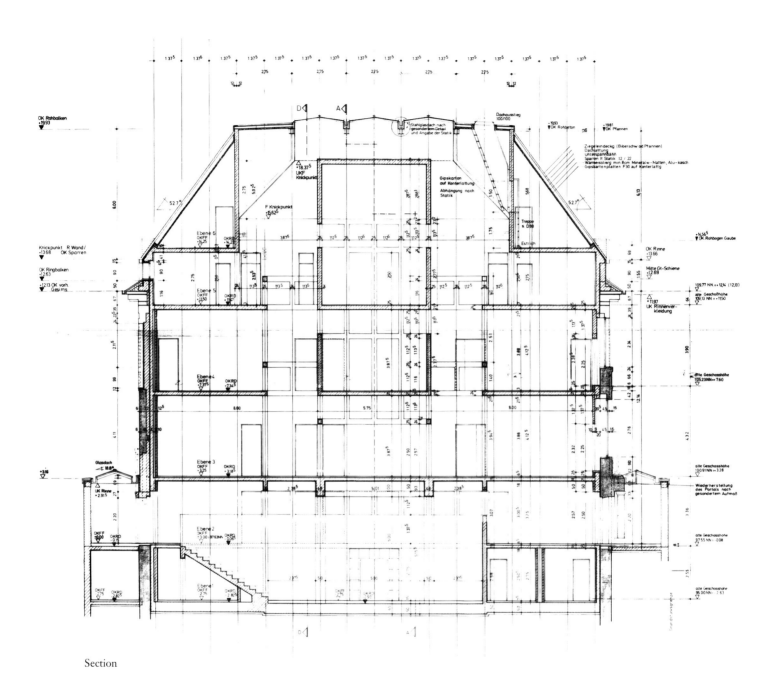

Section

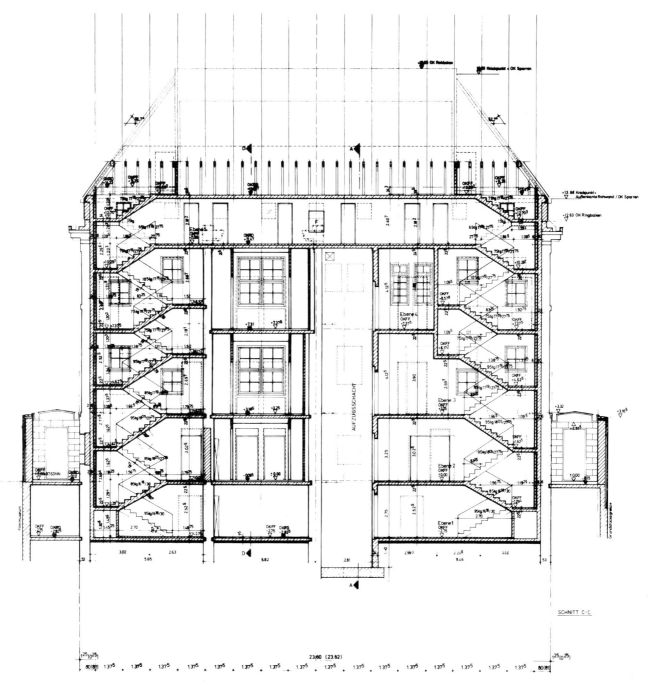

SCHNITT C-C

Section

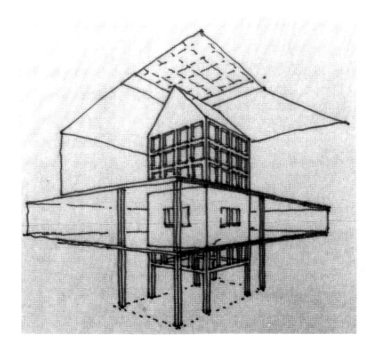

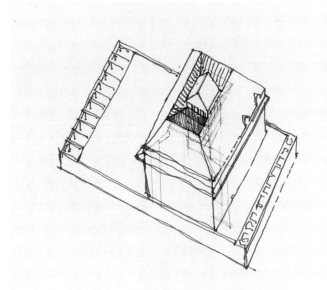

Design sketches for 'house within the house'

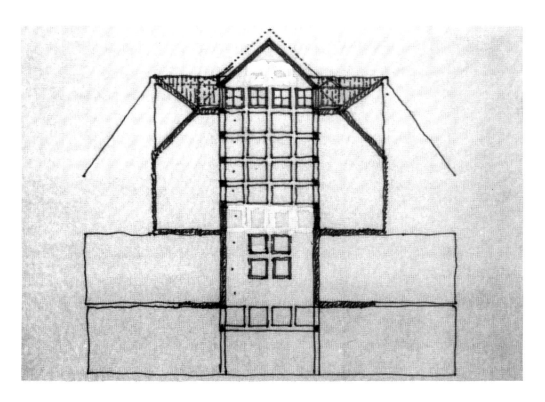

Early sketch of exhibition-hall

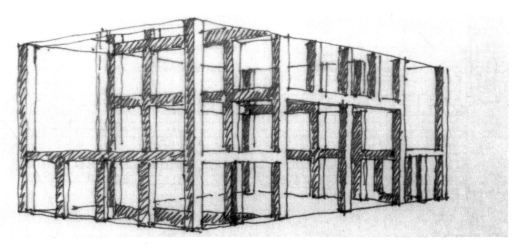

Design sketch for 'house within the house'

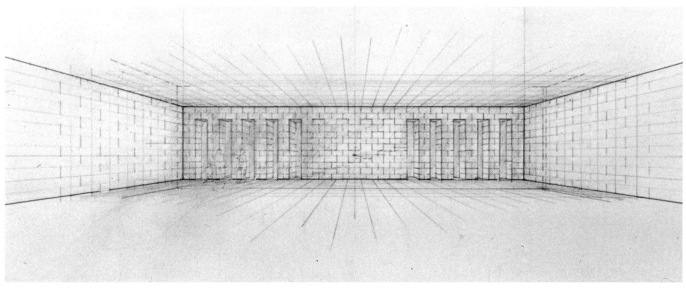

Early sketch of exhibition-hall

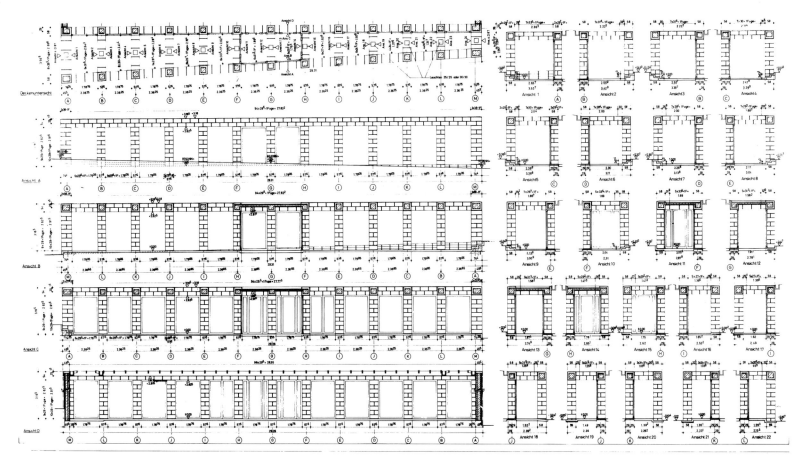

Coursing-plan for arcade

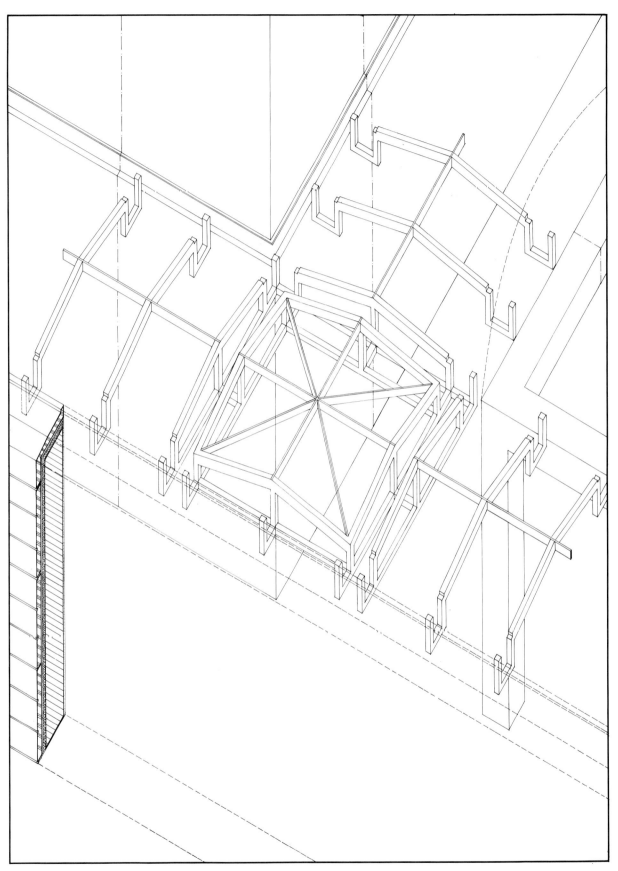

Isometric projection of intersection of glass roofs

City Wall and Adam's House

Heinrich Klotz

O.M. Ungers' building not only provides a home for the German Architecture Museum, it represents in itself what architecture can be.

At a time when the existing heritage of buildings is being discovered as a vital resource it is appropriate to take an old building as the basic element of a new one. Here, a historical villa dating from 1901 is the core of the entire complex. The outer wall forms a contrast to it, running like a rusticated "city rampart" around the site. At the crossing of Schaumainkai and Schweizer Strasse the wall forms a bulwark against the surging traffic and gives the ensemble a definite inward orientation. So as not to discourage the visitor, the rusticated wall opens up on the street front and becomes an inviting loggia, giving a full view right through the building to the rear. At the back, the wall encloses small open courtyards, in which chestnuts and ash-trees grow creating small environments where exhibits can be displayed in the open air. The outer frame of the building may appear to form a cordon against the outside world, yet it is not impermeable, and does in fact allow positive interactions with the surroundings.

The city council had suggested that the entire site be girdled with a wall. O.M. Ungers took the idea further and made a glass-covered surround for the old villa, which now emerges as it were from the glass roofs. These enclose at the front a foyer two bays deep and at the sides corridors, while at the rear an exhibition-hall with "patio" is provided. The patio accommodates a chestnut-tree, whose branches spread out above the hall; this courtyard has the form of a cube, its glass walls articulated in a square grid-pattern and the roof-opening also expressing the architectural figure of the square divided into four. Here, the proportions and dimensions that govern the entire rear hall are evident to the eye; as one moves around, the ceiling-divisions and the spacing of the piers reassert the square-module as determining principle.

The rear hall has its counterweight in the old house, which rises high above the ground-floor envelope. The historicising facade elements, like the Ionic columns and the rounded dormer windows, play a large part in establishing its character. The old rusticated base made the use of rustication appropriate for the new outer wall as well.

On entering the old building one is surprised by the size of the rooms, which permits an inner structure to be erected vertically through the building, a house within the house. On the lower floors, however, this inner core is at first only suggested. In the basement one sees four free-standing supports that form a sort of baldachin with the ceiling-light. A wall-frame perforated by openings encloses this "four-pillar room" like a shell. This is where Ungers starts to articulate the architecture theme and to make manifest his idea of the organization of space via various layers of shells.

The room above, on the ground floor, gives the impression of a hall divided into three aisles. In the centre, however, the room becomes concentrated, for here four pillars are grouped to form an inner compartment. With the girdle of square opening along the top of the walls the articulation scheme of the lower floor is taken up again. This enclosing grid-motif emphasizes the central group of pillars, and the whole represents a more concrete version of the four-pillar room below.

From the first floor, through a gap in the ceiling, one can see that the core-room, the four-pillar baldachin, rises through the upper storeys, becoming more and more enclosed, until finally, on the top floor, it assumes the form of a house with walls pierced by a band of square windows. Now the idea of the whole building becomes clear: not only is this little house the vertical culmination, the final concretisation of the four-pillar room, it also forms the core of the shell-within-shell plan, enclosed by the external wall of the original building, and this again by the rusticated encircling wall. On a second look it becomes clear that another shell has been added, dividing the space between the outer facade of the old building and the inner rooms, so that the service-shafts can be accommodated in this subcompartment as well as the – albeit narrow – stairs and goods-lift. The infrastructure of the building is thus located between the shells of the walls; at the same time, the double wall provides welcome insulation.

As soon as the structure of the building has been grasped, it also becomes clear why Ungers speaks of its "thematic component". It is not the aim of this architecture to fulfil mere functions or act as an abstract space-container to create usable areas. It is rather the illustration of a design-concept – indeed, one could say a story is told about how a building becomes increasingly concentrated towards the inner core and how finally, as symbolization of architecture, a house crystallizes within the house. Its germinal element, the four-pillar room, has the general significance of the protecting roof,

Model

which is supported by four posts. As John Summerson has shown, the four-pillar room as a baldachin has since ancient times been the architectural symbol of the centre of the world. Wherever four posts have been set up, man has placed himself in the centre of the world and found his identity amid the endless expanses of space. Ungers shows how the house evolves from the primordial symbol of the baldachin; and by showing the stages of this evolution from one storey to the next he makes his theme comprehensible and the aesthetic fiction visible. In building this museum Ungers has for the first time realized his architectural theory of the unfolding of a theme, a transformatory morphology. It was not his intention to organize immobile, static space or simply to provide an abstract shell as a protective enclosure; above and beyond its utilitarian function, the architecture has taken on an illustrative character, and it has become the semantic vehicle of a representable fiction. It has assumed a poetic dimension, without the aesthetic aspect being limited to applied ornament. The building is in its entire structure an artistic device, "narrating" the poetic idea of the transformation of the four-pillar room into a house through vertical stages, and at the same time revealing the protective function of multiple enclosure in the horizontal sequence of shells.

Ungers belongs in the tradition of the modern movement in that he rejects applied ornamentation. Looking at the all-pervasive white of the rooms, a white that also covers the floors, one might think that the ideals of the Bauhaus had been followed. The simplicity of all the architectural elements, with their sharp geometric edges and sober lack of ornamentation, seems to confirm the dogma of "New Building". But the white of these rooms is not the symbol of purification that Gropius and le Corbusier aimed for, it is a white that banishes corporeality and suggests weightlessness, as if rooms

Exhibition-room

would be transcended. With an insistence that nearly drove the contractors to despair Ungers managed to create rooms that have seemingly cast off every vestige of materiality and embody what we might call the "metaphysics" of architecture. Only when the partition-walls are put up for exhibitions do the rooms come closer to the reality of the three-dimensional.

This spatial effect is vehemently contradicted by the characteristics of the rear exhibition-hall. Everywhere one encounters the material weight of stone, which finds expression in the embossed blocks of the base of the old building and in the rusticated masonry of the little yards. Bands of rustication are even found along the top and bottom of the side walls; it is almost as if the white hanging-surface had also been rusticated originally. In contrast to the "trans-

cendent" interior world of the old building, the earthly robustness of an outdoor world predominates here, determined by the material tangibility of the "city wall" that runs around the site. One might call the rusticated courses and the sandstone facing of the entrance the "ornamentation" of the exterial area, an expressive device that strictly differentiates the character of the outside from that of the inside. By reasserting the eloquence of architecture and by graphically characterizing the different parts of the building, Ungers has moved far away from the traditional ideas of a modern movement that preached the homogeneity of all parts, so promoting uniformity and an expressionless monotony. The German Architecture Museum has left such a modern movement behind.

Deutsches Postmuseum

German Postal Museum

Architects: GÜNTER BEHNISCH
& PARTNER

Built: 1984–1990

On Schaumainkai, next to the older Städel Art Institute, several new museums have been built: the German Film Museum, the German Architecture Museum, and the Museum of Decorative Arts, to name only three. The German Postal Museum is one of this series of new buildings with which the city of Frankfurt has created a "museum promenade" along the River Main, opposite the skyline of the city centre. Large villas surrounded by gardens formerly lined the river here, and the idea was to preserve these old villas as the characteristic style of the new museum area.

It was thus decided to preserve the villa on the site destined for the Postal Museum, and that is where the museum administration is now housed. For the museum proper only a relatively small part of the site then remained, and the extensive exhibition-space had therefore to be accommodated on two levels under the villa gardens. Above ground level rises a slender structure which is adapted to the cube of the existing villa and also contains exhibition-areas. A glass building, which is a constituent element of the site, links the subterranean parts of the museum with those above ground.

Among other things, the Federal Post Office aims to show the latest communications media here, and the new building is intended to reflect a technically innovative, efficient enterprise.

The area enclosed is 27,444 cubic metres, the main area of use 6,662 square metres. The building costs were DM 38,000,000.

Schaumainkai 53

Photomontage of entrance situation, competition version

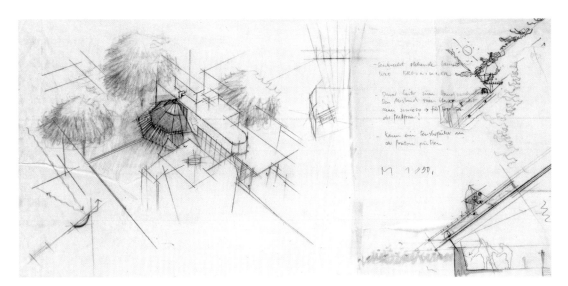

Isometric and detail sketches

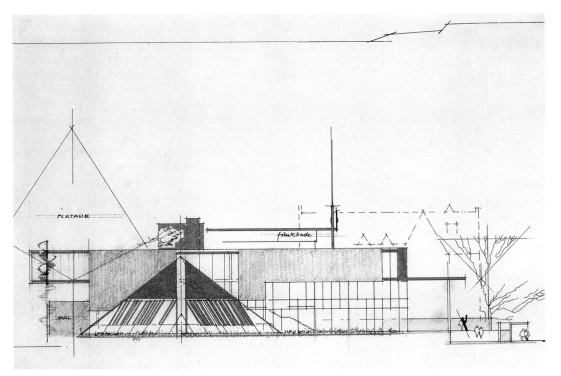

Study for facade

Perspective sketch

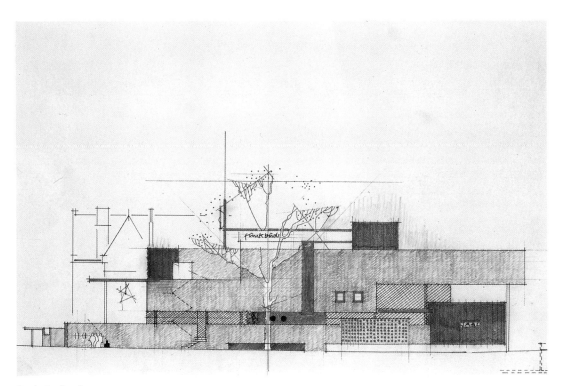

Study for facade

Study for facade of old building

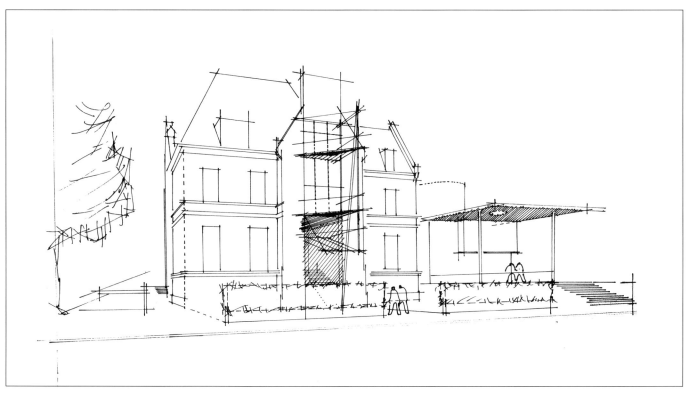

Study for facade of old building

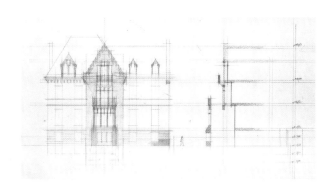

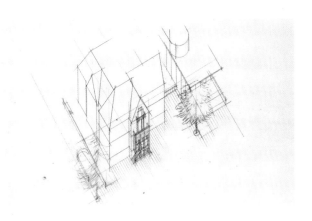

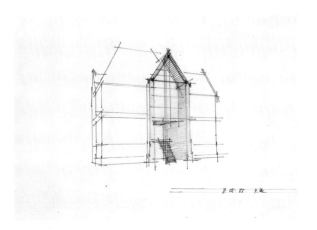

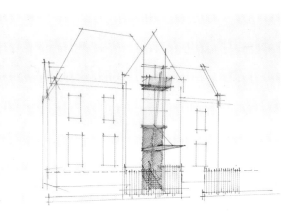

Variant ideas for facade of old building

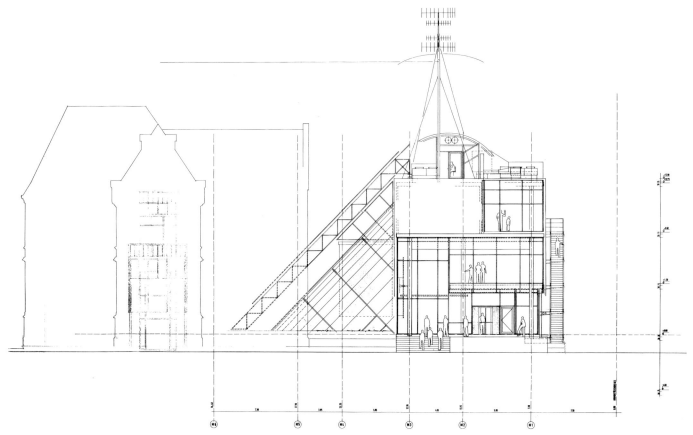

Study for facades of old and new buildings

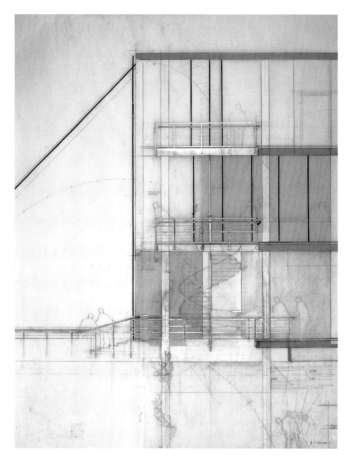

Colour study

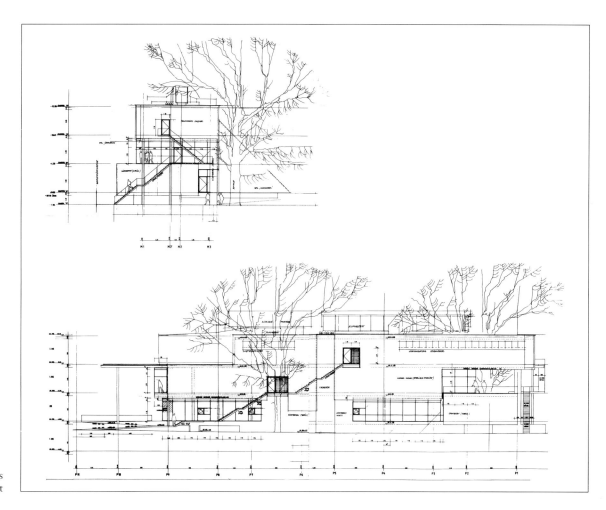

Elevations
from south and west

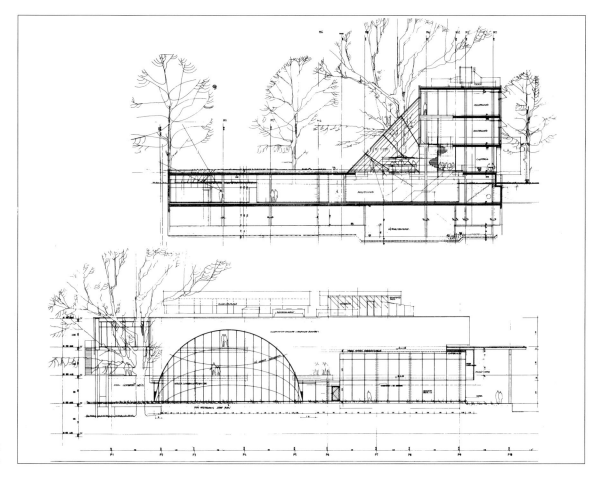

Section and
elevation from east

Deutsches Postmuseum 159

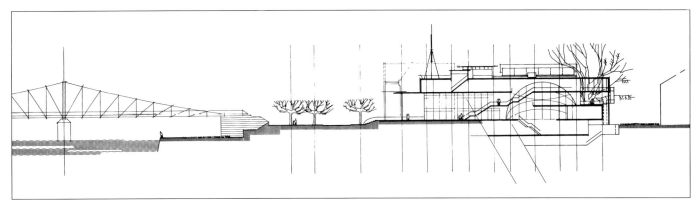

Section with riverbank

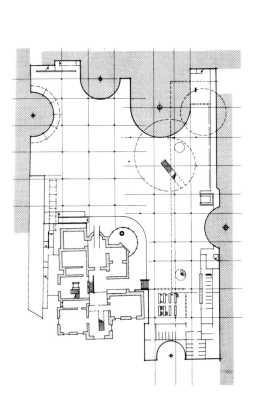

Ground-plan of first basement

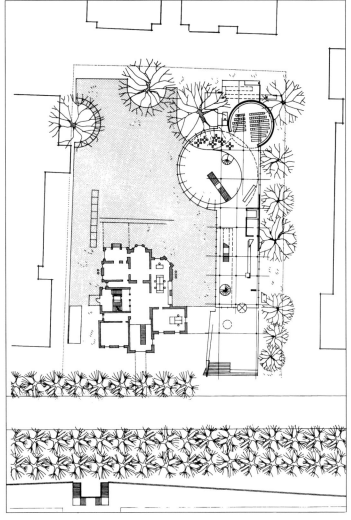

Ground-plan of ground floor

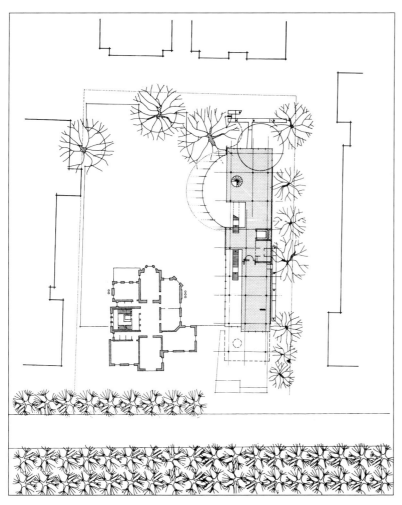

Ground-plan of first floor

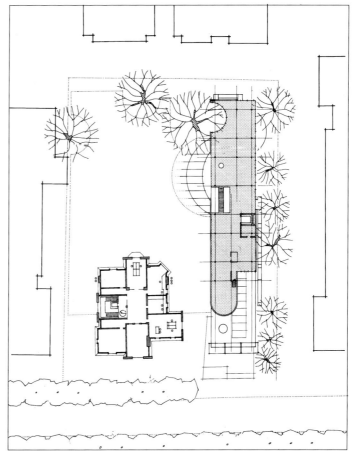

Ground-plan of second floor

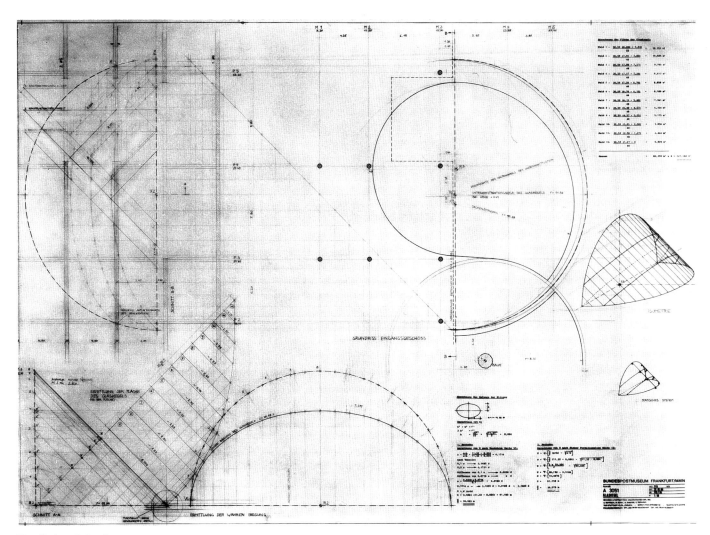

Detail-plan of glass bay

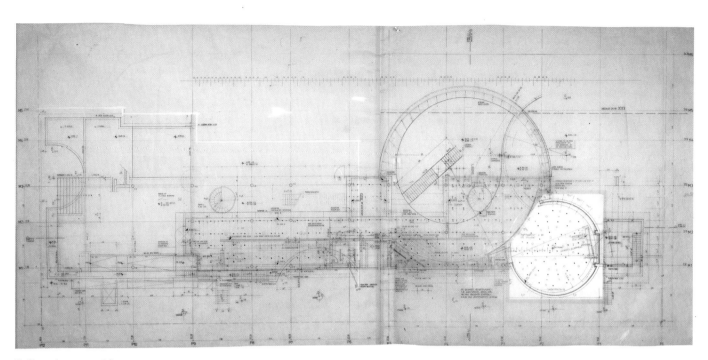

Ceiling-plan, ground floor

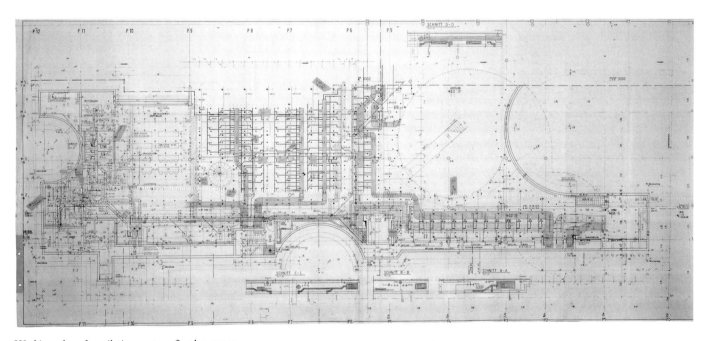

Working-plan of ventilation-system, first basement

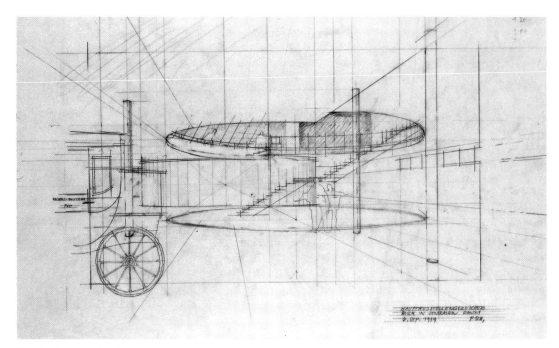

Sketch of interior, first basement

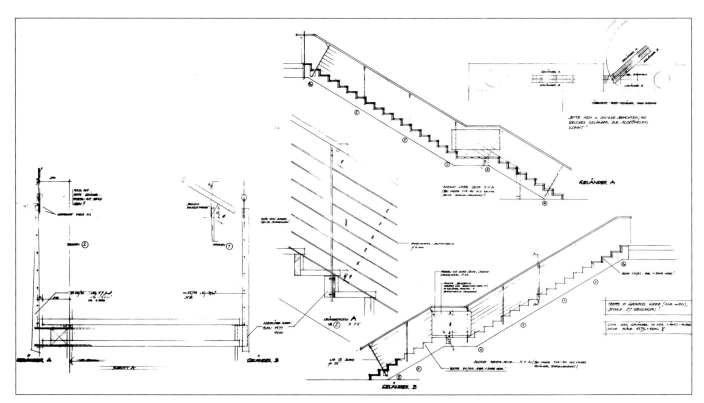

Detail-plan of banisters

Transparent Discipline

Peter Rumpf

Günter Behnisch can always be counted on for surprises. To be strictly correct, one should say Behnisch & Partner, for the finished projects of the last few years, for all they have in common, show clear evidence of different hands. In the German Postal Museum on Schaumainkai the architecture surprises us by its reticence, indeed, by a discipline in the choice of materials and their presentation, which was not always one of the virtues of this office. (How different the partners' work can be is evident from the kindergarten in Untertürkheim, Stuttgart, which was finished at the same time – a highly eccentric structure, sinking obliquely into the ground and bordering on cheap sensationalism.) That the new building on the bank of the Main makes a less startling impact, and reveals all its qualities only on a closer look, is a piece of luck for Frankfurt – and for the Behnisch office.

In this heterogeneous but sensitive ambience, directly adjacent to the sandstone villa with its modest Victorianism and an utterly insignificant commercial building of the 1960s, indeed, in the overall context of the museum strip with its various highlights, the architects of the Postal Museum have not succumbed to the temptation to draw attention to themselves through extremism. The new building is unobtrusive in many ways, but it is definitely not dull.

The design won first prize in a competition open to entrants from Hesse and Baden-Württemberg. That was at the beginning of 1983. The architects on the jury were Max Bächer, Jochem Jourdan, Gerhart Laage and Roland Ostertag. We should remember that around 1980 competitions had produced several prize-winning designs that were to be of great moment not only for Frankfurt but for the evolution of architecture in the Federal Republic as a whole. They included the Römerberg project (Bangert, Jansen, Scholz & Schultes), the German Architecture Museum (Ungers), the German Film Museum (Bofinger), the Museum of Decorative Arts (Meier), the Museum for Prehistory and Early History (Kleihues), and a little later the Museum of Modern Art (Hollein). It is interesting to recall the architectural background – material and theoretical – behind the jury's vote for Behnisch. At hardly any other time before or after was the "Whither architecture?" debate so passionate and the fronts so unremittingly opposed to each other as in these peak years of the post-modern movement. On the one side stood Ungers, Kleihues, and perhaps Meier, on the other Hollein, Bofinger and Stirling (Staatsgalerie, Stuttgart); between these two fronts – or better, opposing both – stood

Model

Model

Behnisch, passionately upholding the tattered banner of a democratic architecture, as he still does today. Well, Behnisch won this competition, with Mutschler, incidentally, in second place.

It was undoubtedly a courageous decision to let Günter Behnisch build between Oswald Mathias Ungers and Richard Meier, and it is to the credit of this controversial architect that he did not let neighbourhood rivalry tempt him into mounting a "demonstration", but fell into line. One result of this was that the building mass specified in the competition has only a modest presence on the relatively small site, thanks to a large part of the exhibition area having been put underground. Only a slender, three-storey longitudinal block is inserted beside the historical villa, and it keeps its distance. A rounded glass outcrop sinking obliquely into the ground points to the hidden areas below.

The decision to use little "new" architecture and so leave the rather plain villa room to breathe, while burying large parts of the structure below ground, meant that a few trees had to be felled for the excavation work. To preserve others on the edge of the site, the subterranean ground-plan has semicircular cutouts to avoid their roots.

The semicircle, an element born of necessity, then becomes the leitmotiv for the entire design. It recurs in the glass bay, in the stairs, the external walls, the aluminium-clad roof superstructure, and in the large circular opening in the projecting porch roof. All the rest is strictly orthogonal, with a consistency quite alien to other recent designs by the Behnisch office.

This severity is, however, limited mainly to the ground-plan. It is countered in the details, the surfaces, and all kinds of transitional elements, where the virtuosity of these architects in handling materials and their inventiveness come to the fore. Piers and profiles are fashioned in consummate slenderness, colour is allotted an independent role, unobstructed views alternate with intersections. What distinguish all the buildings from the Behnisch office, airiness and transparency, are here abundantly present: now particularly, while still empty, the building is filled with sunshine and light.

That brings us to the problems museum curators face in coping with light. A few yards up the river the windows of Meier's Museum of Decorative Arts are well curtained, and the installation of sunblinds on Behnisch's imposing bay window is still causing headaches. But that would mean the

end of all the transparency, and the end of the fascinating opportunity to step out of the building, under the glass canopy, and take in the external facade – which is certainly worth seeing – without leaving the exhibition area.

This is a conflict that is as old as architecture itself: the ambivalence between practical requirements and the intrinsic requirements of the architecture – or, if you like, of the architect. In the ideal case, should a conflict arise, a happy medium will be found. An unusual functional requirement can encourage an architecturally innovative solution, just as an idiosyncratic architectural concept may induce the user to forget his routine expectations. Here in the Postal Museum it is a different matter again: to reduce the building to a "signal", virtually a technical installation, a large part of the exhibition area had to be put underground. There, the architecture had little chance to assert itself against the items on display. Only the opening to the sky, the view into the treetops, the glimpse of the reflecting external skin of glass and aluminium gives the architecture its due. To sacrifice this in the interests of shade would rob the entire concept of an important moment.

The compromise between the need for as

Interior view

much space as possible and the desire for modest architecture is a compromise between two irreconcilables. To be frank, too much was expected of the site – particularly with the wish to preserve the trees. On the other hand, these limitations motivated the architect to exercise self-discipline; and as it turned out, that was not a bad idea. In view of the pleasing and in no way sycophantic result, one could wish to see elsewhere too a return to the virtue of normality, coupled with a wealth of experience in construction and design.

Städtische Galerie
im Städelschen Kunstinstitut

Städel Art Institute, Extension

Architect: GUSTAV PEICHL

Built: 1988–1990

The Städel Art Institute is to receive an annex in the form of a longitudinal building of simple design. Siting, shape and scale derive from the endeavour to integrate the new building into the existing Städel ensemble while preserving the green areas and the sculpture-garden.

The rooms are functional in their arrangement and divisions, and access to them is from a central hall. The plan provides an excellent overview and easy orientation for visitors.

To preserve the solitaire effect of the Städel ensemble, the new structure is separate from the existing buildings; a bridge provides the necessary link.

Despite the spatial separation of the old and new buildings, the two form a recognizable unity. They are related to each other through the fenestration and facing of the annex in natural stone.

The character of the existing architecture and the surrounding area has been preserved by the proportions and choice of materials.

The enclosed space is 18,971 cubic metres, the main area of use 1,382 square metres. The building costs were DM 18,000,000.

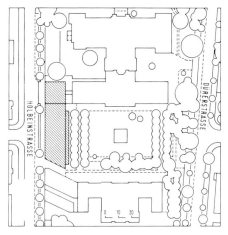

Schaumainkai 63

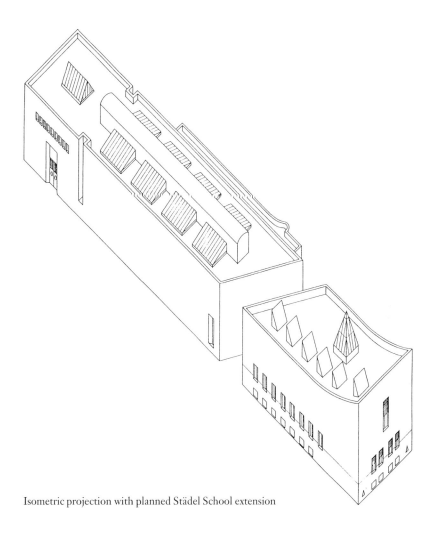

Isometric projection with planned Städel School extension

Perspective sketch
of entrance situation

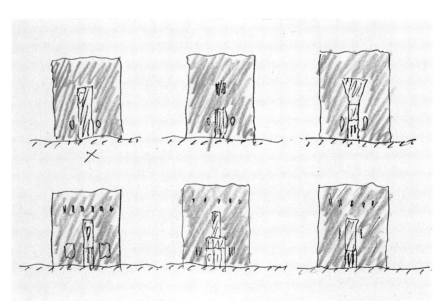

Sketches of
entrance elevation

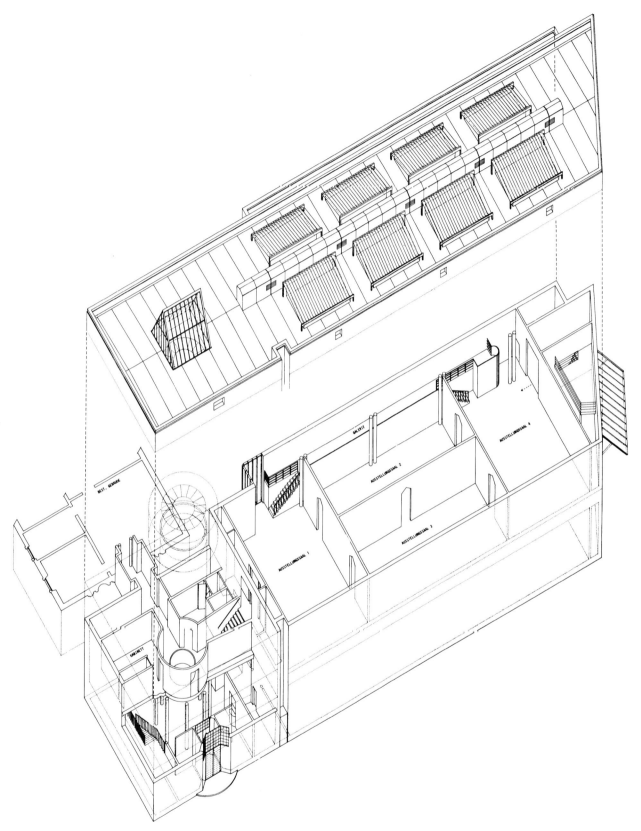

Exploded isometric projection

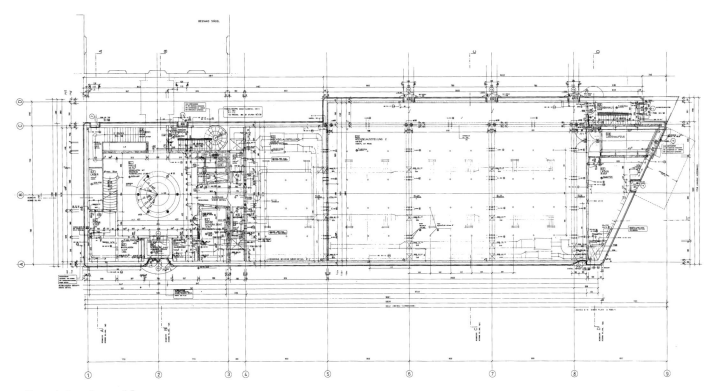

Ground-plan of ground floor

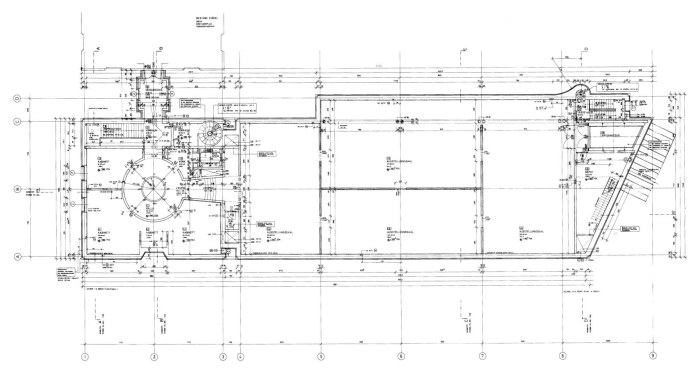

Ground-plan of first floor

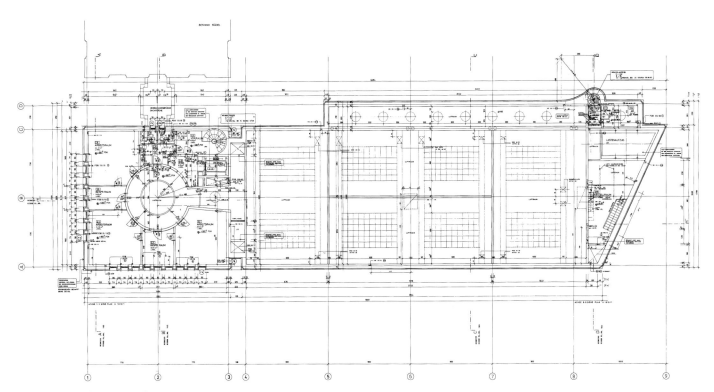

Ground-plan of mezzanine floor

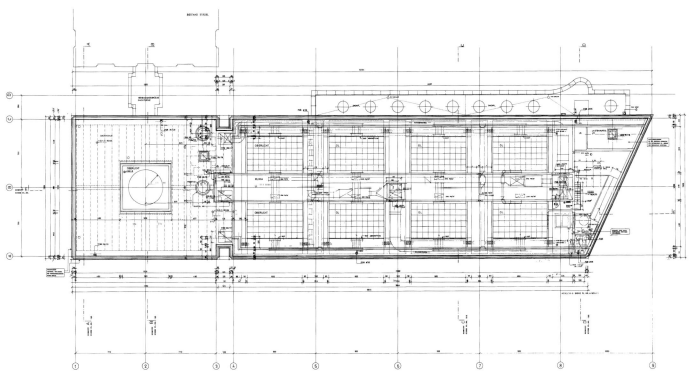

Plan of top-lighting

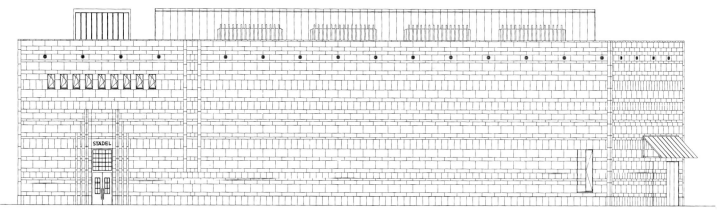

Elevation from west

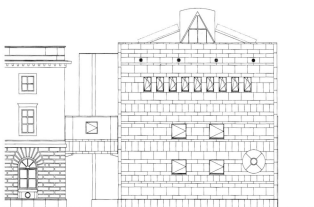

Elevations from north and south

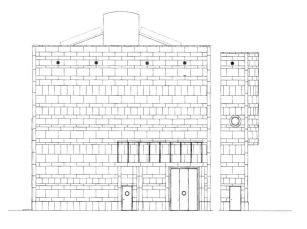

Elevation from east

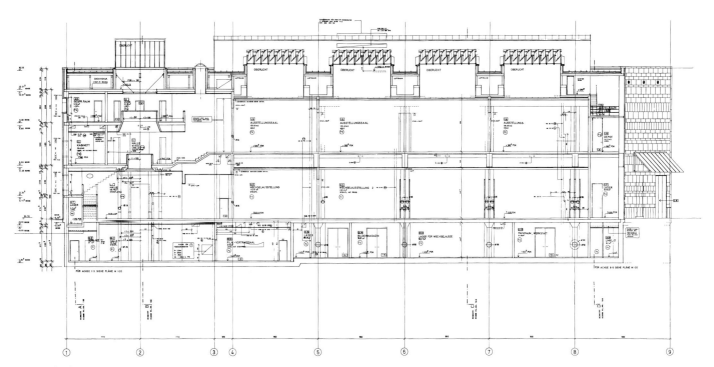

Longitudinal section

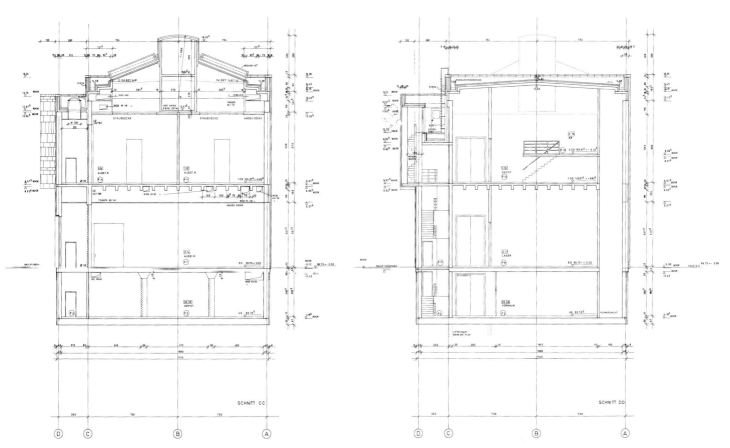

Cross-sections

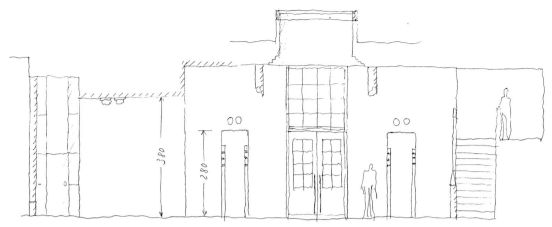

Sketch of interior elevation

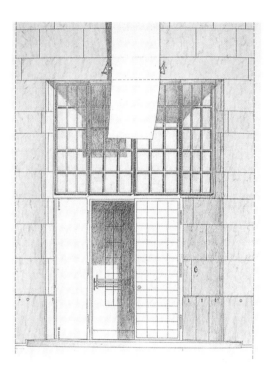

View of entrance

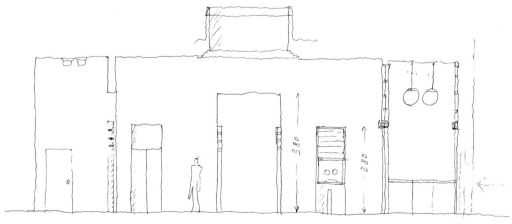

Sketch of interior elevation

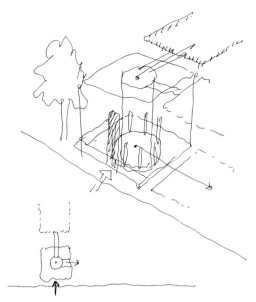

Isometric sketch of access-building

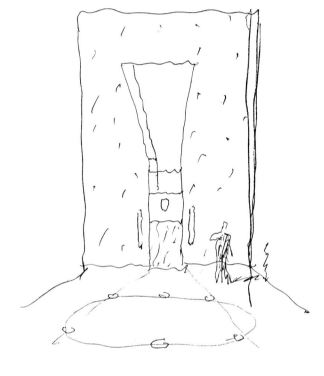

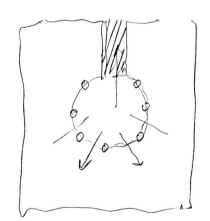

Sketches of access-building: interior and ground-plan

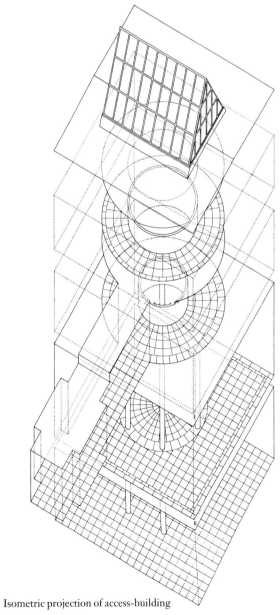

Isometric projection of access-building

Perspective view of interior of access-building

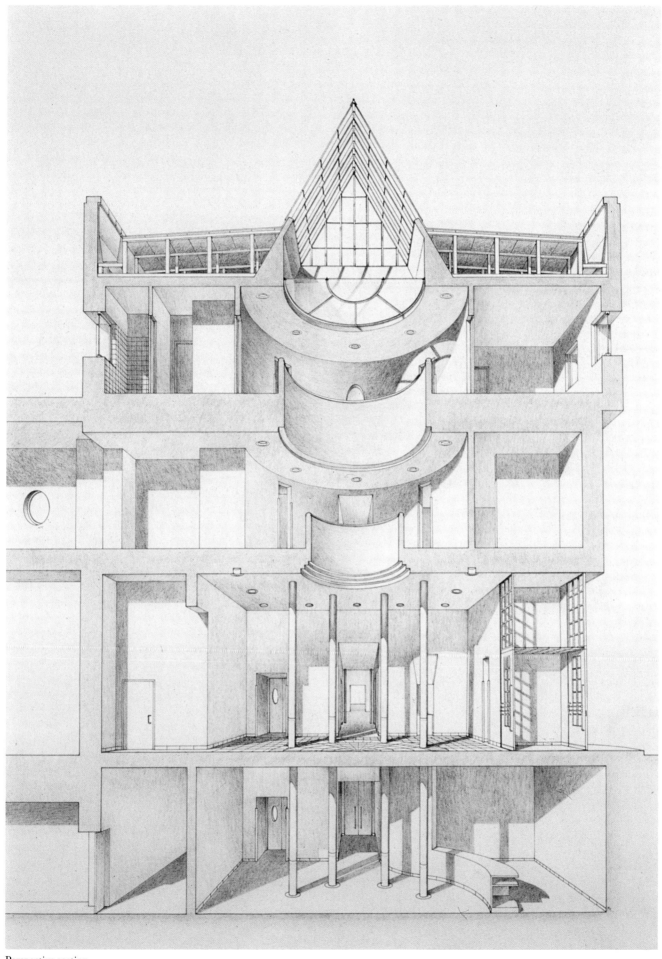

Perspective section

Nothing but Wall, Space and Light

Falk Jaeger

The Städel Art Institute, founded in 1807, had already been collecting contemporary works in the nineteenth century, to promote the understanding of art by showing the relations between new and historical art. In 1907, to revive the somewhat neglected tradition, a municipal gallery was affiliated to the institute, and it soon became necessary to add a first extension at the rear of the edifice, which had been built between 1874 and 1878 by Oscar Sommer. If a new extension, mainly to show the art of the twentieth century, was contemplated only in the 1980s, this is because the museum's stock had suffered a serious depletion in 1937, when about 500 "degenerate" works were removed.

After the war, Johannes Krahn rebuilt the neo-renaissance structure in a somewhat plainer style, and also the neo-classical rear extension that had been added between 1915 and 1926 by Hermann von Hoven and Franz Heberer. The latest extension abuts on to the west end of the latter, and forms a wing extending along Holbeinstrasse at right angles (a symmetrically corresponding block could be put up at some time in the future along Dürerstrasse); so was a tradi-tional multiwing plan, and this was bound to have some influence on the recent design.

Gustav Peichl, who won the restricted competition, and Alan Colquhoun, who came second, both reacted to this circumstance in a particular way, by placing a "hub"-building at the intersection of the two axes. This section, separated from the torso only by a pronounced constriction, offered scope for a distinct design concept. Peichl gave it almost anthropomorphic features, a "face" so to speak. The special status of the "hub" is expressed in the interior as well, for unlike the main part of the building with its large display-rooms it contains the access-hall and a number of small cabinets.

In its cuboid aspect and wall height the extension acknowledges the old building, but facade articulation and materials emphasize autonomy. The "reddish-yellow sandstone" mentioned in the competition entry has been forgotten; Bianco Savanna, a white limestone from South Africa, clads the block-like building in a suitably aloof manner. The flush joints and the lintels over the doors and windows help to avoid the impression of attached stone panels that is so common today with natural stone facades. The lack of a defined base and cornice, however, gives the building an air of stark isolation.

A "simple, unfussy building" was what the architect wanted, "a building that does not broadcast its date of birth". But of course future generations will be able to date it: the fenestration, the accessories, the curved oriel at the back show it to be a child of our time.

A banner over the entrance will advertise the changing exhibitions, which will be shown in a single large room on the ground floor. This is in keeping with the competition instructions, which asked the architects to provide "nothing but wall, space and light". Nothing is to add to or detract from the effect of the art works on show. And so, in designing this room and the four top-lit rooms on the upper floor, the architect has limited himself to the simplest means – "interior, white" was the motto.

The hub-building, however, has an interior architecture of its own. It is entered through the large oak portal from Holbeinstrasse or a walkway from the old building. A circle of round supports (matt-surfaced with steel sleeve) dominates the foyer, creat-

Model with planned Städel School extension

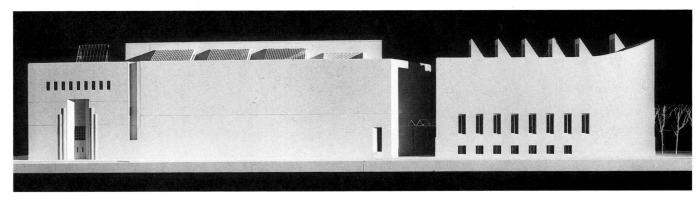

Model with planned Städel School extension

ing a sort of rotunda. An oculus in the ceiling draws the gaze of the visitor upwards towards the generous skylight, and also invites a visit to the upper floor with the cabinets and display-rooms for the permanent collection.

Another opening in the floor would better have integrated the basement, with cinema and toilets, into the whole, but unfortunately this was not to be. And, in the final analysis, the stairways flanking the rotunda are not entirely successful due to the space constraints imposed by the programme.

It was intended to be a "cheerful" building, and many a fine detail and the black and white chessboard floor in the entrance were designed to achieve this. But the paucity of colour accents and the stringent architectural idiom both inside and out allow a degree of gravity to obtain that is certainly no disadvantage for such a museum. In this respect the building is an interesting outsider in the chain of mostly spectacular new museums in Frankfurt.

Liebieghaus
Museum alter Plastik

Liebieghaus (Museum of Ancient Sculpture), Extension

Architects: SCHEFFLER
& WARSCHAUER

Built: 1987–1990

The historicist Villa Liebieg, a listed monument built in 1896, was extended in 1909 when a gallery wing was added. The extension was planned as a triaxial symmetrical building, but only the east wing and the central block were built.

The second extension documented here complexes the original planning concept by adding the missing west wing. It adjoins the central block and exactly reflects the proportions of the east wing. In this design the old villa remains the formative element.

Although keeping to the given framework, the extension plan was not a slavish imitation of the old gallery wing. The same materials were used for the facades as in the old building – plaster, Muschelkalk limestone and basalt lava – but they were supplemented with steel, glass and marble. Above the base-moulding the side aisle walls dissolve into a filigree structure of profile steel supports and pillars.

The side aisle that faces the park culminates in a pavilion-like octagonal tower, which is a formal reference to the tower of the old villa. It houses one of the most valuable items, Myron's Athene.

The enclosed space is 6,935 cubic metres, the main area of use 718 square metres. The building costs were DM 8,300,000.

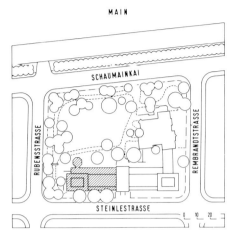

Schaumainkai 71

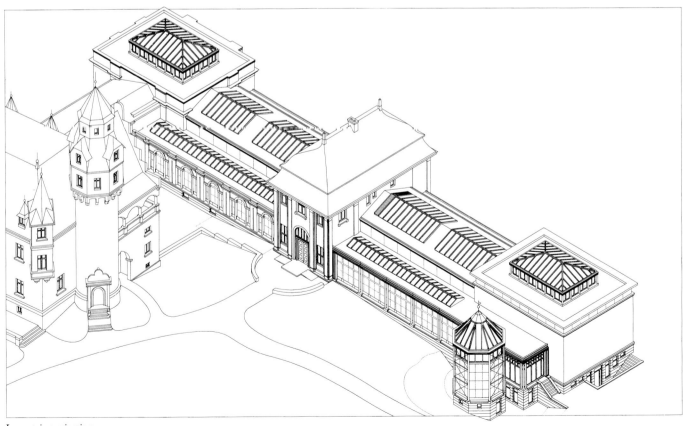

Isometric projection

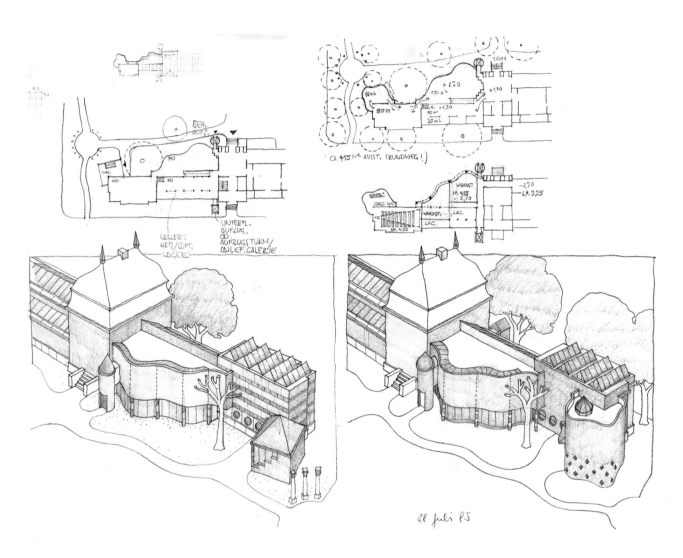

Design sketches

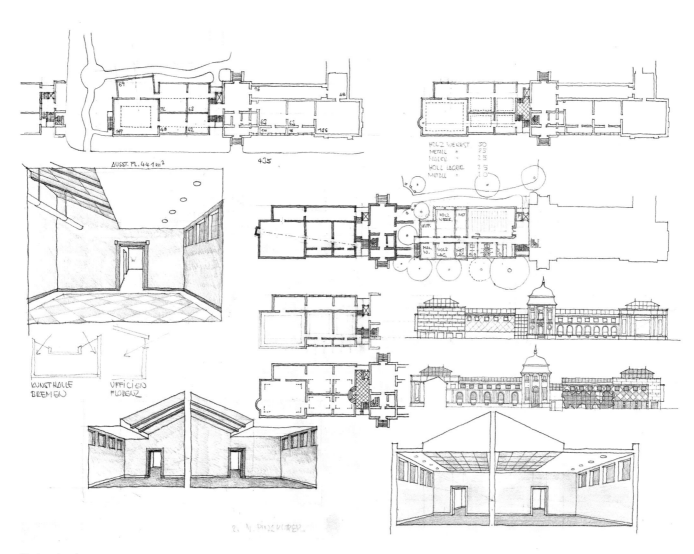

Design sketches

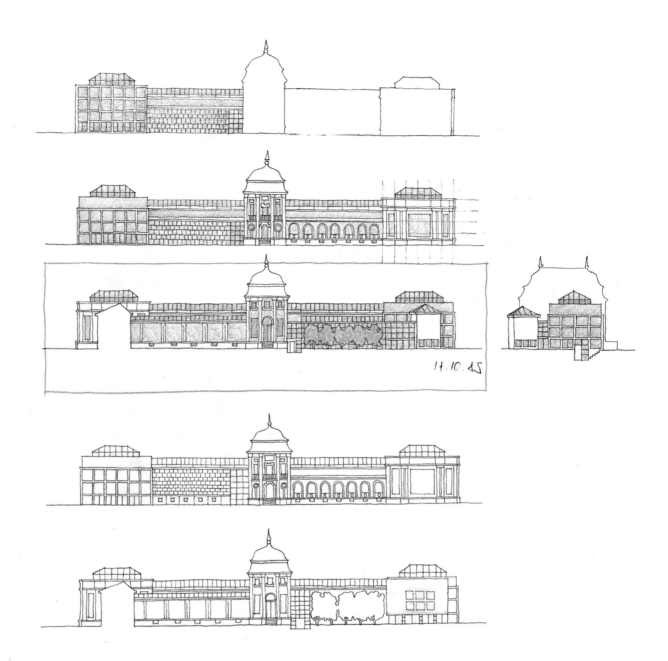

17.10.85

Sketches for facade

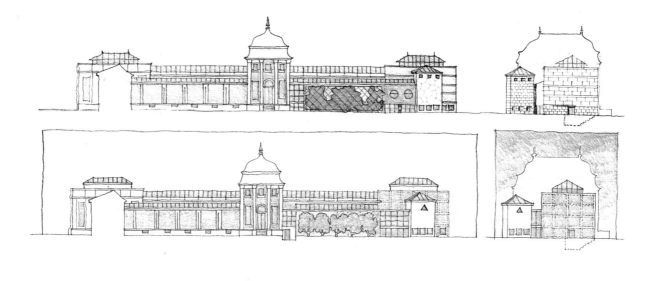

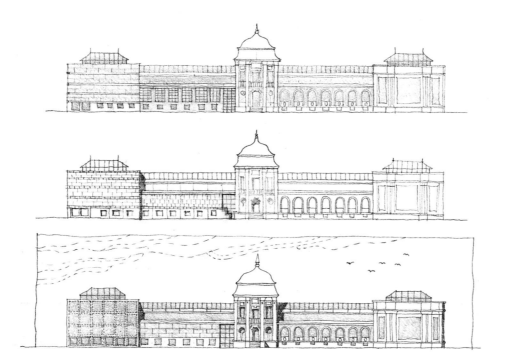

Sketches for facade

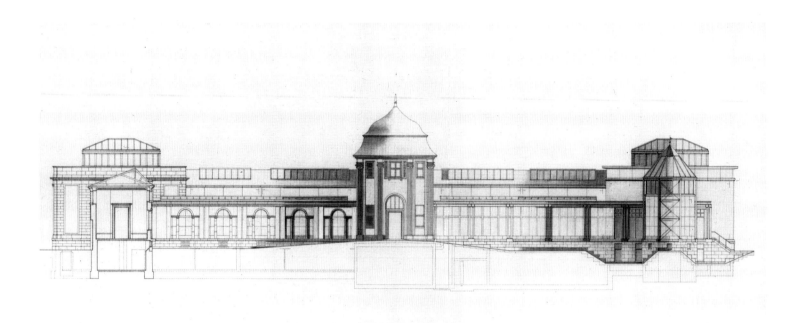

View from north

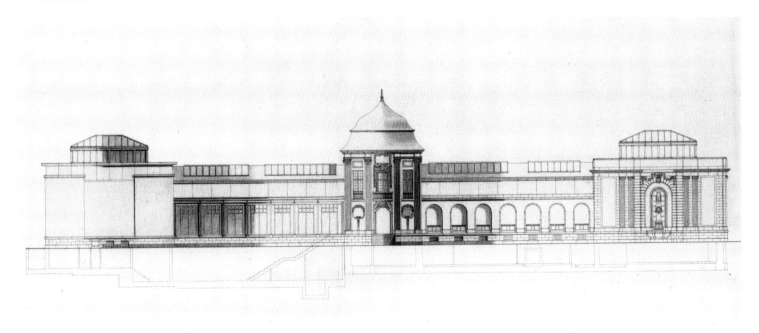

View from south

188 Liebieghaus

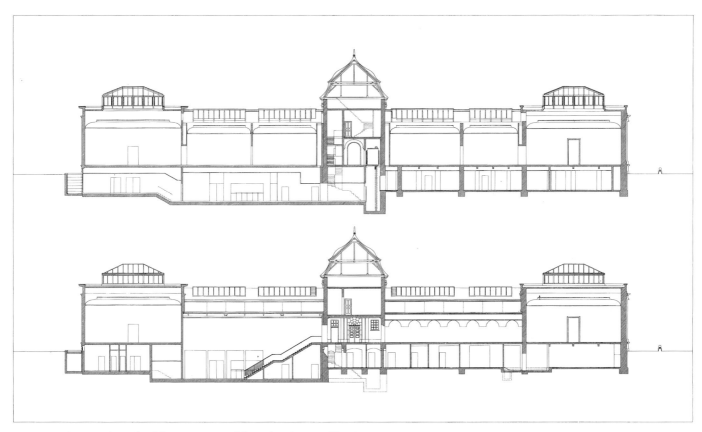

Longitudinal section through exhibition-rooms and through staircase and loggia

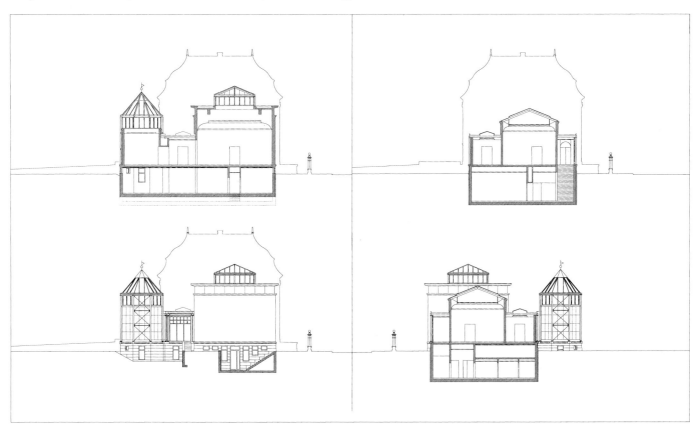

Cross-section and view from west with Athene tower   Cross-sections

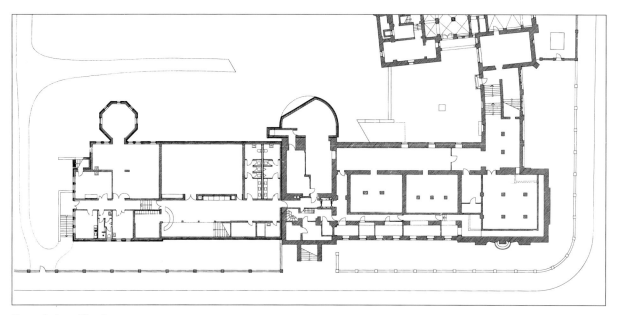

Ground-plan of first basement

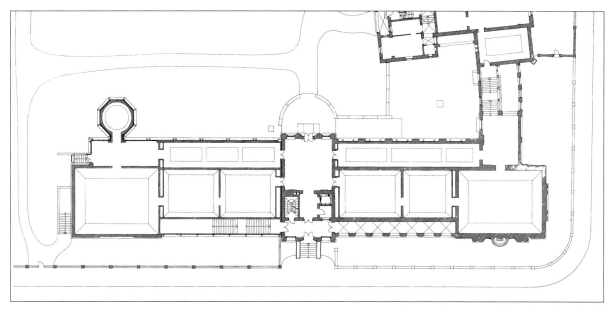

Ground-plan of ground floor

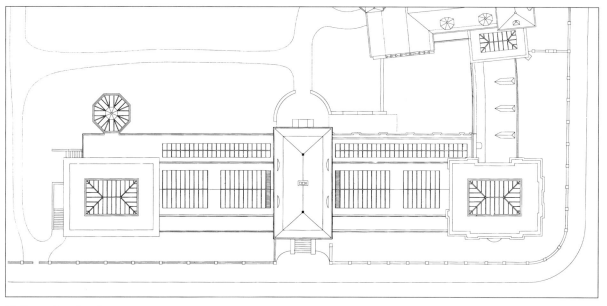

Bird's eye view of roof

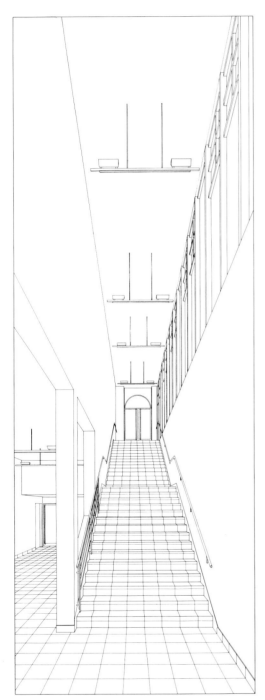

Perspective view of main stairs

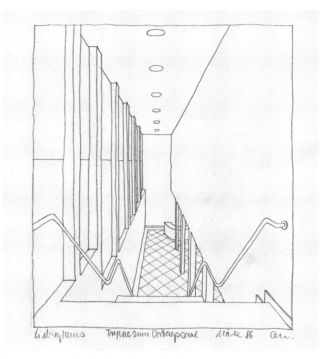

Perspective sketch of stairs to lecture-hall

Perspective sketch of main stairs

Liebieghaus 191

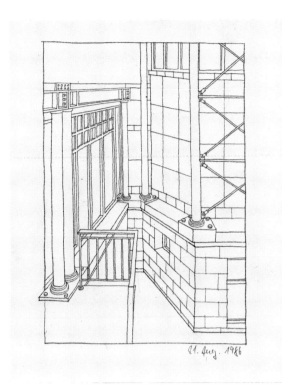

Sketch of facade construction

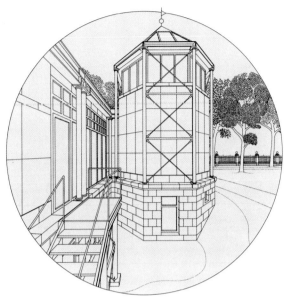

Perspective view of Athene tower

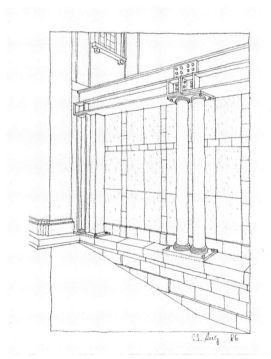

Sketch of facade construction

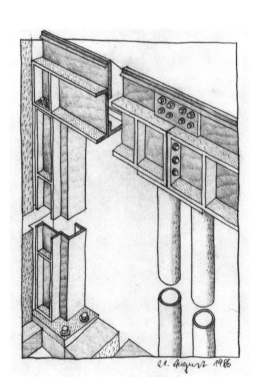

Sketch of facade construction

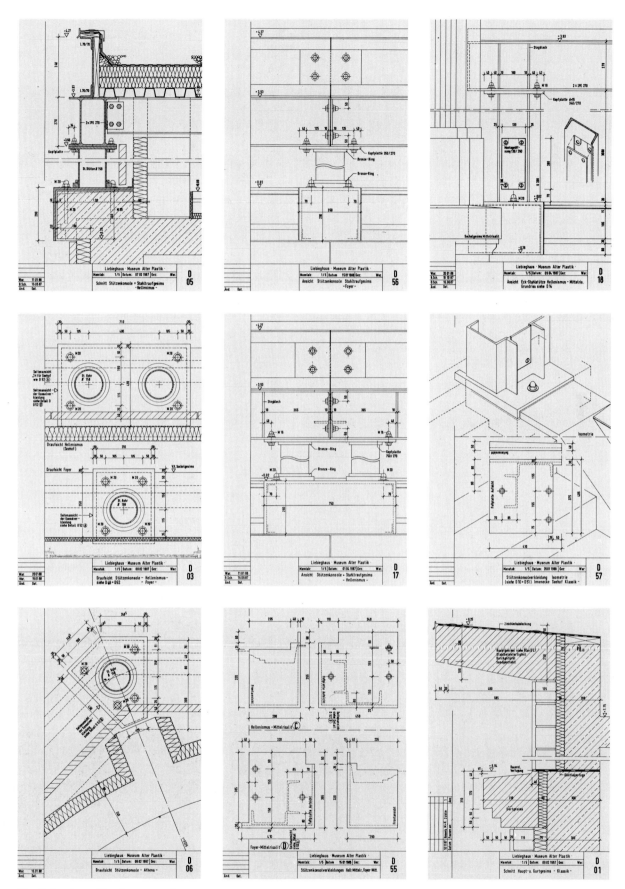

Detail-drawings of facade construction

The Torso Completed

Michael Mönninger

Rodin once said that a sculpture could gain in perfection only if it were sent rolling down a hill, because then everything that was superfluous would break off. His basic tenet was: "More beautiful than a beautiful thing is the ruin of a beautiful thing." Ruin, torso, fragment – not only in sculpture do mutilated or rudimentary figures have an aesthetic value. In architecture, too, we know the fascination of the particulate that is superior to the completed whole. The Liebieg Museum of Ancient Sculpture in Frankfurt was a fascinating torso for eighty years, only a suggestion of the form once intended for it. For eighty years the old museum slumbered like Sleeping Beauty in its wonderful fairytale garden, where time seemed to stand still, until a new building gently brought it back into the present.

If one can hardly tell that the new section of the two-wing building was built three generations later, this is because the complementary fragment, even though it destroys a fine old torso, has been "rolled down a hill", to borrow Rodin's words – that is, it has been through extensive design phases, in the course of which it was freed of all superfluities. Two fragments from completely different ages have grown together, complementing each other. The building that is now complete no longer has the aura of the unfinished, but it stands back to show off the beauty of the torsos and fragments it displays.

The complex dates originally from 1898, when the Bohemian textile manufacturer Heinrich von Liebieg commissioned the Munich architect Leonard Romeis to build a house for him. This building, entirely in the historicizing taste of the turn of the century, has remained unchanged to the present day. It is guarded by a mighty "mediaeval" tower, and with its Romanesque and Gothic elements is like a textbook of architectural styles, its pluralism intensified in the organic sphere by the variety of plants in the garden. In 1906 Liebieg sold his residence to the city of Frankfurt for the establishment of a sculpture museum. Between 1907 and 1909 the house, which was not ideally suited to museum purposes, received an extension in the form of a gallery,

designed by the municipal inspector of buildings, Kanold. The plan was that this orangery-like structure should close off the park to the south along Steinle Strasse; however, only half of the two-wing building, in a neo-baroque Cinquecento style, was completed.

The provision of the missing west wing with terminal pavilion, built by the Frankfurt architects Scheffler & Warschauer between 1985 and 1990, now brings the architectural history of the Liebieghaus to a worthy conclusion. As a conspicuous sign that this is the end of a long evolution, the architects have set a stone exclamation mark at the west end of the building – a little tower abutting on the main corpus, a cross between a pavilion and a belvedere. Like a shrine, the octagon, which echoes the octagonal tower of the main building, is devoted to a single work, the most important item in the collection: Myron's Athene. Apart from this cornerstone and culmination Scheffler & Warschauer's new building deliberately makes no claim to formal autonomy, and only brings to life what was virtually preprogrammed in the old building of 1909. That is also why the new building fits so harmoniously into the park; only four trees had to be felled.

There are numerous examples of building in the historical context today, especially extensions to museums. Either the architects try to achieve as smooth an integration as possible with the existing building by exact

or interpretative imitations, or they choose to make abstract and conceptional references to the context. The latter approach is evident in buildings like Cesar Pelli's glass extension to the New York Museum of Modern Art, I.M. Pei's east wing of the National Gallery in Washington, or, practically on the doorstep here in Frankfurt, the Museum for Prehistory and Early History by J.P. Kleihues and Richard Meier's Museum of Decorative Arts. There are not so many outstanding examples of the imitation and adaptation approach as practised by Scheffler & Warschauer, despite the glut of postmodern nostalgia, but we do have for example the extension to the Tate Gallery in London by James Stirling and the Allen Memorial Art Museum in Ohio by Robert Venturi.

The Frankfurt extension is not only an imitation, it is also a transformation. The volumes and proportions of the old wing provide the binding framework within which a modern neo-classicism can develop. The tripartite division of the facade into base, middle section and cornice was taken as the general articulation scheme of the building, both externally and internally. The basilican plan and section were adopted from the old wing. The geometric rhythm of the facade of the east wing is exactly reflected in the extension – though graphically and structurally rather than plastically. The arcade on the south front was opened up, and in the new wing is transformed into

Model

a glass facade, whose iron columns echo the arch sequence. On the north facade, too, the bays of the old wing, with their Palladio motif of columns *in antis* supporting arches (also now opened up), are mirrored in the new building with double columns instead of pilaster strips. Horizontal steel sections continue the masonry cornice of the old wing at the same height all around.

Only the choice of material, white marble with red Verona Rosso bands, for the panels of the blind windows on the south facade is not appropriate to the reticent modesty of the building, which from the south looks consequently rather like a kitschily restored period trunk. This is a reminder that in the early design phases the architects had rebelled against the strict formal blueprint. Initially, the extension was intended to bulge out into the park (despite the relatively small exhibition area of only 440 square metres) in the form of a strikingly curved glass projection, like the foyer of Stirling's Stuttgart gallery, terminated by an extruded tower at the west end. As the project progressed the overall form became increasingly simplified, and as it now stands it can hardly be seen as the manifestation of "contemporary" architecture; but at least it spares the visitor the sort of Schlumpf or Lego excrescences that are nowadays applied to every parish hall to mask absence of an imaginative architectural concept.

For the exhibition-rooms, which are arranged axially, the museum management had specified uncompromisingly sober forms. The dark terrazzino floors were not to reflect any light and to be on one plane at ground level. The walls, which have the tripartite division into dado, central zone and cornice, culminate in the classical manner in an ample concave curvature which tempers the top-light so that it throws no sharp shadows. The roof was entirely redesigned in both parts of the building. Instead of the wired glass conservatory roofing a

Detail of facade

slate roof with oblique skylights was constructed. The two end-pavilions were given glass superstructures that look like small, compressed penthouses. If the horizontal emphasis and the projecting cornices remind us of Art Nouveau, Frank Lloyd Wright, or even Japanese tea-houses, that is a valid but by no means obligatory interpretation. Such interpretations always tend to offer themselves when a simple and satisfying aesthetic solution has been found.

A reminiscence and a surprise at once is the broad glazed stairway leading down to the lower floor on the south side, where the foyer, catalogue sales-desk, lecture-hall and workshops are located. It recalls the monumental high-walled stairway created by Hans Döllgast when he rebuilt the Alte Pinakothek gallery in Munich.

As a pure sculpture museum, showing works from the third century BC to the middle of last century, the Liebieghaus is unique. Once created to be a branch of and complement to the Städel gallery, the building is now emancipated as a piece of architecture. As a completed torso it owes its charm to the unpretentious way in which the extension respects tradition while meeting modern requirements. It makes no cheap concessions, yet relates to its context through and through, with a felicity unequalled except perhaps in the work of the Eichstätt diocesan architect Karljosef Schattner.

What has been created here is a quiet, contemplative museum that will presumably be spared the invasion of today's culture tourists. Nestling in its enchanted garden, it is a sanctuary for works of art that in their mute expressiveness speak only to those who understand the language of torsos and fragments.

Biographies

Dietrich Bangert

Born in 1942 in Berlin

He studied architecture from 1962 to 1965 at the Technical University in Darmstadt, and then at the Technical University in Berlin. From 1969 to 1971 he worked freelance and from 1971 to 1973 in partnership with J. Ganz, U. Müller and W. Rolles. Since 1973 he has shared a practice with B. Jansen, S. Scholz and A. Schultes.

Joint projects and awards won by Bangert, Jansen, Scholz & Schultes include the Vocational School Centre, Emden, offices for the Protestant Church of Germany, Hanover, the Römerberg, Frankfurt am Main, housing in Linden- and Ritterstrasse, Berlin-Kreuzberg, and the design for a hotel in Budapester Strasse, Berlin. In 1980 Bangert was awarded the "Younger Generation" Prize by the Berlin Academy of Arts.

Günter Behnisch

Born in 1922 in Lockwitz, near Dresden

He studied at the Technical University in Stuttgart. In 1952 he set up an office in Stuttgart with Bruno Lambart and continued to run this alone after Lambart left in 1956. In 1966 he went into partnership with Fritz Auer (who left in 1981), Winfried Büxel, Manfred Sabatke, Erhard Tränker and Karlheinz Weber (left in 1981), as Behnisch & Partner.

In 1967 he was appointed professor of industrial construction and building design at the Technical University in Darmstadt. In 1984 he received an honorary doctorate from the University of Stuttgart. His most important works include the Hohenstaufen Grammar School in Göppingen, the State Technical College in Ulm, the sports building in the Olympia Park in Munich, and the study-centre for the Protestant Church in Stuttgart.

Helge Bofinger

Born in 1940 in Stettin, Pomerania

He studied from 1960 to 1968 at the Technical University in Braunschweig. In 1969 he set up the practice of Bofinger & Partner with Margret Bofinger. In 1972 he was elected to the Federation of German Architects (BDA), serving as a member of the board of the Braunschweig chapter from 1973 to 1979. In 1974 he became a founder-member of the working-group Architecture and Historical Preservation. He has been a guest professor at the University of Venice, the Architecture Academy in Amsterdam, and the University of Rosario, Argentina, and an honorary professor at the University of Buenos Aires. He has been professor of design and architectural theory at the University of Dortmund since 1986. In 1981 he was awarded first prize in a competition (Wilhelmstrasse) at the International Building Exhibition in Berlin. His main buildings and projects include the design of the Palace Park in Braunschweig, a housing-estate in Göttingen, the Lendenhof in Osnabrück, and a design for the Trade Fair Tower in Frankfurt am Main.

Marie-Theres Deutsch

Born in 1955 in Trier

She studied architecture at the Technical Colleges in Trier and Wiesbaden and at the Städel School in Frankfurt am Main under Günther Bock and Peter Cook. In 1985 she started a practice in Frankfurt, and was in partnership with Klaus Dreissigacker from 1987 to 1990. In Frankfurt, as well as the Portikus Exhibition Hall, she designed the foyer of the Harmonie Cinema, the Rückriem Private Museum (with Dreissigacker and Walter & Walter), the Galerie Friedman-Guinness (with Dreissigacker), the music pavilion in front of the Old Opera House (project, first prize in a competition, with Bollinger, Dreissigacker and Grohmann) and the Concrete and Steel Table (with Bollinger). She has had her own office in Frankfurt since 1990.

Klaus Dreissigacker

Born in 1956 in Mainz

He studied architecture at the Technical College in Wiesbaden. In 1980 to 1981 he worked in a number of architects' offices, and made study-tours in the United States, Italy and the Soviet Union. From 1981 to 1985 he studied at the Städel School in Frankfurt am Main under Günther Bock and Peter Cook, followed by a period working with Renzo Piano in Genoa. From 1987 to 1989 he shared a practice with Marie-Theres Deutsch. Major buildings and projects include the Portikus Exhibition Hall, the Rückriem Private Museum (with Deutsch and Walter & Walter), the Galerie Friedmann-Guinness (with Deutsch), the music pavilion in front of the Old Opera House (project, first prize in a competition, with Bollinger, Deutsch and Grohmann) and the Thomas Cook travel agency building. Since 1990 he has had his own office in Frankfurt.

Hans Hollein

Born in 1934 in Vienna

He studied at the Academy of Visual Arts in Vienna under Clemens Holzmeister, at the Illinois Institute of Technology in Chicago, and at the University of California in Berkeley. From 1967 to 1976 he taught an architecture class at the State Academy of Art in Düsseldorf; since 1976 he has been professor at the College of Applied Art in Vienna. He has won numerous prizes and awards, including the Reynolds Memorial Award and the Pritzker Prize for Architecture in 1985. His outstanding works include the design of the Retti candle shop in Vienna, the interior decoration for Siemens AG in Munich, the Schullin jewellery shop in Vienna, the main sales office of the Austrian Travel Bureau in Vienna, the Abteiberg Museum in Mönchengladbach, and a design for the Culture Forum in Berlin for which he won first prize.

Bernd Jansen

Born in 1943 in Büderich
(North-Rhine-Westphalia)

From 1963 to 1969 he studied architecture at the Technical University in Berlin. Subsequently he was engaged in freelance work, including work for the J. P. Kleihues office. In 1971–72 he was in partnership with J. P. Kleihues and A. Schultes. He has been a guest lecturer at the Technical University in Berlin. Since 1973 he has been in partnership with Bangert, Scholz and Schultes.

Josef Paul Kleihues

Born in 1933 in Rheine

He studied at the Technical High School in Stuttgart and at the Technical University in Berlin and at the École des Beaux-Arts in Paris. Since 1962 he has had his own office (until 1967 in partnership with Hans Heinrich Moldenschardt). In 1973 Kleihues became professor at the University in Dortmund, from 1979 to 1987 he was planning-director of the International Building Exhibition in Berlin, and in 1984 he was nominated Distinguished Professor at the Cooper Union in New York. His major projects include the headquarters of the Berliner Stadtreinigung, the hospital in Berlin-Neukölln, the residential and shopping centre in Wulfen, the galleries in Sindelfingen and Kornwestheim, and the designs (not executed) for the Sprengel Museum in Hanover, the North-Rhine-Westphalia State Gallery in Düsseldorf, and the Park Lenné quarter in Berlin.

Ante Josip von Kostelac

Born in 1937 in Zagreb

Studied architecture from 1955 to 1962 in Zagreb. He subsequently worked as architect in Graz, later in Karlsruhe and Darmstadt. From 1971 to 1978 he was a lecturer at the Technical University in Darmstadt, and from 1983 to 1985 guest professor at the Kassel Polytechnic. He has received numerous prizes and awards. His major works include the Malchen House in Seeheim-Jugenheim, residential building on Kurfürstenstrasse for the International Building Exhibition in Berlin, the Grimm House in Mannheim, and the library in Marburg/Lahn.

Richard Alan Meier

Born in 1934 in Newark, New Jersey

He studied at Cornell Universitiy in Ithaca, New York, then worked in the New York office of Skidmore, Owings & Merrill, and with Marcel Breuer. He has had his own office in New York since 1963, Richard Meier & Partners. He has taught at several universities in the United States. Meier became widely known through the exhibition (1969) and the book (published 1972) on the New York Five. His early buildings were mainly one-family homes, and these were followed by large residential complexes. His best-known buildings include the Bronx Development Center, New York (1970–76), the Atheneum in New Harmony, Indiana (1975–79), and the Museum of Decorative Arts in Frankfurt am Main. Since 1976 Meier has been a member of the American Institute of Architects, and since 1986 a member of the International Architects' Academy. In 1984 he received the Pritzker Architecture Prize. He is now working on a project for the J. Paul Getty Fine Arts Center in Los Angeles and the redesign of the cathedral square in Ulm.

Gustav Peichl

Born in 1928 in Vienna

From 1949 to 1953 he studied at the Academy of Visual Arts in Vienna under Clemens Holzmeister. In 1973 he was appointed professor at the Academy. Peichl is an honorary member of the Federation of German Architects and the Royal Institute of British Architects, and he also works as catoonist under the pseudonym Ironimus for *Die Presse* in Vienna and the *Süddeutsche Zeitung* in Munich. Peichl has received numerous awards, including the Major Austrian State Prize, the Reynolds Memorial Award, and the Mies van der Rohe Award. His most famous works include the ORF studios in Linz, Salzburg, Innsbruck, Dornbirn, Graz and Eisenstadt, the phosphate elimination plant in Berlin-Tegel, and the dais for the Pope's visit on Heldenplatz in Vienna in 1984.

Brigitte Scheffler

Born in 1944 in Constance

From 1964 to 1972 she studied architecture in Karlsruhe and London (Architectural Association). From 1972 to 1974 she worked with Braun & Schlockermann. She has submitted designs for competitions and done conversion work. In 1986 she established the architects' office of Scheffler & Warschauer.

Ernst Ulrich Scheffler

Born in 1944 in Ballenstedt

From 1964 to 1972 he studied architecture in Karlsruhe and London (Architectural Association). In 1972 he worked with Braun & Schlockermann, and was appointed to a lectureship at the Städel School in Frankfurt am Main. From 1980 he worked in the planning department of the City Architect's Office in Frankfurt am Main, and had a teaching commission at the Siegen Polytechnic. In 1985 he was appointed professor of basic design at the Technical College in Detmold. In 1986 he set up the architects' office of Scheffler & Warschauer.

Stefan Scholz

Born in 1938 in Königshütte

From 1961 to 1965 he studied at the Technical University in Cracow, subsequently working with L. Martinoia and F. Sironi in Milan. From 1966 to 1969 he studied at the Technical University in Berlin. He worked in J. P. Kleihues's office and with Kriemle, Kreidt & Partner. In 1971–74 he was in partnership with W. Pohl and U. Ringleben. Since 1974 he has been in practice with D. Bangert, B. Jansen and A. Schultes.

Axel Schultes

Born in 1943 in Dresden

He studied architecture at the Technical University in Berlin from 1963 to 1969. From 1969 to 1971 he did competition work, and was project-director for the main workshop, City of Berlin Cleansing Department, in J. P. Kleihues's office. In 1971–72 he was in partnership with J. P. Kleihues and B. Jansen, and since 1973 he has been in joint practice with D. Bangert, B. Jansen and S. Scholz.

Oswald Mathias Ungers

Born in 1926 in Kaiseresch, Eifel

From 1947 to 1950 he studied architecture at the Technical University in Karlsruhe under Egon Eiermann. In 1963 he was appointed professor at the Technical University in Berlin. He has also held chairs at Cornell University, Harvard University, the University of California and the Academy of Art in Düsseldorf. Ungers has practices in Cologne and Frankfurt am Main, among others. In 1978 he received the Major BDA Award and in 1989 the Prix Rhénan d'Architecture, Strasbourg. His most important buildings include Hall 9 and the gallery at the trade fair grounds in Frankfurt am Main, the Alfred Wegener Institute for Polar and Marine Research in Bremerhaven, the Baden State Library in Karlsruhe, and the Gateway Building to the trade fair grounds in Frankfurt.

Thomas Warschauer

Born in 1945 in Wittenberg

From 1962 to 1964 he was apprenticed as an architectural draughtsman. From 1964 to 1971 he studied architecture at the Städel School in Frankfurt am Main. From 1972 Warschauer worked with Göpfert & Hölzinger, Köhler & Kässens, and Braun & Schlockermann. From 1980 he worked in the planning-department of the City Architect's Office in Frankfurt am Main. In 1986 he established the architectural practice of Scheffler & Warschauer.

Architects
and their Team Members

Jüdisches Museum

Ante Josip von Kostelac with Peer Grohmann (Project Manager), Juliane Brandt-Bezzenberger (Museography), Wolfgang Pfortner (Museography)
Further team members: Brigitte Barba, Hans Bezzenberger, Sabine Seum, Kay Wilisch

Museum für Vor- und Frühgeschichte

Josef Paul Kleihues, Mirko Baum (Project Manager)
Further team members: T. Bartels, G. Sunderhaus, S. Ni Eanaigh, J. Kleine Allekotte, H. Rübsamen, H. Schnittmann, C. Wissmann
Structural planning: Rosenboom, Georg Hoyer, Artur Ott, consulting engineers

Kunsthalle Schirn

Bangert, Jansen, Scholz & Schultes with Günther Bender (Project Manager)

Museum für Moderne Kunst

Hans Hollein with Franz Madl (Project Manager)
Further team members: Taro Abe, Heiko Achilles, Shinichi Eto, Finn Erschen, Thomas Herzog-Punzenberger, Toshiko Kawaguchi, Noboru Kimura, Walter Kirpicsenko, Bernd Kretz, Miroslaw Machnacz, Stefan Maisch, Erich Pedevilla, Rainer Pirker, Hans Streitner
Madeleine Jenewein, Dorit Pachler, Elisabeth Rahbari

Ausstellungspavillon am Portikus

Marie-Theres Deutsch & Klaus Dreißigacker with Ulrich Hinrichsmeyer

Ikonenmuseum

Oswald Mathias Ungers with Hikaru Hane (Project Manager)

Museum für Kunsthandwerk

Richard Meier & Partners with Richard Meier, Gunter R. Standke, Michael Palladino (Design Team); Gunter R. Standke (Project Partner)
Further team members: Hans Goedeking, John Eisler, Manfred Fischer, David Diamond, Margaret Bemiss, Geoffrey Wooding

Museum für Völkerkunde

Richard Meier & Partners with Richard Meier, John Eisler (Design Team)
Further team members: Karin Bruckner, Anthony Caradonna, Nancy Clark, Kenneth Frampton, David Ling, Matthew Petrie, Dukho Yeon

Deutsches Architekturmuseum

Oswald Mathias Ungers with K. L. Dietzsch, Barbara Taha and K. Nagel

Deutsches Postmuseum

Behnisch & Partner. Project Group: Peter Schürmann (Project Manager until 7/89), Felix Heßmert (until 10/89), Gotthard Geiselmann (until 8/89). From January 1989 to September 1990 (completion) the project was managed by Christian Kandzia.
Further team members: Martina Deiss Eilers, Jochen Hauff, Margit Schosser Ellensohn
Site supervisors: Rudolf Lettner, Martin Hühn, Uwe Sachs and Sigrid Schäfer
Structural planning: Schlaich Bergermann and Partner, Stuttgart
Sketches by Peter Schürmann and Felix Heßmert.

Städelsches Kunstinstitut

Gustav Peichl mit August Sarnitz (Project Manager), Peter Nigst, Rudolf Weber, Peter Kugelstätter

Liebieghaus

Ernst Ulrich Scheffler, Brigitte Scheffler and Thomas Warschauer with Jan Münchenberg, Sigrun Musa and Klaus Pischulti

Sources of Texts

Dieter Bartetzko's article on the Portikus Exhibition Hall was first published in the *Frankfurter Rundschau* on 12 October 1987. His articles on the Jewish Museum and on the Museum of Ethnology appeared in the same newspaper on 24 December 1988 and 29 January 1990.

Kenneth Frampton's essay has been abbreviated from the brochure *Museum für Kunsthandwerk Frankfurt am Main*, published by the Building-Department of Frankfurt City Council, Frankfurt 1985, pp. 40–46.

Heinrich Klotz first published his text in the *Festschrift zur Eröffnung des Deutschen Architekturmuseums Frankfurt am Main am 1. Juni 1984*, published by the German Architecture Museum and the Dezernat für Kultur und Freizeit, Amt für Wissenschaft und Kunst, Frankfurt 1984, pp. 44–47.

Manfred Sack's critique of the Museum for Prehistory and Early History first appeared in *Die Zeit* on 30 June 1989.

Mathias Schreiber's text on the Schirn Art Gallery was first published in the *Frankfurter Allgemeine Zeitung* on 1 March 1986.

Monika Zimmermann's discussion of the German Film Museum was first published in the *Frankfurter Allgemeine Zeitung* on 7 June 1984.

All the other texts were written specially for this publication. The project-descriptions were written by the architects.

Photocredits

All uncredited illustrations are taken from the architects', the Building Department, and the archives of the German Architecture Museum.

Edelmann, Ursula, Frankfurt am Main
 p. 14

Esto Photographics, New York pp. 114, 115, 122, 123

Göllner, Hans Georg, Frankfurt am Main
 frontispiece, pp. 72, 73, 85

Kleinhans, Lutz, Frankfurt am Main
 p. 105, plate p. 104

Körber-Leupold, Celia, Cologne p. 27

Krase, Waltraud, Frankfurt am Main
 pp. 23, 26, plates pp. 138, 152

Leistner, Dieter, Mainz plates pp. 106, 113

Lillig, Rolf, Cologne p. 146 (center)

Nemec, Ivan, Frankfurt am Main
 cover, plate p. 74

Schilgen, Jost pp. 15, 22

Schwingenschlögl, Vienna pp. 80, 81

Seidel, Peter, Frankfurt am Main pp. 49, 61, 62, 116, 150, 194, 195, plates pp. 34, 50, 96, 182

Seitz-Gray, Ursula p. 16

Walter, Ulrich plate p. 88

Winde, Jörg, Dortmund plate p. 124

Acknowledgements

This catalogue accompanies the first exhibition to take place under my directorship. The conditions were not exactly easy. I am so much the more grateful to all who gave me support and without whose cooperation the undertaking would not have been possible. In the German Architecture Museum it was particularly Volker Fischer and Heike Lauer who organized the exhibition with me; Anna Meseure handled the publicity work, the didactic side, and other tasks; Barbara Schulze helped to design the graphics; Evelin Arnholz and Inge Klietz headed the exhibition secretariat; and Erika Leps and Heinz Jacobs made everything possible that seemed impossible. I am indebted to the staff of the Department of Culture and Leisure of the city of Frankfurt for their ingenuity in helping to overcome the many bureaucratic hurdles; in the Building-Department it was Roland Burgard who willingly provided material and information and gave us the benefit of his experience. My thanks naturally also go to the authors, translators, and editors, who prepared the texts under great pressure of time, and to the architects and photographers who generously provided the material that constitutes the book and the exhibition.

V.M.L.

The original was made possible through the support of the following companies, who also took part in the planning of the museums:

Klaus Fähler Stahl- und Metallbau GmbH, Offenbach

Martin Feicht Natursteinbetrieb GmbH & Co. KG, Munich

Frankfurter Aufbau AG, Frankfurt am Main

Gackstatter und Partner GmbH, Stuttgart

Geocart Ing. ges. mbH., Frankfurt am Main

Gerhardt und Dielmann KG, Frankfurt am Main

Herdt-Stahlbau, Rödermark

Julius Hembus GmbH & Co. KG., Kronberg

Philipp Holzmann AG, head office, Franfurt am Main, Neu-Isenburg

Werner Horn Reparatur und Stahlbau-Schlosserei, Hadamar-Niederzeuzheim

Hans Leitner Baudekoration GmbH, Hammersbach

Müller Stahl- und Metallbau GmbH, Mainz-Hechtsheim

Naturstein-Fassade Günther Gleußner, Eltmann

Josef Reith GmbH & Co. KG, Frankfurt am Main

Rudolff & Sohn, Brechen-Oberbrechen

Karl Sassenscheidt Stahl- und Metallbau GmbH & Co. KG, Iserlohn

Siemens AG, Frankfurt am Main

UHL, Frankfurt am Main

Zeidler & Wimmel GmbH & Co., Kirchheim